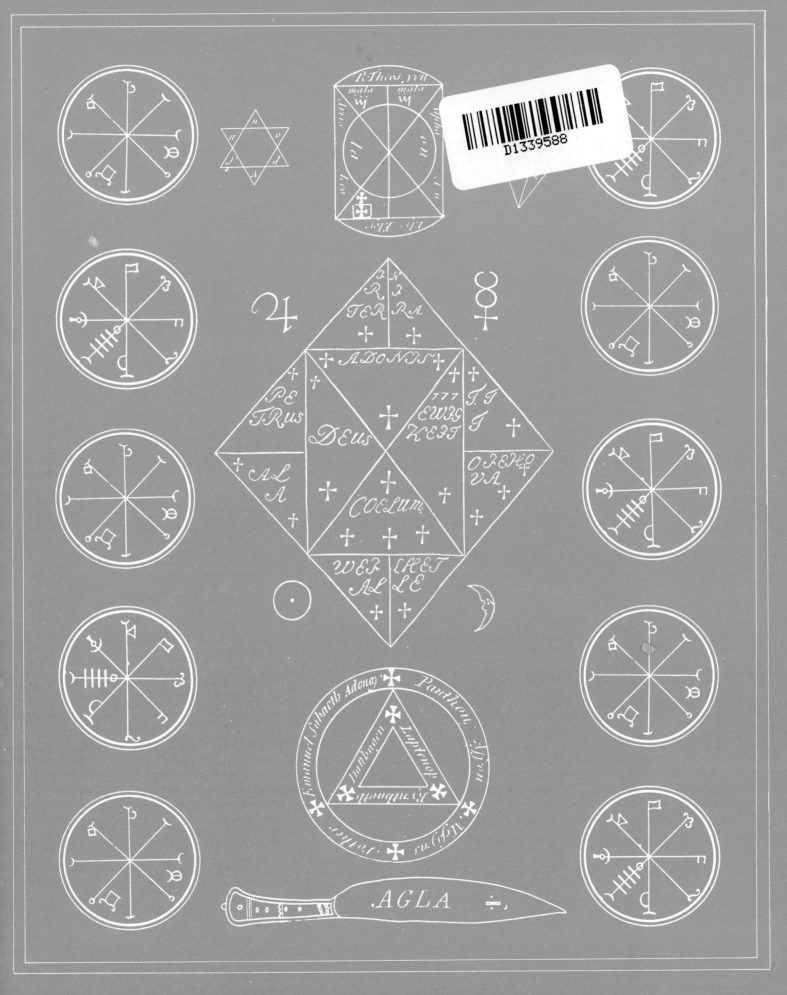

NOSTRADAMUS

PROPHECIES OF THE WORLD'S GREATEST SEER

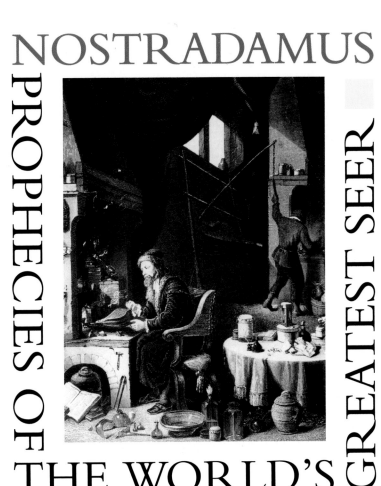

NOSTRADAMUS

PROPHECIES FULFILLED and PREDICTIONS for the MILLENNIUM & BEYOND

PROPHECIES OF THE WORLD'S GREATEST SEER

FRANCIS X. KING
and STEPHEN SKINNER

CARLTON

THIS IS A CARLTON BOOK

This edition published by Carlton Books Limited 1993
Text and Design Copyright © Carlton Books Limited 1993

A catalogue record for this book is available from the British Library.

ISBN 1 85868 014 X

Project Art Director: Bobbie Colgate-Stone
Executive Editor: Lorraine Dickey
Editor: Diana Vowles
Design: Cooper Wilson Design
Picture Research: Emily Hedges

Printed in Spain

CONTENTS

MAGIC, OUR DESTINIES & TIME TRAVEL

We live in a world of high technology, a world in which our everyday realities – from television to transplant surgery and space travel – are what were a century or less ago merely the fantasies of such imaginative writers as Jules Verne and H. G. Wells.

Yet we also live in a pervading atmosphere of mystery and magic, for today many men and women consult professional clairvoyants, astrologers and tarot-card readers in an attempt to find guidance about their emotional lives, financial affairs and the future destiny of humanity as a whole.

Aquarius, bearer of wisdom

What secrets were known to the alchemists?

The methods adopted by those who interest themselves in the latter are many and various. They range from consulting that ancient Chinese oracle book the *I Ching* (Book of Changes) to attempting to attain an altered state of consciousness in which the spirit is liberated from the body and is free to roam throughout all time and space.

None of these techniques is new. One of the most popular of them has been practised, with varying degrees of success, since the middle of the 16th century: the interpretation of the predictive four-line verses (quatrains) composed over 400 years ago by the French prophet Nostradamus – the one seer and astrologer of whom almost everyone has heard. The quatrains, collectively entitled the *Centuries*, were written in a largely coded terminology, the

Precision instruments of a neglected science

6

full understanding of which requires much time and effort. Are those who engage in it and similar pursuits no more than the human relics of a superstitious past, their beliefs outmoded by the development of modern science and technology, their activities utterly futile? Or is it genuinely possible to see the pattern of the future, and did Nostradamus in reality travel through time and discern events that still lie before us?

A recent example of an ancient divinatory art successfully predicting future events

Man's place in the zodiac

is illustrated by the gyrations of prices in 1992 on the high-tech Hong-Kong Stock Exchange and their link with the 'Wind and Water (Feng Shui) Index'.

This Index was compiled in the early part of 1992 by Credit Lyonnais Securities (Asia), on the basis of consultations with three adepts of the ancient Chinese predictive art known as Feng Shui. It successfully forecast the large price rise of March to May 1992, the Hong Kong market's peak in November, and its heavy fall to its

Nostradamus knew the secrets of the Delphic Oracle

low point for the year in early December. However, Credit Lyonnais Securities (Asia) advised its clients on the basis of more orthodox forecasting than that derived from Feng Shui and, while such advice was as excellent as always, it was not nearly as good as that given by the Feng Shui adepts. Maybe ancient arts are not as outmoded by modern technology as some think.

Magician's ritual knife

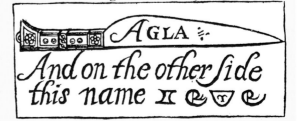

7

THERE ARE AND ALWAYS HAVE BEEN A MULTITUDE OF ALLEGED PROPHECIES WHICH INDICATE THAT THE IMMEDIATE FUTURE IS LIKELY TO BE GRIM. FEW OF THEM ARE WORTH TAKING SERIOUSLY – BUT THOSE OF NOSTRADAMUS ARE TRULY IMPRESSIVE.

It is prophesied that in the seventh month (July) of 1999, or perhaps in early August, just after the end of that seventh month, the 'King of Terror' will descend upon the Earth.

Who – or what – is the King of Terror? Almost certainly an individual who will unleash nuclear war upon our planet or, perhaps, an exceptionally large and destructive fusion bomb (see pages 110–11).

Before and after the coming of the King of Terror 'Mars rules happily' – but not happily for humanity. As Mars is both the name of the Roman god of war and the planet that, in ancient astrological tradition, is the ruler of battle, slaughter and human rage, this phrase means only one thing: that in the months or years before and after the descent of the King of Terror the world will be ravaged by conflict of a previously unknown ferocity.

At the time of the Olympic Games of 2008 a world leader who will be the head of a sinister necromantic cult and may well be the 'King of Terror' will carry out an action of major importance connected with 'setting the East aflame'.

Nostradamians predict an apocalyptic future of plague, famine, war and death

These are not the only events that threaten us in the years that are now imminent. The Four Horsemen of the Apocalypse – plague, famine, war and death – are destined to ride the winds, spreading bloodshed and misery amongst us.

However, not all that lies ahead of us is as gloomy as this; beyond the dark ravine of history through which the human race is destined to travel lie sunlit uplands upon which men and women shall stand, their heads amidst the stars.

All these predictions are derived from the works of the French writer Nostradamus (1503-66), a man often referred to as 'the Seer of Salon' – Salon being the place where he finally settled down after a wandering life during which he had acquired much strange knowledge.

What sort of man was Nostradamus? What is known of the adventures he underwent during his wanderings? And, most importantly, does he have a record of fulfilled prophecy that might induce us to take seriously his predictions for the future of the human race? The first section of this book attempts to answer these questions.

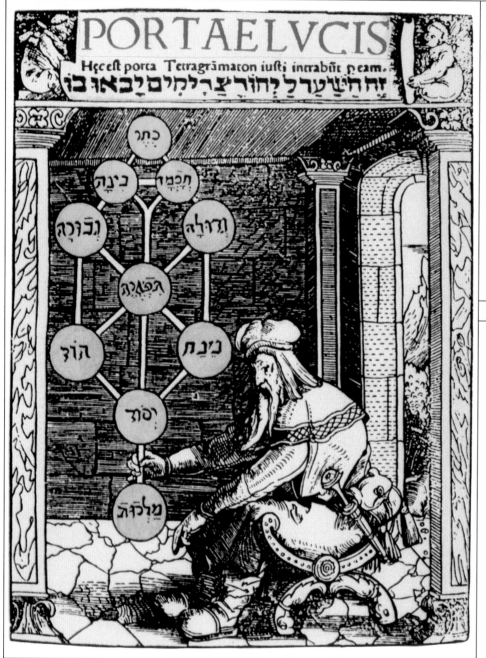

Nostradamus was a student of the mystic cabbalistic diagram known as the Tree of Life

The seer knew the secrets of herbs

Nostradamus was born in the Provençal city of St Rémy on 14 December 1503 to a family of Jewish origin, albeit Catholic converts. According to one tradition his father's ancestors were eminent physicians, renowned for their learning, although there is hard evidence that many of the seer's direct forebears were Jewish traders in the papal enclave of Avignon. This fact does not entirely disprove the tradition, however, for there were plenty of quite humble Jewish trading families in 16th-century Europe who were collaterally or directly descended from learned rabbis, physicians and philosophers and the family of the prophet may have been one of these.

What is certain is that whatever his ancestry may have been, Nostradamus was an intelligent child who by the time he had reached puberty had mastered the rudiments of Greek, Latin and mathematics and had been sent away to study in Avignon.

In 1522, when he was 18 years old, Nostradamus left Avignon and was sent to Montpellier to study medicine. After three years, at the age of only 21, he received a licence to practise the healing art and for some years was a wanderer, specializing in the treatment of what was termed *le charbon*, a disease which was probably a variant of either bubonic or pneumonic plague.

He would seem to have been much more successful in treating victims of *le charbon* than most of his medical contemporaries. This was probably not because of any great virtue in the remedies he used in therapy, the formulae of some of which have survived. One of them, for instance, was compounded of rose petals, cloves, lignum aloes and the dried and powdered roots of iris and sweet flag. It could not have harmed his patients but it is unlikely that it did them any good; he more probably owed his success to the fact that he was opposed to the use of most of the violent treatments then in vogue – bloodletting and the use of violent purgatives, for instance – all of which tended to reduce rather than increase the patient's chances of survival.

It was almost certainly during his years as a wandering physician that Nostradamus began to acquire a knowledge of some of the ancient techniques of prediction that he was later to use in order to tear aside the veils of time and look into the future (see pages 138–9). However, there is no need to assume, as some have done, that because of his abilities as a prophet Nostradamus was years ahead of his time as a medical practitioner.

As far as one can tell, most of the mixtures he prescribed for his patients were quite as odd as any of the remedies commonly practised at the time.

Take, for example, the ointment with which he claimed to have cured the Bishop of Carcassonne of a number of maladies. Its ingredients included powdered coral, lapis lazuli and gold beaten to sheets of such thinness that they were translucent; it could have done no great harm but it is difficult to believe that such a mixture did, as Nostradamus subsequently claimed, 'rejuvenate the person . . . preserve from headaches and constipation . . . and will augment the sperm in such abundance that a man can do as he will without damaging his

The preparation of drugs for medical purposes

health.' There was a distinct element of charlatanry in this claim but, as will be shown in this book, while Nostradamus may sometimes have aped the charlatan he was also an authentic prophet and a practising magician.

NOSTRADAMUS AND THE VIRGIN

After his death, Nostradamus seems to have acquired a reputation as a man who had a sense of humour as well as the ability to perceive what was happening in places separated from him in time and space. Within just a few years of his death, for instance, it was asserted that one day he saw a demure young girl walking towards a locality where the adolescents of Salon were accustomed to meet one another. '*Bonjour pucelle* (Good morning, maiden),' said the seer; '*Bonjour, Monsieur Nostredame*,' replied the girl with a polite curtsey.

An hour later he encountered her once more, still looking as demure as ever. She curtseyed again and repeated: '*Bonjour, Monsieur*

Nostredame' – to which the seer responded with a smile and the words '*Bonjour petite femme* (Good morning, grown up little woman).'

This and similar stories can safely be dismissed as fiction, but their very existence is an indication of the prophet's reputation for being a man capable of freeing himself from the bonds of everyday existence and discerning the hidden realities that lurk beneath outward appearances. This reputation would appear to have been well justified for, as will be demonstrated on numerous subsequent pages, many of his predictions – some of them including both names and implied or actual dates for specific events – have been fulfilled to the very letter.

11

A Renaissance medical consultation

A pictorial atlas of the heavens, showing the constellations as they were conceived by traditional astrologers

For a time Nostradamus abandoned his wandering life, married and settled down in the town of Agen, but he soon began to encounter both ill fortune and personal tragedies. His wife and two children died of plague, his dead wife's family sued him for the return of her dowry and, worst of all, in 1538 he fell under suspicion of heresy because of an observation he had made to someone engaged in casting a bronze image of the Blessed Virgin Mary. He had remarked that the man was 'casting the statue of a devil' – an unfortunate statement, but one which, he insisted, was only intended as a judgement on the artistic merit of the work.

These events led to Nostradamus resuming the life of a wandering physician. Little definite is known of his activities over the next few years until 1544, by which date he was in Marseilles, although there is some evidence that he had previously travelled in Lombardy, in the territories under Venetian rule, and in Sicily.

In 1546 he was invited to Aix, where the plague had broken out in such a virulent form that, so it was said, women attacked by the first symptoms of the disease sewed themselves into shrouds so that their naked corpses would not be on public view when they were carted through the city on their way to the communal burial pits. It would seem that a surprisingly high proportion of Nostradamus's patients recovered and that the grateful citizens of Aix voted him a pension. Nevertheless, he soon moved to Salon de Craux – hence the frequent literary references to him as 'the seer of Salon' – where he married a second wife who bore him a number of children.

Soon after his move to Salon he was summoned to Lyons to help treat the victims of what has been described as an outbreak of a particularly virulent form of whooping cough but was more likely to have been an epidemic of bubonic plague. For some reason his good reputation as a physician declined amongst the citizens of Salon during his absence and it was this, according to one 19th-century source, that induced him to commence a serious study of astrology and other of the occult sciences.

I am somewhat sceptical of this claim, and, as will be made clear in later pages of this book, think that it is likely that Nostradamus's concern with matters esoteric commenced at a much earlier period of his life. In relation to this it is interesting to note

that Théophile de Garencières, a 17th-century student of the life and prophecies of Nostradamus, asserted that the seer took up the serious study of astrology because he was convinced that a truly competent physician had need of some knowledge of it – in which case his practical acquaintance with ancient predictive and other occult techniques may have begun when he was not much more than 18 years old.

Whatever the truth of the matter may have been, it is certain that from 1550 Nostradamus was issuing annual almanacs containing a considerable amount of astrological material and that these enjoyed a surprisingly wide circulation; one of them seems to have been published in English translation as the *Almanacke For 1559* almost as soon as its French original.

In 1555 Nostradamus published the first edition of the *Centuries*, which contained less than 400 quatrains. It attracted wide attention, though some thought its author must be either an impostor or a madman. However, it really made its mark four years later with what was widely regarded as an accurate prediction of the accidental death of King Henri II of France – an event that took place in the summer of 1559 (see pages 16–17).

From that time onward the seer's reputation as a true prophet steadily grew, and by 1566, when he

died (probably of kidney failure resulting from a diseased heart), his fame fully justified the inscription carved upon his memorial:

Here lie the bones of the illustrious Michael Nostradamus, whose near divine pen was alone, in the judgement of all mortals, worthy to record under the inspiration of the stars, the future events of the whole world . . .
Posterity, invade not his rest . . .

Nostradamus certainly did practise astrology and his memorialist claimed that he recorded the future 'under the inspiration of the stars'. However, there is no doubt at all that most of the predictions made in the *Centuries* – both those that have already been fulfilled and those that appear to prophesy a bloody age of force and fire which is close upon us – were arrived at by methods other than astrology. More is said of these powerful (and perhaps perilous) techniques on pages 138–9.

13

Seasonal occupations in relation to the zodiacal signs

The forty-second quatrain of Nostradamus's Century I is of major importance in relation to the nature of the methods used by the seer in order to look down the long vistas of time. In that context its content is examined at length on pages 140–1.

One line of the same quatrain is significant in quite another way: it is evidence that Nostradamus knew of coming events long before they happened. In translation, this line reads, 'The tenth day of the Gothic Calends of April'.

This dating seems simple enough – yet it demonstrates beyond any doubt that the seer was aware of a coming reform of the Christian calendar which did not even begin until 16 years after his death and is still not quite completed.

Nostradamus's use of the word 'Calends' was derived from antiquity. In the Roman calendar the 'Calends of April' was the first of April, 'Calends' simply meaning the first day of any month. So by the phrase 'the tenth day of the . . . Calends of April' Nostradamus meant 10 April, but by qualifying the words with the adjective 'Gothic' he was stating that the date he had in mind was one which 'Goths' called the tenth day of April but was not the true 10 April.

But whom did Nostradamus mean to indicate by his reference to 'Goths', and what was so peculiar about their calendar that they got the days of the month wrong?

What seems certain to be the right answer to this question was given more than 300 years ago by Théophile de Garencières in *The True Prophecies or Prognostications of Michel Nostradamus* (1672). De Garencières pointed out that the Julian calendar, which was in general use throughout Christendom during the lifetime of Nostradamus, ran slightly fast – it contained the occasional leap year too many. Over the centuries the cumulative error

The Great Fire of London in 1666, foretold by Nostradamus and many other prophets

Nostradamus predicted a great plague

had steadily grown until by the 16th century the calendar that was used by all Christians was 10 days behind the true, solar calendar. For instance, what the Julian calendar called mid-summer day (i.e. the longest day of the year) was actually 10 days after what was in reality the longest day.

In 1582, Pope Gregory XIII reformed the calendar by the simple expedient of adding 10 days to the nominal date and arranging that in future an occasional leap year should be omitted. The reform was quickly adopted by the Catholic states of Europe, but the largely Protestant peoples of northern Europe, the 'Goths', meaning non-Latins, retained the old and incorrect Julian calendar until much later. Indeed, at the time that de Garencières published his book England had not yet accepted the Gregorian calendar, which the English seem to have thought of as an unpleasant Papistical innovation, and was not to do so until 80 years later.

The 'Goths' who ruled Czarist Russia (in the 16th century the word Goth was often used as a term for any Christian barbarian) were even more conservative than the English, and Russia did not abandon the Julian calendar until after the 1917 revolution. (The Orthodox and monophysite churches of the world still cling to the inaccurate Julian calendar, which the passage of time has now made no less than 13 days slow.)

A lucky guess on Nostradamus's part? Perhaps. After all, the quatrain contained no names (such as that of Pope Gregory) relevant to the reform nor any indication of the date at which it might begin to be put into action. In any case, at the time when Nostradamus penned his prediction, suggestions for the reform of the Julian calendar had been around for some time and some of the seer's fellow-seekers after hidden knowledge (such as England's John Dee) were keen supporters of the idea.

Yet no hypotheses concerning chance or lucky guesses would seem to explain other of the predictive hits to be found in quatrains of the *Centuries*, such as those which do contain specific names – sometimes in anagrammatic or slightly distorted form – or dates. Take, for instance, the sixteenth quatrain of Century IX, which reads:

> *From Castel* [i.e. Castille, Spain]
> *Franco will bring out the Assembly,*
> *The Ambassadors will not agree and*
> *cause splitting,*
> *The people of Ribiere will be in*
> *the crowd,*
> *And the great man will be denied entry*
> *to the Gulf.*

This quatrain contains references to two names, Franco and Ribiere, which are relevant to its content. It seems to refer to the diplomatic differences which arose in 1940 between Adolf Hitler and the Spanish dictator, General Franco, and denied 'the great man', Hitler, entry to the Gulf – in this context, control of the Straits of Gibraltar.

What of the mysterious person whom Nostradamus referred to as 'Ribiere'? He cannot be identified with complete certainty, but his name bears a resemblance to that of the murdered founder of Spanish fascism, Jose Primo de Rivera – whose 'people', leading officials of the Falange Party, were certainly 'amongst the crowd' at the time of the unsuccessful negotiations held between Hitler and Franco.

These are only two of the fulfilled predictions to be found in the *Centuries*. In the pages which follow readers will learn of many others.

15

The Great Plague of London, 1665

DEATH OF THE LION

While the first edition of the *Centuries* attracted widespread attention, some readers of it considered its contents to indicate that its author was quite mad. Still others believed him to be nothing but a prophetic charlatan – that is to say, someone who wrote allegedly predictive verses that were in reality no more than obscure and almost meaningless nonsense.

In the summer of 1559 at least some of these sceptics changed their minds and concluded that the man they had denounced as either a fraud

A 16th-century barred visor

or a lunatic was truly possessed of authentic prophetic gifts. This reversal of belief was a direct consequence of the accidental death of King Henri II of France as the result of an injury received in a joust.

The fatal accident occurred when the 40-year-old King, who sometimes used a lion as his personal emblem (although for him to do so was not in accordance with the laws of heraldry) was taking part in a three-day tournament which was being held in honour of the joint betrothals of his sister Elizabeth and his daughter Marguerite

A late medieval tournament of the type in which King Henri II met his death

to, respectively, Philip II of Spain and the Duke of Savoy.

On the third day of the tourney the King jousted with the 33-year-old commander of his Scottish guards, a man known as Coryes, or, more commonly, Montgomery. Although the commander bore a Norman name and seems to have been born in France, his ancestors were reputed to have been natives of Scotland, a country of which the heraldic symbol was (and still is) a lion rampant. Montgomery's lance splintered: one portion inflicted a slight wound in the King's throat, while the main part of the head of the lance slipped through the gilded bars of the cage-like visor that covered the King's face and entered one of his eyes. The unhappy monarch's eye festered and, in addition, at least part of his opponent's lance seems to have penetrated his brain. After 10 days of the most excruciating suffering, the King's agonized screams were ended by a merciful death.

It was almost immediately pointed out that the event seemed to have been predicted by Nostradamus in Century I Quatrain 35, which had been published some four years earlier but at the time of its publication had appeared to be meaningless. It reads:

The young Lion shall overcome the old
On a warlike field in single combat,
He will pierce his eyes in a cage of gold,
One of two breakings, then he shall die
a cruel death.

The quatrain was widely regarded as being astonishingly apposite to the circumstances of the King's terrible end. The 'young Lion' was obviously Montgomery, the commander of the Scottish guards. The 'old Lion' who was defeated by him 'on a warlike field in single combat' (that is, a joust at a tournament) was, equally obviously, King Henri II, whose eye was pierced even though it was protected by a 'cage of gold' – his gilded visor – and who did indeed 'die a cruel death' as the consequence of 'one of two breakings' of his opponent's lance.

A PREDICTIVE JOKE

The immediate results of Nostradamus's successful prediction of the death of Henri II included his appointment as one of the physicians-in-ordinary to King Charles IX of France and an increase in his reputation as a seer among the nobility, many of whom consulted him in relation to both their physical health and their personal affairs. This reputation was to prove an abiding and increasing one, both during and after the seer's death, not only among the nobility but also among peasants, tradesmen and even, it would seem, treasure-hunters and tomb-robbers.

It may have been the case that Nostradamus even predicted his posthumous fame, for, according to a story first printed in the early 18th century, he engaged in a practical joke that would not be fully effective until he had been long dead and tales had begun to be spread concerning manuscripts or treasures allegedly interred within his tomb.

Tales such as this were very common in relation to the graves of holy men, seers and wizards and they were widely circulated regarding the sepulchre of Nostradamus by, at the latest, the 1690s. So strong was the belief in these legends that in 1700 the grave was opened by a gang of daring tomb-robbers.

The robbers found neither treasure nor documents containing hitherto unknown Nostradamian revelations – but the tomb contained, as well as the bones of the seer, a thin, gilded medallion. On it were the letters MDCC – the Latin equivalent of 1700, the year in which the thieves committed their act of sacrilege. Nostradamus seems to have had a sense of humour!

17

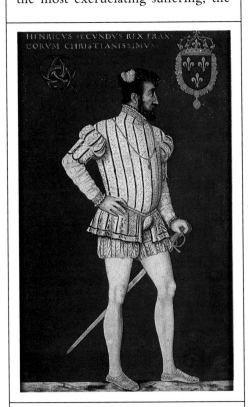

King Henri II of France

The serpent's brood – members of the family of Catherine de' Medici

Catherine de' Medici

After the death of Henri II (see pages 16–17) Francis II, one of Henri's seven children by Catherine de' Medici, succeeded to the throne.

Catherine was a cultured and intelligent woman but one who seems to have had no real principles, her only true desire being to maintain the power of her children and, more especially, herself. In pursuit of these ends she was both ruthless and treacherous, displaying all the merciless cunning that is traditionally attributed (although most unfairly) to snakes.

Oddly enough – and with exquisite suitability – after the death of her husband she changed her heraldic emblem to a serpent with its tail in its mouth. Nostradamus predicted this in the first two lines of Century I Quatrain 19, which read:

When the snakes encircle the altar,
And the Trojan blood is troubled . . .

The second line offers a good example of how Nostradamus often saw fit to convey his meanings by obscure allusions rather than direct statements. Here and elsewhere in the *Centuries* he used the phrase 'Trojan blood' as a coded term for the French royal family, alluding to a medieval legend that the family were descendants of a mythical Francus, supposedly a son of Priam of Troy.

The period of 30 years or so during which the doings of the serpent and her brood – Catherine de' Medici and her children – were of major importance in French history seems to have been the focus of many of Nostradamus's visions. Except for the period of the French Revolution and the First Empire which was its culmination (see pages 42–53), no other epoch had so many quatrains devoted to it by the seer. This may have been because he was fascinated by the character of Catherine de' Medici, to whom he made factual but prejudiced references in more than one of his

'Mendosus' is one of the many partial anagrams that Nostradamus employed; it stands for 'Vendosme' – that is, Henri of Navarre, who had inherited the dukedom of Vendosme from his father. 'Nolaris' was the word, based on another partial anagram, which the seer often employed to mean Lorraine, the traditional home of the Guise family. Consequently, the first two lines of the verse can be paraphrased as:

Henri of Navarre will soon come to his great reign,
Leaving the Guises in the rear . . .

The opening words of the third line, 'the pale red one, the one of the time between kingdoms', is equally easily interpreted. In December 1585, almost four years before the death of Henri III, an agreement had been made at Joinville between King Philip of Spain, the Pope and the Guises with the object of preventing Henri of Navarre from ascending to the throne. It had been arranged that upon the death of Henri III one of the Guises, Charles, the aged Cardinal of Bourbon, should be proclaimed King of France and that he should then make a will recognizing Henri of Guise as his successor.

It was the Cardinal of Bourbon who was termed 'the pale red one' by Nostradamus. This was because red is the colour of a cardinal's hat and the old man was pallid with age – and, perhaps, also with approaching death. While the aged cleric was indeed proclaimed as King Charles X towards the end of 1589, he was never to rule, for all throughout his phantom reign he was the prisoner of Henri of

Protestant leader Martin Luther

Navarre and he died soon afterwards.

As for 'the one of the time between kingdoms', the 'timid youth' and 'Barbaris', these were all coded Nostradamian references to other rivals who challenged Henri of Navarre's right to the throne – the first one being the Duc de Mayenne, the second the younger Duc de Guise, and the last King Philip of Spain, whose personal claim was never taken very seriously, not even by himself.

Henri of Navarre not only had to fight hard to gain the throne of France but was also forced to change his religion (see pages 26–7). Nevertheless, he eventually attained his goal, destroying the pretensions of his only serious rivals, the Duc de Mayenne and the timid young Duc de Guise, as had been prophesied by Nostradamus in Century X Quatrain 18:

The House of Lorraine will make way for Vendosme,
The great will be abased and the humble exalted,

The son of Mamon [or Hamon – in either case a heretic is indicated] will be chosen in Rome,
And the two great ones will be defeated.

The significance of the seer's use of the words 'Lorraine' and 'Vendosme' has already been explained, so it will be seen that the quatrain's first line means 'The Guises will have to give way to Henri of Navarre'. The content of the second line is apparent; the third means that the Pope would eventually recognize Henri as the rightful king; and the two defeated great ones of the verse's last line were the two Pretenders, the dukes of Mayenne and Guise.

Nostradamus made at least one other specific reference to King Henri IV (albeit one of some obscurity). In the forty-fifth quatrain of Century X, he predicted:

The shadow of the King of Navarre is false,
It will make a strong man a bastard [or unlawful]
The vague promise made at Cambrai,
The king at Orléans will give a lawful wall [boundary].

It seems likely that in this quatrain Nostradamus was referring to irregularities in Henri's personal life rather than to political events of major importance, for Henri certainly had numerous mistresses, including the wife of the Governor of Cambrai, and was reputed to have fathered a number of illegitimate children. However, the second line of the verse could have been a reference to one of the Pretenders to the throne having been made 'unlawful' by Henri.

23

The Europe of Nostradamus's time was a continent dominated by theological disputes over such matters as free will and predestination, the nature of the presence of Christ in the bread and wine of the Eucharist, and the Papal supremacy. Such disputes were almost inextricably entangled with the dynastic ambitions of some and the economic designs of others. For example, the struggle of the Calvinists and other Protestants of the Netherlands to practise their religion freely was entwined with both the first stirrings of a sense of national identity which led to a resentment of 'the Spanish yoke' – the Low Countries' subjugation to the King of Spain – and economic tensions derived from the increasing mercantile importance of the northern areas (roughly speaking, modern Holland)

and the relative decline of Antwerp.

Nevertheless, while purely political and economic factors were of real importance, it was religious differences that were at the root of the whole series of conflicts, uprisings and wars which inflicted enormous damage upon Europe and its peoples over a period extending from the third decade of Nostradamus's own century until the middle years of the succeeding one.

Being both a man of his own times and a devoted Catholic (see panel opposite), Nostradamus tended not only to interpret his visions of the conflicts of the near future in purely religious terms but to do so with a markedly pro-Catholic bias. This bias is apparent in almost all the quatrains that in any way relate, even marginally, to the Church and those who

rebelled against it, but nowhere is it more blatant than in Century III Quatrain 67, which reads:

A new sect of philosophers
Despising death, honours, gold and
other riches
Will not be limited by the borders
[literally, mountains] of Germany [in
this context all German-
speaking areas]
Their supporters will be multitudinous.

This is a somewhat vaguely worded prediction to almost anyone who reads it at the present day. However, to those Catholics who came across it in the three or four decades after its first publication it was a grimly fulfilled prophecy of the way in which the doctrines of Calvin (Calvinus – literally 'the bald man') had spread right throughout Europe from their

As had been foreseen by Nostradamus, Calvinism inspired the Netherlands to its victories

German-speaking stronghold of Geneva. One of the places in which these doctrines took root was Lausanne, whence, as Nostradamus had somewhat inelegantly predicted in the first line of Century VIII Quatrain 10, 'a great stink will come' as the consequence of the activities of Calvin's disciple Theodore Beza.

Nostradamus's Catholic bias was such that he had no hesitation in publishing prophecies relating to Protestantism that could be described as libellous – that is to say, predictions in which he falsely attributed to all Protestants the intemperate opinions of only a small proportion of them. The second line of the quatrain quoted above provides an example of

Calvin at the Council of Geneva in 1549

this, with Nostradamus implying that all Protestants shared the communistic opinions of such violent extremists as Jan of Leyden. Some Nostradamian

commentators have even alleged that the seer quite deliberately published false prophecies of mass conversions from Protestantism to the Church. As an example of this mendacity they point to Century III Quatrain 76, which reads:

In Germany will arise various sects
Which will resemble a happy paganism,
The heart enslaved and little received,
They will return to pay the true tithe.

To the present writer, however, it seems likely that Nostradamus was innocent of the imputation of falsehood and that the above quatrain refers to Nordic neo-pagan sects which came into existence in the period 1890-1945.

CATHOLICISM AND REINCARNATION

25

While at one brief period Nostradamus came under suspicion of heresy, it is certain that throughout his life he regularly attended Mass and performed the other religious duties of a loyal son of the Church.

Some have suggested that the seer's Catholicism was feigned, simply a device to ensure freedom from unwelcome ecclesiastical attention, and that Nostradamus's religious views were in reality extremely unorthodox, extending to a belief in reincarnation. As evidence for these assertions they have instanced Century II Quatrain 13, which reads:

The soulless body no longer at
the sacrifice,

At the day of death it is brought
to rebirth.
The Divine Spirit will make the
soul rejoice,
Seeing the eternity of the Word.

The first line of this quatrain, so it has been argued, means that Nostradamus privately rejected the Christian doctrine of the resurrection of the body while the second line demonstrates that he believed in reincarnation.

In the opinion of the present writer, all such arguments are based upon a misunderstanding of the content of Century II Quatrain 13, for, while the verse undoubtedly did carry a personal religious significance for its author, its content is impeccably

orthodox. All that the seer was expressing in this quatrain was his assurance of salvation and his doggerel can be paraphrased thus:

After my death my body will no
longer be present at the Sacrifice of
the Mass, my soul will be reborn
into heaven, where I shall view
eternity with the Holy Spirit [i.e.
the Logos, literally 'Word', of
St John's Gospel].

There seems to be no good reason to doubt Nostradamus's Catholicism – although, like a number of other occultists throughout the centuries, he appears to have found his faith quite compatible with the practice of ritual magic and other of the forbidden arts (see pages 136–9).

Henri of Navarre's accession to the throne of France had been predicted in the *Centuries* of Nostradamus (see pages 22–3). So were at least some of the military and diplomatic struggles he had to undertake before he was secure upon the throne that rightfully belonged to him – for example, in Century III Quatrain 25, which reads:

*He who holds [or inherits] the Kingdom of Navarre
When Naples and Sicily are joined,
He will hold [or grasp] Bigore and Landes through Foix and Oloron,
From one too strictly conjoined with Spain.*

The prophecy is somewhat vague but, read in conjunction with one another, its first and second lines enable one to date the events to which Nostradamus was referring with a reasonable degree

King Henri IV triumphed over his rivals

of accuracy – for while the kingdoms of Naples and Sicily were, in practice, conjoined with one another for centuries there were only three historical occasions on which their unity was formally proclaimed.

The last two of these occasions were in the 19th century, by which time the tiny kingdom of Navarre had long since ceased to exist as an independent state. Consequently, the quatrain could not possibly relate to either of them. This leaves only the first occasion – in 1554, when Philip of Spain asserted the unity of the two kingdoms. And it was in 1562, during the reign of Philip, that the future Henri IV of France inherited the throne of Navarre. We can be sure, then, that it was him rather than some other ruler of Navarre whom Nostradamus had in mind when he wrote the words of Century III Quatrain 25.

The names in line three are all those of places in Navarre, but one of them, Bigore, is of significance in a different context – that of the battles between the Protestant soldiers of Henri IV and their Catholic opponents, for 'Bigorro' was a word that was chanted in conflict by Henri's Protestant infantrymen.

The meaning of the last line of the quatrain is vague – many of Henri's enemies were too closely allied with Spain for his comfort – but from the verse one thing seems to be definitely established: Nostradamus knew a great deal about the struggles between Henri and his opponents long before they began!

Although Henri was a soldier of genius his military successes were not enough to secure his throne fully. To do that he had to change his religion, adopting the Catholic faith because,

King Henri IV's victorious entry into Paris on 22 March 1594

as he himself cynically put it, 'Paris is worth a Mass'. However, while he abandoned Protestantism Henri did not abandon the Protestants who had fought for him, and by the Edict of Nantes in 1598 the French followers of Calvinism were granted an almost complete religious toleration and exactly the same civil rights as the King's Catholic subjects.

Predictably, the Edict of Nantes was not looked upon with favour by the more extreme, and largely pro-Spanish, Catholics; it was one of these who, in 1610, murdered Henri IV – yet another future event of which Nostradamus obviously knew a great deal (see panel below).

THE LOPPING OF THE SACRED BRANCH

The execution of King Henri IV's assassin

In the spring of 1610, as the consequence of a complex dispute which involved the succession to the throne of the small state of Julich-Cleves, Henri IV was making preparations to go to war against the Hapsburgs.

It was a serious and dangerous course for the French king to consider embarking upon and, had it been proceeded with, it would have meant France was at loggerheads with half of Europe – for one branch of the Hapsburg dynasty ruled still-mighty Spain while another ruled the sprawling Holy Roman Empire, which included within its boundaries Bohemia, Moravia, and all the German-speaking lands of Middle Europe with the exception of Switzerland.

The war did not take place, for on 14 May 1610 Henri IV was stabbed to death by a pro-Spanish assassin named François Ravaillac, to be succeeded by his youthful son, Louis XIII. The new King's mother, appointed as Regent, gave in to the pro-Spanish party – men who were 'more Catholic than the Pope' – and arrived at a rapprochement with the Hapsburgs.

Henri's murder was predicted by Nostradamus in Century III Quatrain 11, which reads:

For a long season the weapons fight in the sky,
The tree fell in the midst of the city,
The sacred branch lopped by a sword opposite Tison,
Then the monarch Hadrie succumbs [falls].

The first line of the verse, with its reference to a 'fight in the sky', makes it sound as though the quatrain applied to the 20th century or later. However, the last line shows that this is not the case, for Nostradamus's various mentions of the code name 'Hadrie' all seem to apply to Henri IV. In fact, the first line refers to the fact that at the time of the assassination of Henri there were reports, very similar to those circulating at the outbreak of the English Civil War, of spectral armies seen in the heavens.

The sacred branch lopped off in the midst of the city was Henri himself – as an anointed king his person was considered sacred – and his murder took place not far from the Rue Tison (see line three of the quatrain).

Yet again, a strangely worded quatrain was destined to be fulfilled by the course of history.

27

The first husband of Mary Stuart, perhaps more often referred to as Mary Queen of Scots, was the Valois monarch Francis II (see page 19), son of Henri II and his queen, Catherine de' Medici.

The marriage of Francis and Mary and its brief duration, which ended with her widowhood, was accurately predicted in Century X Quatrain 39, which reads:

> *The first son, a widow, an*
> *unlucky marriage,*
> *Childless, two islands [kingdoms?]*
> *in discord.*
> *Before eighteen years of age, a minor,*
> *Of the other the [age of] betrothal will*
> *be even less.*

In spite of its curious wording and odd syntax the predictive significance of this quatrain was immediately apparent to the French court at the time the events to which it pertained took place; it was rightly regarded as a notable prophetic hit and helped to make Nostradamus's reputation as a seer.

Francis was the eldest son of the French monarchs, and his wife Mary – spelt in this English/Scots manner, not in the French form of 'Marie', by Nostradamus in Century X Quatrain 55 (see below) – was left a childless widow by his death. Furthermore, Francis had still been a minor of less than 18 years of age at the date of his betrothal, and the consequences of Mary's return to Scotland after the early death of her husband were to be the cause of much discord in both England and Scotland.

Mary Queen of Scots prepares to set forth for her execution

The last line of the quatrain was also of significance to Nostradamus's contemporaries; they took it as a direct reference to the betrothal at the age of 11 of Francis's brother Charles to Elizabeth of Austria.

Nostradamus made a second reference to Mary's unlucky first marriage in Century X Quatrain 55:

> *The unlucky marriage will be celebrated*
> *With great joy, but the end will*
> *be unhappy.*
> *The mother [of the husband] will*
> *despise Mary,*
> *The Phybe dead and the daughter-in-*
> *law most piteous.*

The predictive meaning of the first two lines was easily apparent and rapidly fulfilled. The third line would also appear to have had an obvious meaning and to have proved accurate, for Catherine and Mary disliked one another – indeed, Mary was reported to have dared to go so far as to make a rude allusion to the (distant) bourgeois origins of the Medici family, referring to her mother-in-law as 'the merchant's daughter'.

The first three words of the fourth line of the quatrain seem meaningless on a first reading, but are explicable by two of the many tricks involving word games with classical languages in which Nostradamus indulged. 'Phybe' is a compound of two letters of the Greek alphabet, the first being phi, pronounced 'F', and the second being Beta, which was used in ancient Greece to represent the number two. So 'Phybe' meant no more than 'FII' – in other words, Francis II.

MARRIAGE, MURDER AND THE CASKET LETTERS

The second and third marriages of Mary Queen of Scots were even more unfortunate, both for her and for others, than the first. Her second husband was Henry Stewart, Lord Darnley, whom she married in the chapel at Holyrood in the summer of 1565. At the time of the marriage Darnley was a good-looking young man – after their first meeting Mary described him as 'the best proportioned lang [i.e. tall] man I have ever seen' – and, while the Queen probably chose her husband largely on political grounds, she also seems to have looked upon him with real affection. Certainly the relationship between them was close enough for her to become pregnant by him with the child who was in the course of time to become James I of England and James VI of Scotland.

However, by the time of the child's birth the Queen already looked upon his father with utter loathing and contempt. He had been responsible for the murder of Rizzio, Mary's Italian secretary; he had lost his youthful good looks; he was suffering from the ravages of tertiary syphilis; and Mary was in the process of falling in love. The object of her affections was the Earl of Bothwell who, most probably with the connivance of Mary, murdered Darnley and married his widow a few weeks later.

The discovery of some letters and other documents in a casket led to Mary's alleged involvement in the murder of her second husband becoming generally accepted as fact. The result of this was a rebellion against her in Scotland, whereupon she took flight to England in order to take refuge with Queen Elizabeth I, her first cousin once removed.

This refuge proved to be only a temporary one. Mary had a genealogical claim to the English throne and she now began to conspire against her cousin. Her plots were ingenious but they always failed, and she became a prisoner, rather than a guest, of Queen Elizabeth who, in 1587, had her beheaded.

Nostradamus made no prediction of this, but seems to have accurately prophesied the finding of the 'Casket Letters' in the mysterious Century VIII Quatrain 23, which reads:

Letters are found in the Queen's caskets,
Without signature and the writer nameless,
The trick [or the government] will hide the offers,
So that they do not know who is the lover.

Queen Elizabeth I of England, who ordered the execution of her cousin Mary

29

THE ENGLISH REVOLUTION

A surprisingly large number of the quatrains of the *Centuries* have been taken as referring to the English Revolutionary period – that is, to the years of the struggles between Crown and Parliament, the first and second Civil Wars, the personal rule of Oliver Cromwell as Lord Protector, and the events resulting in the Stuart Restoration of 1660.

To the present writer some of these referrals seem somewhat far-fetched, based upon a twisting of the meanings of the prophet's obscurely worded predictions rather than on scholarly attempts at unravelling their often coded content. Take, for example, Century III Quatrain 81:

The bold and shameless great talker,
Will be chosen as head of the army,
The audacity of his contention,
The broken bridge, the city faint
with dread.

It has often been argued that the person described in the first two lines of this quatrain as an audacious and unabashed orator who becomes head of the army was Oliver Cromwell. And 'the city faint with dread'? That, it is said, was the Royalist stronghold of Pontefract – the name of the town being derived from two Latin words meaning 'bridge' and 'broken' – which underwent two major sieges during the Civil Wars.

Perhaps – but the verse could equally well be interpreted as referring to the Kronstadt revolt of 1921 against the Bolshevik government led by Lenin, in which case the bold orator would be Trotsky, the head of

Nostradamus predicted the rise of Cromwell, whose 'Ironsides' army would be decisive in the ensuing bloody struggle between King and Parliament

the Red Army, the fearful city would be Kronstadt itself, and the 'broken bridge' would be the shell-shattered ice-link with the mainland over which Trotsky's troops advanced when storming the rebel stronghold.

Another dubiously interpreted 'Cromwellian' quatrain (Century VIII Quatrain 56) is alleged to have been predictive of Cromwell's victory over the Scots at the Battle of Dunbar. However, this verse, which contains a typically Nostradamian partial anagram of Edinburgh, seems to be more applicable to the battle of Culloden (1746) than to Dunbar.

In spite of the existence of such over-enthusiastic Cromwellian interpretations of particular verses of the *Centuries* there seems little doubt that Nostradamus knew a good deal about the English Civil War almost 100 years before it took place. Indeed, he specifically predicted that 'the Senate [i.e. Parliament] of London will put their King to death' in Century IX Quatrain 49 (see pages 32–3). The numbering of this quatrain may be significant, for it

suggests that the seer may have even known the year in which this event, the execution of Charles I, was destined to take place – 1649.

In reading the quatrains that certainly, probably, or possibly refer to the men and events that dominated English history in the period 1641-1660 one is conscious of an intense anti-Parliamentarian bias that was responsible, for instance, for the seer's unflatteringly negative view of the character of Oliver Cromwell (see panel below). A similar bias is apparent in quatrains pertaining to other epochs of revolution and social turmoil.

When he looked in psychic vision down the years Nostradamus was always on the side of the rulers, never the ruled; it was as if a haze of blood distorted his clairvoyant perceptions. He always saw the sufferings of royalty and the nobility, and rarely those of the common people; in viewing the cycles of change and revolution he tended to pity the plumage and forget the dying bird.

That pity was expressed in several of the quatrains in relation to Charles I, whom he saw as an innocent man whose blood was shed for no good reason (see pages 32–3).

Oliver Cromwell, Lord Protector of England

CROMWELL AS BUTCHER

Nostradamus would seem to have disapproved of Cromwell almost as much as he did the leaders of the French Revolution (see pages 44–9), referring to him as a 'meat basket' (butcher) and a 'bastard'. The latter term, found in Century III Quatrain 80, which is largely concerned with the character of Charles I, would appear to have been applied metaphorically, in the sense of 'ignoble', rather than literally. The former is to be found in Century VIII Quatrain 76, which reads:

More a basket of meat than a king in England,
Born in obscurity he will gain his rank through force,
Coward without [the Catholic] faith he will bleed the land;
His time approaches so near that I sigh.

The reference to Cromwell as a butcher has a double application of the sort to which Nostradamus was inclined. On the one hand it referred to the butchery of camp followers which invariably followed upon Cromwell's victories; on the other to a legend that in the 15th century his ancestors had been butchers and blacksmiths. In reality Cromwell's origins were obscure (see line two of the quatrain) only in the sense that he was not of noble blood and that prior to the outbreak of the Civil War he lived the life of a quiet country gentleman.

The 'nearness' of the approach of Cromwell referred to in the quatrain's final line was about 40 years – that is to say, the period between the first publication of the quatrain and the year of Cromwell's birth (1597).

31

THE BLOOD OF THE JUST MAN

Nostradamus was a conservative in the primary sense of the word – that is to say, he was a man who was attached to tradition and disapproved of all change unless it seemed quite certain to him that such change would be for the better.

This conservatism, combined with a typically 16th-century reverence for the principle of hereditary monarchy, was reflected in many of the quatrains predictive of events involving social upheaval. Thus, for instance, those many verses of the *Centuries* which would appear to refer to the French Revolution (see pages 44–9) are often notable not only for their accuracy but for their disapproval – implicit and explicit – of the revolutionaries and all their doings. Such a note of censure is particularly marked in those quatrains that are thought to relate to the execution of Louis XVI and his Queen; it is clear that Nostradamus believed in the sacredness of the Blood Royal.

His attitude towards an earlier act of regicide, the beheading of King Charles I by his English subjects on 30 January 1649, was equally condemnatory. Indeed, the seer's predictions concerning the two major disasters that were to take place in the London of the 1660s make it obvious that he regarded them as being in the nature of divine retribution. London, he predicted, was going to receive punishment for its sinful part in the King's execution.

The quatrains in which these disasters were foretold by the seer – Century II Quatrain 51 and Century II Quatrain 53 – are examined in relation to London's 'punishments' and to one another on pages 34–5. Here we are concerned with those parts of them that were predictive references to the execution of King Charles – namely the first line of Century II Quatrain 51, which reads 'The blood of the just shall be required of London', and the third line of Quatrain 53: 'The blood of the just [man] condemned for no crime'. In the latter quatrain Nostradamus made no specific mention of London, but he did refer to the place where the unjust condemnation took place as being 'a maritime city'. No major port other than London experienced similar disasters to those which are dealt with on pages 34–5 at the date indicated by the seer, so we can be quite sure that England's capital was the location where he

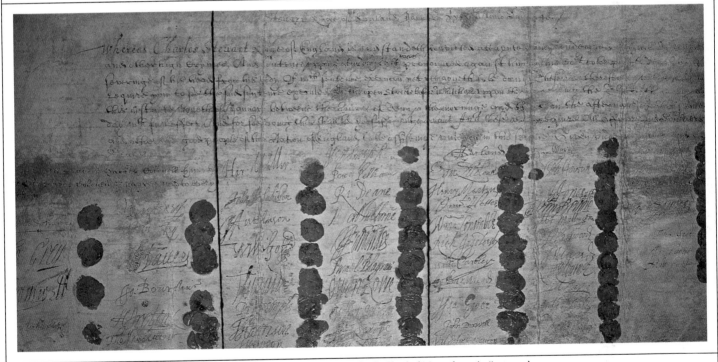

The death warrant of Charles I, calling for the blood of Nostradamus's 'just man'

foretold that the just man's blood was destined to be shed.

It is fairly obvious that the two lines quoted in the preceding paragraph were intended, like the two relevant quatrains in their entirety, to be read in conjunction with one another – in which case the 'blood of the just man' who was described by Nostradamus as being destined to be condemned for no crime could only have been that of King Charles the Martyr, executed at the orders of those who had illegally tried him and sentenced him to death. In both quatrains the French word Dame was used to mean Saint Paul's Cathedral – described as 'outraged' in the last line of Century II Quatrain 53 because at the time of the King's judicial murder its lawful occupants, clerics loyal to the Church of England, had been expelled and replaced by sectaries of one sort or another.

Surely, it might be asked by the sceptic, there were 'just men' other than Charles I who were executed in London prior to the disasters which Nostradamus foretold? Why should 'the just man' of the quatrains be identified with the martyred King?

There are three good reasons for making the identification. First, the reference to St Paul's Cathedral as being occupied by 'pretenders', by which term Nostradamus was indicating ministers of religion who were sectaries rather than mere schismatics. The latter term, not the former, was the one normally applied by Catholics to Anglican priests and bishops in the lifetime of Nostradamus – Anglican orders were not formally condemned by the Holy Office until 1896. As schismatics, Anglican clerics were considered to be

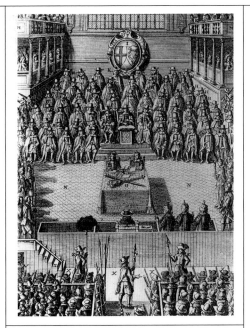

The trial of Charles I, foreseen by Nostradamus

in a state of mortal sin but not as pretenders to a priesthood they did not possess. The only period between the publication of the *Centuries* and our own lifetimes when the Cathedral was wholly or partially occupied by those whom Nostradamus called 'pretenders' was between 1641 and 1662, so it must have been during those years that the blood of the just man was shed.

Secondly, the phrase 'the just man' was used by English royalists to refer to their former monarch – the form of words had a textual significance derived from the King James translation of the Bible and was, in any case, a safer phrase to use than its alternative, 'the Royal Martyr'.

And thirdly, in the third line of Century IX Quatrain 49 Nostradamus specifically predicted that 'the Senate of London will put their King to death'.

Read together, the two quatrains suggest that Nostradamus certainly had visions of events that were to take place in London in the years 1649-66. The first two of his clairvoyant glimpses of London's future were, in chronological order, one of 'pretenders' in Saint Paul's Cathedral and one of the execution of King Charles I.

The second two were of the disasters described on pages 34–5. Being a man of his own time, when it was accepted that heaven was constantly intervening in the affairs of earth, the seer drew the conclusion that the latter two of the four events were inflicted upon London as punishments for the part that its citizens had played in the first two of them.

33

The execution of Charles I at Whitehall on 30 January 1649

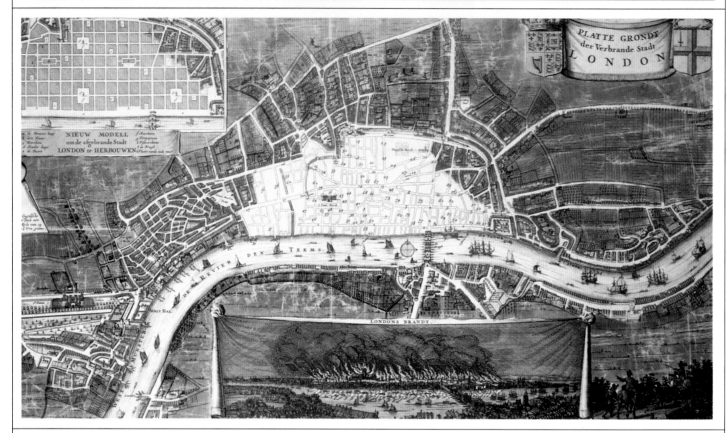

A plan for rebuilding London after huge areas of the City were destroyed by the Great Fire

Both the outbreak of bubonic plague that swept London in 1665 and the Great Fire that succeeded it in the following year are believed to have been prophesied by Nostradamus. For the latter event he went so far as to give the relevant date, for Century II Quatrain 51 reads:

The blood of the just shall be required of London,
Burned by fire in thrice twenty and six,
The ancient Dame shall fall from her high place,
And many of the same sect shall fall.

The coded significance of the first line of this verse was dealt with on page 32; the literal meaning of the second is apparent – much of London burned to ashes. The only dates on which great fires took place in London were 1941, the result of German bombing, and 1666, when a conflagration which began in a bakery raged for many days, destroying huge areas of the City. Clearly the fire to which Nostradamus referred, the one predicted to break out in 'thrice twenty and six', was the latter.

The 'ancient Dame' would seem to have been Saint Paul's Cathedral – the word 'Dame' was frequently employed by the seer in the sense of 'church' – and the 'many of the same sect' predicted to fall were, it can be presumed, the more than 80 London churches that were destroyed in the Great Fire.

Like so many other of the seer's prophecies, this prediction could not have been made on the basis of astrology. While there were, and are, predictive methods which supposedly enable astrologers to make tentative prognostications such as 'at such-and-such a date the opposition between Mars in such-and-such a degree of Aries to Jupiter combined with the square of the sun in Gemini to Saturn indicate a risk of serious fires breaking out in London', there never has been an astrological technique capable of making such a detailed forecast as that contained in Century II Quatrain 51.

The plague which preceded the Fire would seem to be referred to in Century II Quatrain 53, which reads:

The Great Plague of the maritime city
Shall not lessen until death has
taken vengeance,
For the blood of the just [man]
condemned for no crime,
The great Dame is outraged
by pretenders.

For reasons that were explained on page 32 it is likely that the maritime city referred to in this quatrain was London, and it seems to be relevant to the plague outbreak of 1665, which temporarily reduced the City of London to something like a ghost town with grass growing in the streets and all those of its inhabitants who could afford to do so taking refuge in the countryside. It is thought virtually certain that the two quatrains were intended to be read in conjunction with one another as referring to events close in time to one another.

The monument that was erected in memory of the Fire of London

To the present writer, it seems that the two quatrains were likely to have been based upon a vision or a series of visions experienced by the seer in which he saw, in the mind's 'psychic eye', four separate events taking place in a city which it was apparent to him was London in the years 1649-66. The first two of these were dealt with on pages 32–3. The third (judging from the order in which the quatrains were first printed) was the Great Fire of 1666; and the fourth was the outbreak of bubonic plague in 1665.

35

BURIED TREASURE

Nostradamus was not the only seer who seems to have successfully foretold both London's outbreak of bubonic plague and the Great Fire that succeeded it in the following year. Another was the Englishman William Lilly (1602-81), a man who was, like Nostradamus, best known as an astrologer and physician but also practised a number of other occult arts and took an interest in every aspect of the supernatural – on one occasion going so far as to express the opinion that a creature reported to have vanished 'with a most melodious twang' was a fairy.

His mystic pursuits were typified by an adventure which he undertook one night in the early 1660s. In company with other occult experimenters, he used 'the Mosaicall Rods' – which seem to have pertained to ritual dowsing – in order to seek buried treasure in London's Old St Paul's Cathedral. The attempt was unsuccessful; the treasure seekers only managed to annoy some guardian spirits who raised such a tempest that they feared the Cathedral roof might crash upon their heads.

Similar storms were encountered by other seekers of buried treasure.

Dr John Dee, mathematician and geographer to Queen Elizabeth I, used his divining rod 'to find things that might be missing and with his rod did bring back to many persons silver and such objects which had been missing sometimes over years'. On one such occasion, Dee discovered gold in a pool in Breconshire in Wales. His activities, noticed by the local village folk, were followed by such a severe storm at the critical harvest time that it was said 'people had not known the like.' Dee and his colleagues were arrested as conjurors and suspected of worse by the irate villagers.

The Sun King of France – Louis XIV, with solar sceptre and lunar Queen

Charles II, the Stuart king who was restored to the thrones of England, Scotland and Ireland in 1660, and his younger brother, James, had endured unhappy early lives. As children they had experienced the alarms and upheavals of the Civil War; as adolescents they had known the agony of learning of the trial and execution of their father, Charles I – the 'just man' of the *Centuries* (see pages 32–3); as young men they had lived with those loyal to them in poverty-stricken exile, utterly dependent on meagre financial help supplied by French and Dutch sources.

The early years of the Stuart Restoration were happy enough; the compliant Cavalier Parliament was more obliging than any with which their father had had to deal and they were popular among all sections of the community save those that were firmly attached to the 'Good Old Cause' – Protestant Republicanism.

It was all too good to last. London was devastated by plague and fire (see pages 34–5), Parliament grew critical – the royal family seemed to have an insatiable appetite for money and was also suspected of Catholic sympathies – and an unpopular war against the Netherlands saw defeats at sea and a humiliating Dutch incursion into the Thames, in the course of which many English ships were destroyed or towed away captive.

By 1670 the Treasury was empty and both Charles II and his brother James, the Duke of York, began to look to the example set them from across the Channel. It was a decision that was eventually to prove disastrous: it led to James, who inherited the throne from his brother in 1685, losing his crown and then, in 1714, the replacement of the Stuart dynasty by the stolid Hanoverian line. All of these events had

36

been predicted by Nostradamus, but in 1670 they still lay in the future and it seemed to make good sense for the Stuarts to ally themselves with France. This Charles did by signing the Treaty of Dover, an agreement which had appended to it secret protocols, not revealed until over a century later, under which Charles was to receive large subsidies in return for converting to Catholicism and making Britain's policies, both foreign and domestic, subservient to French interests.

In France itself, Louis XIV, the 'Sun King' who was destined to dominate the political life of Europe for half a century, had begun his personal rule in 1661 and had already greatly increased the power and reputation of his country. France had left behind the internal conflicts of the preceding 20 years and had embarked upon a period of material prosperity and physical transformation which had been prophesied by Nostradamus in Century X Quatrain 89:

*The walls will be transformed from
brick to marble,
Fifty-seven [or seventy-five]
peaceful years.
Joy to all people, the aqueduct
renovated,
Health, the joy of abundant harvests,
honey-sweet times.*

The first line of this quatrain is of particular interest as it makes a similar allusion to Louis XIV as was made by the Roman historian Suetonius to the Emperor Augustus (63BC–AD14), whom he claimed had described himself as 'finding Rome brick and leaving it marble'. The semi-identification of the two rulers was particularly

significant as Louis was referred to as the 'Sun King' and Augustus was posthumously deified as an avatar (an incarnation) of the 'Invincible Sun'.

However, while the quatrain was accurate enough in essence it displayed the Nostradamian bias in favour of powerful French monarchs which is apparent throughout the *Centuries*, for while the years of Louis

Charles II, Louis XIV's satellite

XIV's rule were peaceful enough at home (save for those of his subjects who clung to the Protestant faith) his foreign policy was belligerent in the extreme. In fairness to Louis it has to be admitted that his warlike policies were, in the early years of his personal rule at any rate, a natural reaction to the environment of foreign and civil war into which he had been born and in which he had spent his childhood.

This period of turmoil in France had been foreseen by Nostradamus,

who described it in Century X Quatrain 58:

*At a time of mourning the
feline monarch,
Will go to war with the youthful
Aemathien,
Gaul shivers, the barque [of Peter]
in danger,
Marseilles tested and talks in the West.*

The phrase 'youthful Aemathien' in the second line of the quatrain is obviously a reference to Louis' transmutation into the Sun King, for in classical mythology Aemathien was the child of dawn and can therefore be identified with the sun. The 'feline monarch' of the preceding line was the cunning Philip IV of Spain, who actively waged war against France during the period of mourning which followed the death of Louis XIII in 1643. And 'Gaul shivered' (see line three) because of the Fronde (the rebellions against excessive tax demands and the administration of Cardinal Mazarin) and the other civil struggles and upheavals that marked the years of the minority of Louis XIV.

The phrase 'the barque [of Peter] in danger' in the third line has a dual meaning of the type that is often met with in the *Centuries*. First, it applies to the difficult position of the Gallican Church during the years 1643–61; secondly, to the later disputes between Rome and Louis XIV. The former was the consequence of the fact that during the years in question the Church was hampered in its often difficult relations with the state because Louis XIV's chief minister, Cardinal Mazarin, was himself a prince of the Church. The latter are described on page 38.

37

In Century X Quatrain 58, Nostradamus predicted that the policies of Louis XIV, the Sun King, would place the Catholic Church – 'the barque [of Peter]' – in danger. As Louis XIV was a fanatical Catholic (albeit not always a devout one) this might be dismissed as one of Nostradamus's predictive misses. In reality the forecast was surprisingly accurate,

which the King asserted belonged to him. The French Assembly of the Clergy agreed, and by the four Articles of 1682 Louis and the Assembly proclaimed that the papacy had power over spiritual matters only and that the rules of the French church were inviolable. The Pope responded by refusing to authorize the consecration of bishops who had

The arms of England included the leopards

The Sun King's navy destroyed many ships – but not the barque of Peter

for at the very moment that Louis reached a pinnacle of both diplomatic and military success that led sycophants to hail him as 'the Glory of Europe' a long-festering dispute between the King and the papacy finally erupted.

The quarrel was about the ownership of the material benefits and the spiritual rights of vacant bishoprics,

been nominated by Louis, and the complicated in-fighting which ensued weakened both church and state.

Louis had persuaded the Assembly of the Clergy on to his side in this matter by going along with the rigid approach of the French clergy towards native Protestantism. French Protestants, men and women who were devoted to the rigidly logical theology

of Calvinism, had been granted full toleration by the Edict of Nantes in 1598 (see page 27). From 1651 onwards, however, the Catholic clergy of France in general, and a group called the 'Company of the Holy Sacrament' in particular, had done all that was within their power to nullify the effects of the Edict by the use of a narrowly legalistic interpretation of its articles.

Desirous of having the Gallican Church on his side in his approaching struggles with Rome, Louis supported this policy of religious confrontation from the commencement of his personal rule in 1661. Between then and 1685 the Huguenots (French Calvinists) were subjected to a process of attrition which successively deprived them of their schools, colleges and hospitals. Large fines were imposed upon them and, when these proved ineffective in producing conversions to Catholicism, violent and brutal soldiers were billeted upon them. Finally, in 1685, Louis simply revoked the Edict of Nantes and embarked upon a policy of outright persecution that was ultimately to result in an eight-year guerrilla war which had been successfully predicted by Nostradamus almost 150 years earlier (see panel below).

Three years after the Revocation, the efforts that Louis had been making since 1670 to ensure Catholic rule in England (see page 37) collapsed into utter ruin. That collapse, and the identity of the man whose doing it was – William, Prince of Orange – had both been discerned in advance by Nostradamus, who spoke of them in Century II Quatrains 67, 68 and 69.

William of Orange was the son-in-law of James II of England – the former Duke of York and younger brother of Charles II. At the invitation of a large number of eminent Protestants he invaded England and, with his wife, Mary, seized the English throne. It was a major blow to Louis, which had been accurately predicted by Nostradamus:

Prince William of Orange conquers the three leopards

A Gallic king from the Celtic right [i.e. Holland],
Seeing the discord of the Great Monarchy,

Will flourish his sceptre over the three leopards,
Against the Cappe [Capet, i.e. French king] of the great Hierarchy.

39

GUERRILLA WARFARE

When Louis revoked the Edict of Nantes in 1685, he thought that he was putting an end to French Calvinism; in reality, while his action ensured both mass conversions and a mass emigration, Huguenot organization managed to survive, most notably in the mountainous area of the Cevennes.

In 1703, driven to desperation by brutality and bloodshed, the Protestant mountaineers rose in revolt and for eight years waged a brave but ultimately unsuccessful guerrilla war against the royal armies. This courageous struggle and its unhappy ending were foretold by Nostradamus in Century III Quatrain 63 and Century II Quatrain 64. The relevant lines of the former read:

The Celtic [in this context Gallic, i.e. French] Army against the mountaineers,
Who will become known, and trapped,
Will perish by the sword . . .

This is a somewhat vague prediction, and it could be argued that it is easily applicable to a French army defeating mountaineers. However, Century II Quatrain 64, with its references to the followers of Calvin and the Cevennes, is specific:

The people of Geneva [i.e. the Calvinists] will dry up with thirst and hunger,
Their hopes will fail;
The law of the Cevennes will be at breaking point,
The fleet cannot enter the great port.

The only line that requires any explanation is the last, which seems to be a reference to the failure of international Calvinism to deliver effective help to the Camisards, the Protestant guerrillas.

BLOODSHED

REVOLUTION

& THE ATOM

NOSTRADAMUS LIVED IN AN AGE WHEN MONARCHS RULED THE WORLD AND A GALLOPING HORSE WAS THE FASTEST MEANS OF LOCOMOTION - YET, TRAVELLING THROUGH TIME, HE FORESAW SPACE TRAVEL, REPUBLICAN REVOLUTIONS AND THE CONQUESTS OF MODERN TECHNOLOGY.

Revolutions, the rise and fall of the Napoleonic Empire, the evil politics of Adolf Hitler, famine, bloodshed and modern technology are the predominating themes of this section. Before beginning upon these themes, however, readers should keep in mind some important points.

The initial reaction of most people on reading the *Centuries* in either its original form or in translation is usually one of bewilderment, for, as readers of this book will by now have appreciated, the quatrains were largely written in an oblique and coded language in which anagrams and classical neologisms (invented words derived from Greek and Latin) abound and individuals are referred to by allusive names – Henri of Navarre as 'Vendosme', for instance. Even the title is misleading, for the word 'Centuries' suggests that Nostradamus wrote his prophecies in accordance with some sort of chronological structure – that is to say, that the predictive quatrains at the commencement of the book would deal with events close to the seer's own times and those at its end with the far-distant future.

Revolution is one of the major themes in the Centuries *of Nostradamus*

Alas, it is not so. The *Centuries* seems to be the record of a series of visions which were not entirely under the control of the seer and gave him a random selection of glimpses into the future – and of the past, for there are a few quatrains which seem to be 'retrospective predictions'.

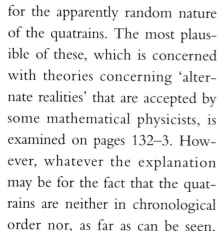

There are other explanations for the apparently random nature of the quatrains. The most plausible of these, which is concerned with theories concerning 'alternate realities' that are accepted by some mathematical physicists, is examined on pages 132–3. However, whatever the explanation may be for the fact that the quatrains are neither in chronological order nor, as far as can be seen, arranged in any structured pattern, Nostradamian interpreters have to accept it as fact and endeavour to cope with it as best they can.

Nowhere is the problem greater than in interpreting the predictions dealt with in this section. Quatrains which pertain to Napoleon, for instance, are to be found in almost all of the 10 sections of the *Centuries* and yet there seems to be no doubt that these scattered verses do refer to the same man.

The harvest of victims of the French Revolution

very strong evidence that he did. Take, for instance, the content of Century IX Quatrain 20:

At night will come through the forest of Reines
Two partners, by a roundabout way, the Queen, the white stone,
The monk-king in grey at Varennes,
The elect Capet, resulting in tempest, fire, bloody slicing.

At the time it was first published the meaning of this quatrain was not known, but by the early years of the 1790s its significance became apparent and what had looked like near gibberish had been transformed by history into something important and evidential of Nostradamus's ability to see into the future.

The most remarkable thing about this quatrain is that it should actually

'How much the greatest event it is that ever happened in the world! and how much the best!' wrote Charles James Fox (1749–1806), leader of the radical wing of the Whig Party in the British House of Commons and perhaps the greatest English parliamentary orator of all time, when news of the outbreak of the French Revolution reached England.

Nostradamus, who died more than 200 years before the event on which Fox was commenting in a letter to his friend Richard Fitzpatrick, took a very different point of view of the matter. As far as he was concerned the French Revolution was one of the worst events in human history, not the best; almost all of the references to the Jacobins and other revolutionaries that appear in the quatrains of the *Centuries* are uncomplimentary in the extreme.

But, it might be asked, did Nostradamus really make specific references to the Revolution more than 200 years before it occurred? There is

Bloody slicing – the execution of Louis XVI

mention the name of Varennes, for this somewhat insignificant commune has only one association of any historical importance whatsoever – the fact that it was there, in 1791, that the attempt to escape the Revolution made by Louis XVI and his Queen, Marie Antoinette, was foiled.

The two did indeed make their way to Varennes by a somewhat roundabout way through the forest of Reines, Louis does seem to have been clad in quiet grey rather than the scarlet and gold more usually associated with 18th-century monarchs, and the capture of the royal pair certainly resulted in tempest (in the sense of social turmoil), the blazing up of the fire of revolution, and 'bloody slicing' in the most literal sense – both Louis and his Queen were sent to the guillotine.

Two phrases used in the quatrain – 'the elect Capet' and 'the white stone' – require explanation.

By using the term 'elect' or 'chosen' Capet, Nostradamus was almost certainly referring to Louis XVI himself. Strictly speaking, the name 'Capet' should only have been used in reference to monarchs of an earlier French dynasty than the Bourbon family of which Louis XVI was the head. However, the word was often employed in a looser sense, meaning any reigning king of France.

The 'white stone' of the quatrain is not quite so easy to explain, although many commentators have attempted to do so. It has been suggested, for instance, that these words refer to a curious scandal of the 1780s termed 'The Affair of the Diamond Necklace' which did much to bring the monarchy into disrepute, and involved

a diamond necklace, a senile and gullible cardinal, Marie Antoinette and the occult adventurer who called himself Cagliostro – a man who had a large element of the charlatan in his character but may also have had certain predictive abilities.

It is possible that those who have identified the 'white stone' of Nostradamus with the diamond necklace of the scandal are right, although to the present writer such an interpretation seems strained. In a sense, however, the question is of no great moment. The real significance of Century IX Quatrain 20 is that it would appear to provide hard evidence that in the 1550s Nostradamus was aware of obscure details of an event that did not take place until 1791.

PROPHETIC OBSCURITIES

The doomed King and Queen return from Varennes

The task of interpreting the predictive quatrains of Nostradamus is made even more difficult than would otherwise be the case by the seer's deliberate use of crabbed and obscure phrases, neologisms (invented words) derived from Greek and Latin, and anagrams, sometimes complete (such as substituting the word 'Rapis' for Paris, for example), but more often only partial.

The original French of the quatrain predicting the flight of Louis XVI and his consort contains two typical partial anagrams. One of these is 'Herne', a partial anagram of Reine (Queen) with a transmutation of the letter 'i' into an 'h', the preceding letter of the alphabet, while the other is 'noir' (black), a distortion used more than once in the *Centuries* to convey the French word for a king – *roi*.

43

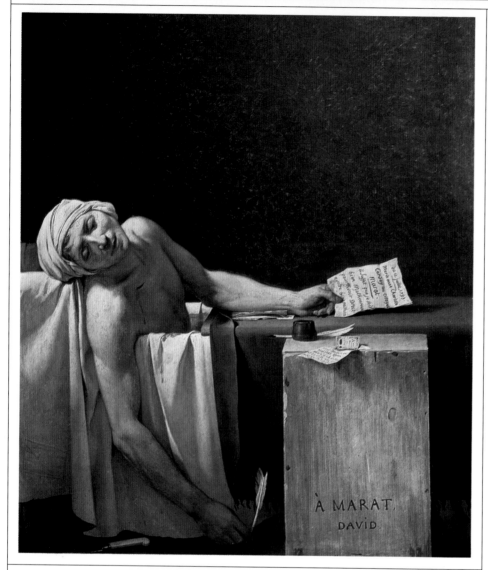

Death of the Jacobin leader Jean Paul Marat

sequent to the year AD 3000, it is an astonishingly high proportion.

Not all of these 40 'revolutionary quatrains' are as specific as Century IX Quatrain 20 (see page 42) or other predictions considered on later pages. Some of them are fairly general in nature – that is, while they seem in every respect to be applicable to the Revolution it is just possible that they relate instead (or also – Nostradamus had a trick of writing prophecies relating to more than one event) to events in French history that still lie in the future. Typical of such a verse is Century VI Quatrain 23, which reads:

Defences [of the realm] *undermined by the spirit of the Kingdom,*
The people will be stirred up against their King,
Peace made newly, Holy Laws degenerate,
Never was Rapis [Paris] *in such great tribulation.*

The verse fits the early years of the Revolution better than any other time, but it could be a double or even a treble prediction, one applicable not only to the early years of the Revolution but also to events that took place during the minority of Louis XIV and to things destined to happen in our future.

Another double prediction is to be found in Century I Quatrain 53, which would appear to be predictive of very similar events that took place as consequences of the French and Russian revolutions. In loose translation this double prophecy reads:

Nostradamus's fulfilled prophecy of the attempted escape of Louis XVI and Marie Antoinette from France (see pages 42–3) was by no means the only prediction in the *Centuries* and other writings of the seer that pertained to the French Revolution of 1789 and the events that succeeded it in the years from 1790 to 1815. Indeed, if any one theme is dominant in the *Centuries* it is the Revolution. Of the fewer than 1000 quatrains which made up the final version of that strange work, at least 40 seem to be relevant to French history during the period of the First Republic and the Napoleonic Empire which succeeded it.

This is only just over four per cent, of course – but as the years in question only amounted to around a quarter of a century and the *Centuries* dealt with events forecast to take place between the seer's own lifetime and a date sub-

We will see a great people tormented,
And the Holy Law in utter ruin,
Christendom under other laws [than
Christian ones]*,*
When a new source of gold and silver
[i.e. money] *is found.*

The quatrain seems to refer to both the suppression of Catholicism in the France of the early 1790s (see panel below) and the even more savage suppression of Russian Orthodoxy following the Bolshevik Revolution of 1917. The last line is also of significance in that the French and Russian revolutionaries found 'a new source of money' by printing quantities of paper money which rapidly depreciated and eventually became almost worthless.

Was the double meaning of this quatrain – the reference to similar

Robespierre on his way to the guillotine

events in two different revolutions – intended by Nostradamus? Or does it show that Nostradamian commentators twist the meaning of the verses to

make them fit specific events?

The answer to the first question would appear to be 'yes', that to the second an equally decisive 'no', for Nostradamus made it clear in the two lines that follow immediately upon Century I Quatrain 53 that he had been making reference to two revolutions:

Two revolutions will be caused by the
evil scythe-bearer,
Making a change of kingdoms and
centuries . . .

By 'the evil scythe bearer' the seer meant the planet Saturn – the 'Great Malefic' of 16th-century astrology – whose symbols are the hour-glass and the scythe. In these two lines he was claiming that, in the final analysis, Saturnian influences caused both the French and Russian revolutions.

45

BEESWAX AND HONEY

Nostradamus made a further prediction relating to the persecution of the Catholic clergy of France during the early 1790s in Century I Quatrain 44. This reads:

In a short time [non-Christian]
sacrifices will be revived,
Those opposed will be martyred.
There will no longer be monks,
abbots or novices,
Honey will cost more
than beeswax.

Traditionally, the price of beeswax had exceeded that of the honey it contained, so by the last line of the verse Nostradamus was implying that the price of beeswax would fall during a period of religious perse-

Robespierre, sworn foe of Christianity

cution because it would no longer be in such demand for the manufacture of votive and altar candles. The previous line pertains to the suppression of the monastic and

other religious orders as a consequence of the adoption of the Constitution of 1790 and other legislative innovations. Those who opposed these changes were indeed martyred, as predicted.

The mention of pagan sacrifices being reinstituted with which the quatrain opens is a reference to the pseudo-religious rites that were temporarily introduced into France by the more extreme of the revolutionaries. The most notable of such ceremonies were the honouring of the 'goddess of Reason' (10 November 1793) and the absurd 'Festival of the Supreme Being' that was orchestrated by Robespierre.

FIGHTING AT THE TUILERIES

While many quatrains of the *Centuries* may have seemed obscure to earlier interpreters, they were subsequently to be clarified by the passage of historical events. One such is Century IX Quatrain 34, which reads:

The solitary marriage partner will be mitred
On return, fighting will proceed at the thuille,
By five hundred one dignified will be betrayed,
Narbone and Saulce, we shall have oil for knives.

While 'Narbone' might mean the city of Narbonne, to early Nostradamians 'thuille' seemed to be either one of the seer's neologisms or an unusual version of a word meaning tiles – or, alternatively, tile kilns. In either case, no commentator on the quatrains could possibly make sense of this pre-diction until some 250 years or so after its first publication.

One 17th-century student of Nostradamus made a brave attempt at interpretation. Taking thuille as a slightly distorted version of a French word meaning roof tiles, he translated the verse as:

The separated husband shall wear a mitre,
Returning battle, he shall go over the tyle,
By five hundred one dignified shall be betrayed,
Narbon and Salces shall have oil by the quintal.

His interpretation of this was as fol-lows: 'The verse signifieth, that some certain man who was married shall be parted from his wife, and shall attain to some ecclesiastical dignity . . . coming back from some place or enterprise, he shall be met and fought

The 'betrayal' predicted by Nostradamus gained momentum after the National Assembly took the oath of allegiance to the revolutionary cause

with, and compelled to escape over the tiles of a house . . . a man of great account shall be betrayed by 500 of his men . . . when these things shall come to pass, Narbon and Salces . . . shall reap [i.e. harvest] and make a great deal of oil.'

Ingenious, of course – but pretty unlikely. Odd as the church may have been in some respects in the 17th century, it was fairly improbable that a man, subsequent to separating from his wife, would attain to high office in it and then 'be met and fought with', retreating from his assailants by cavorting about on the rooftops.

However, the seemingly meaningless obscurities of this quatrain ceased to be meaningless in 1791 and 1792. In the June of the former year, the King of France, Louis XVI, and his consort, Marie Antoinette, made their attempted escape from revolutionary France (see pages 42–3). The venture was bungled right from the start, with the entire royal party, including the King and Queen, travelling together in an enormous lumbering coach that was almost bound to draw attention to its occupants en route.

At the small municipality of Ste Menehould a man named Drouet noticed that one of the men in the coach had a face reminiscent of the appearance of the King as portrayed on a 50-livre assignat (paper money secured on seized church lands). At Varennes the entire party was stopped and arrested, largely as the result of the activities of a man named Saulce, a chandler, grocer and oil merchant – whose name and occupation suggest the Salces mentioned in the last line of the quatrain in association with oil.

Five hundred Marseillais federals joined the citizens of Paris in sacking the Tuileries

The rest of the quatrain also applies very neatly to the flight of Louis XVI and the events following close upon it. The first line reads 'The solitary marriage partner will be mitred', and after his return to Paris from Varennes the King was both 'mitred' and a 'solitary marriage partner' – the latter because he was politically more and more isolated from his own advisers and, increasingly, from Marie Antoinette, who was herself the puppet of her reactionary Swedish adviser Count Hans Axel von Fersen, a man whose political influence was disastrous. He was enmitred in a literal way on 20 June 1792, when a mob invaded the Tuileries palace and compelled their monarch to don the bonnet rouge, the red cap of Liberty, modelled on the Phrygian mitre of antiquity.

What, then, of the meaning of next lines of the quatrain, 'On return, fighting will proceed at the thuille' and 'By five hundred one dignified will be betrayed'?

As described on pages 48–9, the scene of the fighting that took place on 10 August 1792 and resulted in the overthrow of the King shortly afterwards was the palace of the Tuileries. This palace, not under construction or even, as far as is known, planned at the time of the first publication of the *Centuries*, was erected on a site that had formerly been occupied by at least one tile-firing kiln – the thuille of the quatrain.

So fighting did proceed at the tile kiln following the return of Louis XVI to Paris after his failed escape. At what had been, two centuries earlier, a place where mounds of clay had been fired into coverings for the rooftops of Paris, a new ideology which had been moulded by Jacobin theorists was fired in the heat of battle into a French Republic.

And the 'five hundred' who were predicted to betray 'one dignified'?

The one dignified was the King; the 'five hundred' who betrayed him were probably the Marseillais 'federals' who took part in the fighting at the Tuileries. For, according to the 19th-century historian Louis Thiers (1797-1877), 'ils étaient cinq cents' – there were five hundred.

47

The destruction of the emblems of monarchy – the symbolic ending of the ancien regime *in France*

Nostradamus prefaced the first edition of the *Centuries* with an apocalyptically worded Epistle to Henri II. Such is the tone of the language in which much of this is couched that sceptics assert that it is nothing more than a vague, even meaningless, catalogue of disaster, whole sections of which can be distorted by ingenious interpreters so that they can be applied to any unpleasant event which has taken place within the last 400 years or so.

However, there are significant and absolutely specific prophecies in the Epistle that have definitely been verified by the course of history. One in particular is of enormous interest because it gives a specific year – 1792 – for a predicted major event. The relevant passage reads as follows:

Then will be the beginning [of an era] *that will include within itself* [patterns of behaviour and thought, the way in which people look at the world] *which will last long, and in its first year there shall be a great persecution of the Christian Church, fiercer than that in Africa* [almost certainly a historical reference to the savage Vandal persecution of the church that took place in North Africa in the fifth century]*, and this will burst out during the year One Thousand, Seven Hundred and Ninety Two.*

It cannot really be denied that Nostradamus's prediction that the events taking place in the course of 1792 would inaugurate a new era was correct. If any one year can be regarded as marking the beginning of the age in which we live at the present day it was 1792 – far more so than other candidates for that doubtful honour, such as 1776, when Britain's North American colonies declared their independence from the Motherland, or 1789, when Louis XVI of France summoned the Estates General. The event which, above all else, marks 1792 off from all other years took place on 10 August, when the so-called mob attacked the Tuileries, which had become the

The National Guard, formed from the citizen army that grew out of the revolution, was part of the new era

French royal family's home after they had been removed from Versailles. In actuality the attack was a carefully organized affair, brilliantly planned by an insurrectionary committee, largely under the control of Jacobins, the extreme left of the revolutionary movement, which worked in close collaboration with extremist groups from Brest and Marseilles.

The immediate consequences of the attack included the deaths in hand-to-hand fighting of 400 insurrectionaries and 800 royal troops; the King being first suspended from the throne, then deposed, and eventually executed; the ghastly September massacres in which many hundreds of imprisoned ecclesiastics, men and women of the aristocracy, rank and file royalists – even prostitutes and minor criminals – were butchered by the sans-culottes allies of the middle-class Jacobins; and the Paris commune becoming, in all but name, the central government of France.

The eventual consequences of the successful insurrection which took place on that hot afternoon in August 1792 have affected, and are still affecting, the lives of each and every one of us. To make any sort of attempt to recount them in full would be quite outside the scope of a book such as this. It suffices to say that those events that took place in Paris in 1792 – events of which Nostradamus seems to have had psychic intimations some 250 years earlier – directly led to the emergence of the ideologies that have largely dominated world politics for over two centuries: secularism, nationalism, revolutionary democracy and socialism.

There is a further point worth making in relation to the prediction that 1792 would mark the beginning of a new era.

In that year France's Jacobin revolutionaries introduced a new calendar. The traditional names of the 12 months of the year, their names derived from classical mythology and history and thus looked upon by the more radical revolutionaries as outmoded relics of the past, were abandoned and the number of the year was changed so that it could no longer be regarded as based upon a Christian chronology.

At midnight on 21-22 September 1792 'Year I of the Republic' began. It ran for a full 365 days and was made up of 12 months, each of 30 days plus 5 additional days. The new months were given what were considered to be 'rational' names; thus, for instance, the month thought likely to be usually the hottest – the one that began on what most people still thought of as July 22 – was called 'Thermidor' (heat).

Thus, in September 1792, the prognostication made by Nostradamus was fulfilled to the very letter. Or was it? After all, the seer predicted that the new era would 'last long', and one does not meet people complaining of 'a very cold Thermidor' or 'a wet Prairal'. However, anyone who reads the theoretical literature of contemporary Marxism continually comes across references to that calendar in the use of such hackneyed phrases as 'a Thermidorean reaction'. In one sense at least the revolutionary calendar, like the new social era inaugurated in 1792, is still with us.

49

Louis XVI's son died in prison aged only 10

The European turmoil that was begun by the outbreak of the French Revolution was no passing phase, and the First Republic that succeeded the reign of Louis XVI existed in a state of perpetual change. Robespierre and his allies replaced the more moderate Republicans, only to be themselves supplanted by the corrupt Directory, which was in turn succeeded by the Consulate and the Empire of Napoleon Bonaparte.

The rise and fall of Napoleon was predicted by Nostradamus; indeed, there are so many quatrains which would seem to refer to Napoleon, the obscure Corsican artillery officer who became a great emperor, that it is impossible to give a detailed interpretation of more than a few of them. Perhaps the best-known is Century VIII Quatrain 57, which reads:

*From a simple soldier he will attain
to Empire,
He will exchange the short robe for
the long,
Brave in arms, much worse towards
the Church,
He vexes the priests as water soaks
a sponge.*

The phrase 'short robe' was one of the seer's double allusions, for by it he signified both the cloak that the future emperor wore when he was a mere military cadet and the robe he wore on formal occasions when he held the office of First Consul. The 'long robe' for which he exchanged the latter was the Coronation robe he donned when crowned emperor by Pope Pius VII in 1804. The meaning of the third line is apparent, and the way in which Napoleon 'vexed the priests' as prognosticated in line four is described on page 55 with reference to two other quatrains.

Not only was Nostradamus aware that a 'simple soldier' would 'attain to Empire', he may even have had a fair idea of that soldier's name – or so it has been argued on an ingenious interpretation of Century VIII Quatrain 1, which reads:

*PAU, NAY, LORON, will be
more of fire than blood.
To swim in praise the great man will
swim to the confluence.
He will deny the magpies entrance.
Pampon and the Durance will keep
them confined.*

Emperor Napoleon I

Napoleon's coronation at Notre Dame cathedral, 1804

The three names with which line one begins are all those of small and historically insignificant towns in the west of France. However, Nostradamus thought fit to have these names printed in capitals, which is almost always an indication that the words capitalized were used by the seer in a secondary sense – usually one involving an anagram or some other variety of wordplay.

An anagram found in these names by one usually reliable French interpreter of the *Centuries* is NAPAULON ROY – that is, 'King Napoleon'. As the same commentator pointed out over a century ago, in Napoleon's

Napoleon's destiny is foretold

own lifetime the spelling of his unusual name with an 'au' instead of an 'o' was common – and, in any case, Nostradamus may have been hinting

at the way in which the Emperor changed the spelling of his surname from the Corsican 'Buonaparte' to the more Gallic 'Bonaparte'.

That this was perhaps the case is suggested by the fact that in Century I Quatrain 76, one of those strange dual quatrains in which Nostradamus would appear to have been making a prophecy applicable to two different men, he gibed at the 'barbaric' surnames of both Napoleon and Adolf Hitler.

Nostradamus may or may not have known Napoleon's surname – but it seems a certainty that, as described on the next two pages, he knew of the Emperor's final destiny.

THE EAGLE, MILAN AND PAVIA

Napoleon's rising military reputation was thoroughly established by the victorious whirlwind of his Italian campaign of 1796-7. Two of the outstanding episodes in this, the first and in some ways the greatest of Napoleon's military triumphs, were referred to by Nostradamus in Century III Quatrain 37, which reads:

Before the assault a speech [or prayer] is orated,
Milan, deceived by the ambuscade,
is captured by the Eagle,
The ancient walls are breached by artillery,
In fire and blood only a few are granted mercy.

The 'Eagle' of line two who captures Milan is Napoleon – referred to as the Eagle in several of the

Napoleon halts the pillage of Rome

quatrains – but to which of the two Napoleonic captures of Milan (1796 and 1800) does the verse refer?

Clearly the first, for the speech to which the quatrain refers was that all-important one made by the future Emperor to his troops at the beginning of the Italian campaign of 1796-97: 'Soldiers,

you are starving and almost naked . . . I will lead you into the most fertile plains in the world . . . There you will find honour, glory and riches . . . will you be wanting in courage?'

With the occupation of Milan and other nearby cities the soldiers of the French army found the riches that their General had promised them. Alas, their exactions were on such a scale that the citizens of Milan, Pavia and Binasco broke into an open revolt in which they allied themselves with the peasantry of the surrounding countryside. The insurrection was suppressed with the utmost brutality, most notably in Pavia, and, as predicted in the last line of the quatrain, little mercy was given by Napoleon's men to those captured in arms against them.

51

By the time that Napoleon was crowned Emperor of the French (see pages 50–1) he dominated the whole of continental Europe west of the Russian border. Not since the time of the Emperor Charles V had any one man wielded such power in the western world.

Britain was the only dangerous and powerful enemy still threatening him; its fleet still dominated the seas, and its commercial wealth was employed to subsidize any European state bold enough to oppose his seemingly unstoppable armies. Napoleon felt that

Britain was the one remaining major obstacle which must be removed from his path; he had to destroy its naval supremacy and, if possible, invade its territory.

He attempted to do both, and failed – as Nostradamus had accurately predicted would be the case in, respectively, Century I Quatrain 77 and Century VIII Quatrain 53. The former reads:

Between two seas stands a promontory,
A man who will die later by a horse's bridle [or bit],

Neptune unfurls a black sail for his man,
The fleet near Calpre [Gibraltar?] and Rocheval [Cape Roche].

While this verse was obviously intended to prophesy some sort of naval battle in which one of the opposing fleets would have a 'black sail' unfurled for it (i.e. be decisively defeated) it seems, on first reading, to be as obscurely worded as almost any quatrain in the *Centuries*.

However, its second line, 'a man who will die later by a horse's bridle',

The defeat of the combined French and Spanish fleets at Trafalgar, prophesied by Nostradamus

gives a clue which enables the event to be identified with some certainty as the Battle of Trafalgar – the decisive naval battle in which the English destroyed the combined French and Spanish fleets and finally thwarted Napoleon's ambition to be as supreme at sea as he was on land. For while few naval commanders of any historical importance can have been killed by a horse's bridle, Villeneuve, the admiral who commanded the French fleet at Trafalgar, does seem to have died in this curious fashion. Taken prisoner at the battle, he was released and returned to France in the following year – only to be strangled in mysterious circumstances at an inn in Rennes. According to contemporary reports, the assassin had used a horse's bridle as his chosen weapon.

The rest of the quatrain is easily understandable – the 'promontory between two seas' being Gibraltar, which stands between the Atlantic and the Mediterranean.

Napoleon's failure to invade England and the way in which he used his untested army of invasion after he withdrew it from its lines near Boulogne some two months before his navy was smashed at Trafalgar was predicted by Nostradamus in Century VIII Quatrain 53, which reads:

Within Bolongne [Boulogne] *he will want to wash away his faults,*
He cannot do so at the Temple of the Sun,
He will haste away to do great things,
In the hierarchy he was never equalled.

The 'faults' which Napoleon wished to wash away were not moral failings; they were his successive misjudgements

Napoleon retreats from Russia

of the importance of Britain's naval supremacy and economic strength which had largely negated his military successes ever since his Egyptian campaign of 1798. But what was the 'Temple of the Sun' in which Nostradamus said that Napoleon would, metaphorically speaking, be unable to wash away his faults?

The phrase simply meant Britain, for by employing the words 'Temple of the Sun' the seer was making two of the classical allusions of which he was so fond. First, he was referring to the writings of a pre-Christian Greek geographer who described what was almost certainly Stonehenge as a temple of the sun god Apollo; secondly, he was alluding to a traditionally held belief that Westminster Abbey, where English monarchs have been crowned since Norman times, was built on the site of a Romano-British sun temple.

After Napoleon abandoned his invasion barges on the Channel coast in

the summer of 1804 he marched his army eastwards, occupying Vienna and smashing the combined Austrian and Russian armies at Austerlitz. In other words, he hastened away from Boulogne to do 'great things' – just as Nostradamus had foretold. But Britain continued to forge against him coalitions of which it was the paymaster.

After his invasion of Russia ended in disaster and he was defeated at the Battle of Leipzig Napoleon was forced to abdicate as Emperor in 1814. He was exiled to the mini-state of Elba, of which he was given sovereignty. Inevitably the tiny island was too small for him; he escaped and returned to France, where he was proclaimed Emperor. However, after a rule of only 100 days he was defeated by the British and Prussians at Waterloo and exiled to the windswept island of St Helena in the south Atlantic Ocean, where he died in 1821.

These latter events seem to have been the subjects of more than one of Nostradamus's visions, for they are described, under the usual veils of allegory and symbol, in several quatrains. For instance, both Century II Quatrain 66 and Century X Quatrain 25 describe in symbolized yet easily interpreted outline some events of the brief restoration of the Napoleonic Empire, and Century I Quatrains 23 and 38 were both prophetic of the Battle of Waterloo. The last two quatrains were written in the symbolic quasi-heraldic terminology so beloved of the seer – but both are meaningful and the first gave a clear prediction that the heraldic Leopard of England would triumph over the Eagles of Napoleon's Grand Army.

53

In the *Centuries* there are to be found numerous references to the papacy and to individual popes. It would seem that, as might have been expected of a man of his times – when the Pope was a temporal as well as a spiritual ruler, generally considered by western Christians to be the most important man in the world – Nostradamus sought many visions pertaining to the papacy and particular persons destined to occupy the 'Throne of Peter'.

Some of the 'papal quatrains' relate to events that have not as yet taken place, and it is to be presumed that in these either Nostradamus prophesied falsely or, more likely, that they will take place at some time in the future – probably the very near future (see pages 82–3). Others are so specific and fit the facts of history so neatly that one can take it as reasonably certain that they are notable examples of Nostradamian predictive hits – for instance, the prognostication of the circumstances in which that rarest of post-medieval ecclesiastical creatures, an exiled pope, would meet his end (see panel opposite).

Another very specific Nostradamian prediction concerning the papacy is to be found in Century V Quatrain 29, which reads:

Liberty will not be recovered,
It will be occupied by a [man who is]
black, proud, fierce and evil,
When the matter of the Pope is opened
By Hister, the Republic of Venice will
be vexed.

Taking the last line of this verse in its literal sense, it would appear that the prediction must relate to the 18th century or earlier, for the patrician Venetian Republic ceased to exist as an independent state as a consequence of the conquests made by the armies of revolutionary France. However, it has long been the consensus of opinion among Nostradamian interpreters

54

St Peter's in Rome – the seat of papal power, of pivotal importance to Nostradamus

that in this quatrain the seer was using the phrase 'Republic of Venice' in a semi-allegorical fashion, implying by it something like 'popular liberties in the Italian peninsula and the Pope's freedom of action'.

If this interpretation is accepted – and the arguments for it are varied and ingenious – its relevance seems to be to the period 1939-45 and the predicted 'Hister' is none other than Adolf Hitler. Under this interpretation, the unrecovered liberty of line one had a double meaning for Nostradamus. On the one hand it was the political freedom of the Italian people which had been lost as a result of the seizure of power by Mussolini – who was the black [shirted] evil man of line two. On the other, it was the temporal freedom of the popes which had been lost in 1870, when Rome was forcibly incorporated into the Kingdom of Italy; it was not really regained as a consequence of the concordat between Mussolini and the Vatican, and the burdens inflicted upon the papacy as a consequence of its loss of temporal power were made even more onerous by the interference of Hitler in the affairs of both Italy and the Vatican.

All very ingenious, but in the opinion of the present writer it may be just too ingenious an interpretation of prophecy – one of those occasions in which legitimate speculation has crossed the boundaries of common sense. It has to be admitted, however, that several quatrains in the *Centuries* mention 'Hister', and that what is said of him seems generally compatible with events in the life of Adolf Hitler.

THE VEXED PRIESTS

As was said on page 50, in the fourth line of Century VIII Quatrain 57 Nostradamus prophesied that Napoleon Bonaparte would 'vex the priests as water soaks a sponge'.

The seer's prophecy was accurate, for in one way or another Napoleon vexed a very large number of the Catholic clergy, both before and after he became Emperor. They included not only humble parish priests, but also bishops (and at least one former bishop, the aristocratic Talleyrand), cardinals and two popes, Pius VI and Pius VII.

As one of the consequences of the French successes that followed upon Napoleon's Italian triumphs (see page 51), Pope Pius VI was taken to France as a prisoner of the French and subsequently died at Valence, vomiting and spitting blood, in the late summer of 1799. Nostradamus may have

The Pope blesses the ground

rather vaguely prophesied this death on foreign soil in the last line of Century I Quatrain 37, which mentions 'Pope and . . . sepulchre both in foreign lands'. A much more specific prediction was given in Century II Quatrain 97, which reads:

Roman Pontiff, beware of approaching
The city with two rivers.
You will spit your blood in that place,
You and yours, when the roses
bloom.

The successor of the pope who died spitting blood when the roses of both summer and the Revolution were in full bloom was Pope Pius VII, who entered into a concordat with France in 1814 but was, nevertheless, held captive by Napoleon for almost four years. Nostradamus allusively predicted this captivity in both line three of Century I Quatrain 4 – 'At this time the barque of the Papacy will be lost' – and in the first two lines of Century V Quatrain 15, which read as follows:

While travelling [literally 'navigating' or 'sailing'] *the Great Pontiff will be captured, The efforts of the troubled clergy fail . . .*

55

'The populace dying through evil' during the siege of Paris in 1870

Nostradamus is perhaps the best-known prophet of the future in the world – certainly the Western world – but he was not always correct in every detail of his predictions. Thus, for instance, his prophecy of the murder of the Guise brothers in Century III Quatrain 51 (see page 21) was right in almost every particular save those relating to the last line.

In this line, which reads 'Angers, Troyes and Langres will do them a disservice', he was clearly predicting that the cities mentioned would be hostile to the cause with which the Guise brothers were associated – the supremacy of the Catholic faith in France. In reality none of those who governed these places displayed any notable sympathy for the Protestant cause in the French Wars of Religion – one of them stayed more or less neutral and the other two supported the Catholic League.

There are several such largely, but not entirely, correct predictions relating to events that took place in the 19th century. These may be examples of Nostradamian errors – but the present writer suspects that in at least some of them the errors have arisen from mistaken interpretations rather than from psychic clouds obscuring Nostradamus's visions of the future.

One outstanding example of a probably misinterpreted prophecy is provided by Century X Quatrain 8. The first two lines of this have been applied to the baptism of the son of Napoleon III in the summer of 1856 and its third line to Napoleon III's wife, the Empress Eugenie; the fourth line of the verse has been assumed either to have not been fulfilled at all or to be so obscure in meaning that no one can appreciate just how it has been fulfilled. The quatrain reads:

With first finger and thumb he will sprinkle the forehead,
The Count of Senegalia to his own [god]son,
Venus through several in short order,
In a week three are mortally wounded.

There is no difficulty at all in arriving at a Napoleonic interpretation of the first two lines – clearly a baptism was being described at which a 'Count of Senegalia' would be the foremost godfather of the child. As the godfather of Napoleon III's son was Pio Nono (Pope Pius IX), who was the son of Count Mastoi Feretti of Senigallia, the quatrain fits well enough. However, there seems to be no good reason to assume that the quatrain is predictively associated in any fashion whatsoever

Napoloeon III, subject of many quatrains

with either Napoleon III or his family. Pope Pius IX stood as godfather to a great many children both before and after his elevation to the 'Throne of Peter' and the verse's prophetic significance may be relevant to the lives of individuals whom history has forgotten.

The Napoleonic misinterpretation (if misinterpretation it be) of Century X Quatrain 8 arose as a result of the overeagerness of 19th-century French students of the prophecies of Nostradamus to interpret obscure quatrains to fit events with which they were

familiar or which they were hoping would happen in their own lifetimes – for example, a Bourbon Restoration after the fall of the Second Empire and the proclamation of the Third Republic (1870).

Not all the 19th-century applications of Nostradamian predictions to incidents in the life of Napoleon III have been based on such dubious reasoning as that of Century X Quatrain 8. Century IV Quatrain 100 and Century V Quatrain 32 both seem to have been predictive of the Franco-Prussian War which resulted in the abdication of Napoleon III, the end of his empire, the proclamation of the Third Republic and a bitter internecine struggle between its army and the forces of the Paris Commune.

The former quatrain is especially applicable to these events. It reads:

Fire will fall from the sky on the royal building
When the fire of Mars is weakened:
For seven months a mighty war, the populace dying through evil,
Rouen and Evreux will not fail the King.

During the 1870 siege of Paris, when the seven-month-long Franco-Prussian war was drawing towards its close ('the fire of Mars . . . weakened') that 'royal building' the Tuileries (see page 47) was destroyed by heavy, and high-elevation, artillery fire. During the siege the evil of famine and resulting disease killed even more Parisians than did the military activities of the Prussians. And after the proclamation Rouen, Evreux and other cities of Normandy did not 'fail the King', for they were centres of legitimism, the

cause of those who wanted the Second Empire to give way to a Bourbon, not a Republican, restoration.

In the case of this particular 19th-century interpretation there seems to have been no ingenious deformation of the meaning of the relevant quatrain. However, it has to be borne in mind that in every century, not just the last, there has been an understandable and almost inevitable tendency among commentators on the *Centuries* of Nostradamus to unconsciously tailor

Pope Pius IX, godfather to Napoleon's son

quatrains to fit recent events. Those who interpret Nostradamus at the present day cannot entirely escape following the same pattern, however hard they may try to do so.

Readers of some of the pages that follow (particularly pages 68-71) should, therefore, always be conscious of the possibility that sometimes the present writer may have fallen into the same trap as did the 19th-century commentator who first applied Century X Quatrain 8 to the baptism of the son of Napoleon III.

57

would go to war with France and Britain over Poland?'

It is likely that Goebbels already knew something of this prediction, for it would seem that four different members of the Nazi Party had already sent him copies of the book that had so excited his wife. Nevertheless, he looked at the passage to which she had drawn his attention and was immediately struck by its potential value as propaganda, for it did seem to accurately foretell both the date and the cause of the war that had broken out some three months or so previously. Perhaps, he thought, the author of the book knew of other prophecies which might serve to convince the enemies of the Reich of the inevitability of a German victory.

The book was entitled *Mysterien von Sonne und Seele* (Mysteries of the Sun and Spirit). It had been written by a certain Doktor H. H. Kritzinger, and had been published in 1922, 17 years before the outbreak of war. The prediction which so excited Magda Goebbels and the four other Nazis who had drawn her husband's attention to it was based upon a particular, and extremely ingenious, interpretation of Century III Quatrain 57. This interpretation was not originated by Doktor Kritzinger – indeed, some elements of this particular piece of prophetic exegesis can be dated back to at least 1715, when an English interpreter of Nostradamus, a man who wrote under the pseudonym of 'D. D.', turned his attention to this quatrain, which reads:

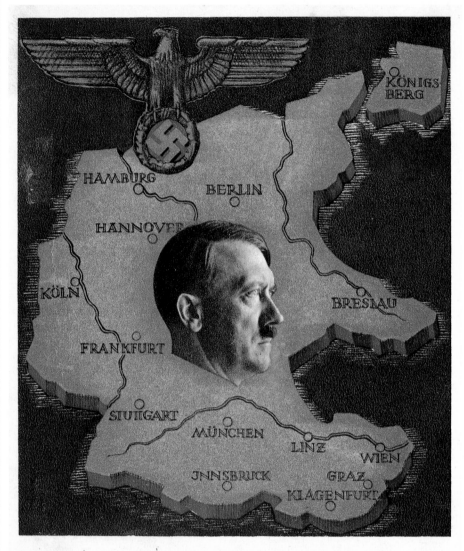

Nostradamus predicted Hitler's incorporation of neighbouring countries into a Greater Germany

One evening in the winter of 1939–40, during the period of military inactivity preceding the German blitzkrieg that resulted in the fall of France, Magda Goebbels, wife of Hitler's brilliant but totally amoral Minister of Propaganda and Enlightenment, was reading in bed. Suddenly she called out to her husband in great excitement, 'Did you know that over 400 years ago it was prophesied that in 1939 Germany

*Seven times you will see the British
nation change,
Tinged with blood for two hundred and
ninety years:
Not at all free through German
support,
Aries fears for his 'pole' Bastarnien.*

D. D. gave it as his opinion that the phrase 'tinged with blood for two hundred and ninety years' referred to a period beginning with the shedding of the Blood Royal by the execution of King Charles I in 1649. This gave D. D. the date 1939 as the year of some notable event in British history. The first line of the quatrain was interpreted by D. D. as seven dynastic or quasi-dynastic changes – such as, for instance, the Restoration of the Stuart monarchy in 1660.

Between 1715 and 1921 other students of Nostradamus extended D. D.'s theories. The last of these, a Herr Loog, combined all these interpretations into

Magda Goebbels, wife of Hitler's propaganda chief

one and added to them his own explanation of the last line of the quatrain, 'Aries fears for his "pole" Bastarnien'. This he took to mean 'France doubts (or fears for) her subordinate ally, the land of the Bastarnae (Poland)'.

Why should Herr Loog have taken Aries to mean France? Was he just making a wild guess? No, he was not – for as long ago as the 17th century Théophile de Garencières had written in relation to this particular quatrain

that Aries signified France because 'the sign of Aries doth govern France'.

Loog followed earlier commentators in interpreting 1939 as the year to be 'tinged with blood' and, on this basis, forecast for it war involving Poland, France, Germany, and Britain – the prediction which was inserted by Doktor Kritzinger into his book.

Was this fulfilled prediction of Nostradamus just a lucky hit, as sceptics have claimed? To this question the unbiased observer can only reply that if the prediction that seems to have been fulfilled by Hitler's invasion of Poland and the outbreak of World War II in September 1939 was just a lucky hit, then it has to be admitted that the seer had an extraordinary capacity for making lucky hits. For, as readers of this book will appreciate, there are numerous examples of the same sort of fulfilled predictions to be found in the *Centuries* and other writings of Nostradamus.

59

The conquering German army marches through the streets of Warsaw in 1939, the year Nostradamus foresaw as 'tinged with blood'

Josef Goebbels recognized the potential propaganda value of Nostradamian predictions

As was pointed out on page 44, Nostradamus sometimes wrote prophetic verses of a double nature – that is, predictions which, without being exceptionally vague, do seem to fit more than one person or event. The sceptic's explanation for the aptness of such quatrains is that the seer never made a genuinely fulfilled prophecy, that interpreters have simply twisted the meanings of the components of the *Centuries* to fit their own preconceived ideas, and that the existence of quatrains with more than one supposed meaning does no more than illustrate the fact that two or more Nostradamian commentators have arrived at different interpretations.

It is an ingenious and, in some ways, a persuasive argument – but it is based on the premise that none of Nostradamus's predictions were ever genuinely fulfilled. To the present writer

and many others this position seems quite untenable in view of various prognostications which were explicitly or implicitly dated by the seer (see pages 34 and 48 for example). A more likely explanation for the double-meaning quatrains is that in vision Nostradamus discerned two separate individuals whose lives were separated in time, who may well have been very different from one another in character, but who had certain things in common that enabled him to write a prophetic verse that pertained to both.

A good example of such an ingeniously worded double prediction is provided by Century I Quatrain 76, which seems to apply to both Napoleon Bonaparte (see page 51) and the equally – to any German of the 1920s not born on the borderlands of Slavdom – 'barbarically named' Hitler. The meaning of this quatrain is apparent. It reads:

This man will be called by a barbaric name
Which the three sisters will have received,
He will speak to a great people in words and actions,
He will have fame and renown beyond any other man [of his time].

It seems likely, however, that some quatrains that have been applied to more than one person have been misinterpreted by over-credulous interpreters. One such is Century II Quatrain 70, applied to Napoleon by some, but very probably prophetic of the character and death of Heinrich Himmler, leader of Hitler's SS, who ended his life while talking – just as did the 'human monster' in the verse in question, which reads:

The dart from heaven will make its journey,
Death while speaking, a great execution;
The stone in the tree, a proud race abased,
Talk of a human monster, purge and expiation.

Another quatrain which has been applied to Napoleon but seems far more apposite in the context of Nazism is Century III Quatrain 35, which reads:

In the farthest depths of Western Europe,
A child will be born of a poor people,
Who by his speeches will seduce great numbers,
His reputation will grow even greater in the eastern domain.

This seems to be another reference to Adolf Hitler, for his parents were a good deal poorer than those of Napoleon, he was born on the eastern boundaries of western Europe, his rise to power came about as a consequence of his oratory 'seducing many', and his drive for Lebensraum was primarily directed towards the 'eastern domain' of the Soviet Union.

Of the numerous quatrains that have been applied to the Nazis over the last 50 years or so, some seem dubious in the extreme – but it is hard to doubt many of them. For instance, Century IX Quatrain 90 accurately predicts the disastrous effects upon Hungary of that country's ruler, Admiral Horthy, accepting the 'help' offered by Hitler:

A captain of Greater Germany
[i.e. Hitler]
Will deliver counterfeit help,
A King of Kings to support Hungary,
His war will cause great bloodshed.

According to the Nazis, the writings of Nostradamus predicted a German victory

Similarly, Century V Quatrain 29 obviously applies to Hitler, Mussolini and the Papacy (see page 55), Century V Quatrain 51 to the activities of the two dictators at the time of the Spanish Civil War, and Century VI Quatrain 51 to the unsuccessful attempt that was made upon Hitler's life in November 1939.

The conquests made by Hitler the following spring also seem to have been perceived by Nostradamus who, in Century V Quatrain 94, wrote:

He [presumably Hitler] *will transform into Greater Germany, Brabant, Flanders, Ghent, Bruges and Boulogne . . .*

61

THE SIGN OF THE SWASTIKA

The swastika, or *hakenkreuz* (literally, 'hooked cross'), is now forever associated in the minds of most of us with the Nazis and the terrible crimes that they committed in World War II. Originally, however, the symbol had a purely spiritual significance in both the eastern and western hemispheres of our planet; indeed, at the present day the swastika symbol is still to be found in many Hindu temples.

Prior to the outbreak of World War I, the swastika was regarded in

Germany as a symbol of the god Thor (or Thunor) and for this reason the Freikorps – the armed

groups who defended Germany after the war – adopted it. In the early 1920s Hitler reversed the position of the arms of the swastika and made it the badge of his movement.

Nostradamus seems to have predicted the future notoriety of both the swastika and the Nazi leader in Century VI Quatrain 49, which reads:

The great Priest of the Party of Mars [i.e. Hitler]
Who will subjugate the Danube,
The cross harried by the crook . . .

Spanish Fascists under General Franco (centre) survived the defeat of Hitler – the allies' 'uncertain victory'

Describing the Nazi leader as a 'bird of prey flying on the left', Nostradamus wrote prophetically of European perceptions of Adolf Hitler in the period 1933-39 in Century I Quatrain 34, which reads:

The bird of prey flying to the left
Makes [warlike] preparations before
combating the French:
Some will regard him as good, some as
evil, some as ambiguous,
The weaker party will regard him as a
good augury.

The first line's description of Hitler as 'flying to the left' was a typical piece of Nostradamian wordplay. His primary reference was to the fact that the word 'sinister' is derived from the Latin word for left; his secondary one

was that Hitler, as he explained in his book *Mein Kampf*, deliberately modelled his propaganda methods on those used by Marxists and that many members of his storm troops, the SA, had been recruited from the ranks of former communists.

The second line of the quatrain requires little clarification – Hitler's war preparations against France were such that in the summer of 1940 hundreds of thousands of refugees were to jam that country's roads (see panel opposite) – but the third does need some explanation .

To us, with all the advantages of hindsight, it seems obvious that Hitler was a megalomaniac warmonger with a desire to dominate the world and to destroy any individuals or peoples who

either stood directly in his way or were considered by him to be racially undesirable. In the 1930s, however, none of this was quite so apparent. On the right, Soviet Communism was seen as the major threat to European stability and peace and it was generally thought that the Nazis had 'saved Germany from Bolshevism'. And on both the liberal left and the right it was quite widely believed that for all his firebreathing oratory Hitler did not really desire war, but that he was prepared to use the threat of it in order to remedy the injustices that Germany had suffered under the provisions of the 1919 Treaty of Versailles.

So attitudes towards the Führer were, as Nostradamus had predicted, very mixed. Some, like British Liberal leader

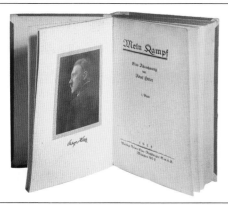
Hitler's own work of prophecy – Mein Kampf

Lloyd George, for a time regarded him with admiration; others discerned his evil nature at an early stage of his career; others were unsure. The 'weaker party' of the quatrain's fourth line who the seer foretold would regard the coming to power of Hitler as a 'good augury' was, rather surprisingly, the KPD, the German Communist Party, whose Stalinist leaders argued that a phase of Nazi rule would precede the German proletarian revolution.

There are several quatrains in the *Centuries* referring to somebody or something named 'Hister', almost all of which bear the double predictive meanings in which Nostradamus, so to speak, specialized; that is to say they all refer to both the river Ister, a classical name for the Danube, and to Adolf Hitler. One of them is Century II Quatrain 24. This would appear to relate to both the imprisonment of Hungary's leader, Admiral Horthy, by 'Hister' in its Hitlerian sense and to the eventual defeat of the Wehrmacht in Hungary and its panic-stricken retreat across the 'Hister' in its Danubian sense. It reads:

Beasts mad with hunger will swim
across the rivers,
The most part of the battlefield will be
against Hister.
In an iron cage the leader will be
dragged [by him?],
When the child of Germany follows
no law.

Nostradamus prophesied Hitler's defeats in western Europe as well as those on the Danube and Century II Quatrain 16 is clearly relevant to the 'new tyranny' of Italian fascists and their German patrons, the Allied invasion of Sicily in 1943, and the intense air and naval bombardment ('great noise and fire in the heavens') which preceded it. The quatrain reads:

In Naples, Palermo, Syracuse and
throughout Sicily
New tyrants [rule], great noise and fire
in the heavens,
A force from London, Ghent, Brussels
and Suse,
A great slaughter, then triumph
and festivities.

The final line was a foretelling of Allied victory – but elsewhere, in Century I Quatrain 31, the seer made it apparent that he knew that this victory would be to some extent a hollow one for the Allies, with Spanish fascism still in power, new threats from the Soviet Union, and an awareness by the 'three great ones, the Eagle [the USA], the Cock [France] . . . the Lion [Britain]' that they had enjoyed at best 'an uncertain victory'.

63

THE FEAST OF THE CARRION

The flight of the unhappy French refugees who, bombed by Stukas and raked by fire from fighter aircraft, made their way along the roads leading south as the Wehrmacht advanced upon Paris in the early summer of 1940 was predicted by Nostradamus in Century III Quatrain 7, which reads:

The refugees [literally, fugitives],
fire from the sky on their weapons,
The next battle will be that of the
carrion crows,

St Lo, witness to 'fire from the sky'

They [the refugees] call on earth
and heaven for relief
When the warriors draw near
the walls.

The 'fire from the sky' was that which came from Luftwaffe aeroplanes and was so effective that men, women and children were killed and – as the seer had foretold – carrion crows battled with one another for their share of the human flesh upon which they were able to feast.

Nostradamus seems to have had visions of aerial combat, of 'noise, shouts, battles seen in the heavens'

For a period of more than 400 years students of prophecy and the predictive arts have brooded upon the tortuous and often obscure verses which collectively make up the *Centuries* of Nostradamus. Some of them, such as the late James Laver, have merely wanted to discover examples of fulfilled prophecy; others have also wanted to interpret the quatrains with the object of finding out what the future holds in store both for them and for their descendants. Still others have studied the *Centuries* with quite a different end in view: they wish, for reasons which can only be surmised, to discredit prophecies in general and those of Nostradamus in particular.

Most of these professional sceptics have rejected all examples of fulfilled Nostradamian predictions – even including those in which specific dates were given by the seer – as either coincidental or as the product of what could be termed 'delusional hindsight', by which is meant the ingenious twisting of the content and import of particular quatrains in order to make them fit a past event. There is no doubt at all that this has sometimes been done, both by over-enthusiastic Nostradamians and by those wanting to carry out an amusing hoax.

Thus, for instance, one American commentator (who it is to be hoped was a hoaxer rather than a man who wished to contribute towards a serious commentary upon the *Centuries*) went to considerable trouble to reinterpret a quatrain usually held to be a fairly clear prediction of the 18th-century invention of balloon flight by the Montgolfier brothers. According to him, the quatrain in question had been misunderstood; it was in reality a revelation of the result of a US Open golf championship that took place in the 1920s (see page 77).

Amusing as it is that such a ludicrous interpretation can be made, it is usually by no means easy to twist the quatrains of the *Centuries* to a particular purpose. In relation to this it is interesting to note a circumstance connected with the German army's advance into France in the early part of the summer of 1940.

The 'black propaganda' section of either the Wehrmacht or the Propaganda Ministry was anxious to find a Nostradamus quatrain of which the meaning could be perverted in order that it could be used to encourage French civilian refugees to take to, and thus block, the roads leading towards the south-west of France. The idea was that leaflets containing a suitably interpreted quatrain should be dropped by the Luftwaffe over areas in which there were known to be refugee concentrations.

However, in spite of the 'black propaganda' experts calling on the assistance of various Nostradamian experts – at least one of whom, Karl Krafft, was a committed Nazi – they totally failed to find a quatrain that would suit their purpose. There was, of course, the quatrain described in the panel on page 63, but as it suggested that those who took to the roads might well end up being eaten by birds of prey it hardly suited German intentions. Instead, the Nazis were forced to rely on dropping crude

Is this the 'pig-like half-man' of the seer's vision?

forgeries from the air. These were attributed to Nostradamus, but they in no way resembled genuine quatrains in either style or content.

It is likely that Nostradamus would not have been particularly surprised if he had known that almost 400 years after his death verses attributed to him were destined to be dropped from the air from flying machines – for, although he lived in an age in which

the fastest mode of transportation was a galloping horse, he seems to have experienced visions of aerial combat. One such vision would appear to be described in Century I Quatrain 64, which reads:

*At night they will think that they have
seen the sun,
When they see the pig-like half-man,
Noise, shouts, battles seen in
the heavens:
Brute beasts will be heard speaking.*

This suggests a description of an air battle such as might have taken place at any time between the beginning of World War I and the Gulf War of 1991. If such an interpretation is to be accepted, the sun at night would be the glare of exploding anti-aircraft shells or missiles, the 'pig-like half-man' would be a pilot or navigator wearing flying helmet and oxygen mask, these in appearance vaguely resembling a porcine snout. And the 'brute beasts' heard speaking would be the 'half-men', i.e. the airmen, communicating by radio with their bases and one another.

MODERN TECHNOLOGY

Many of the quatrains which seemed to be no more than a string of incomprehensible phrases to those who read them in the 1690s, the 1790s and the 1890s appear to have a fairly clear meaning to those of us who attempt to interpret them in the 1990s. Much of the Nostradamian verse which in, say, the 1890s seemed to be meaninglessly symbolic,

vaguely mystical stuff now makes sense as a record of a vision interpreted by a man living in the 16th century – a man who was trying to describe a technology of which he knew nothing.

Century I Quatrain 64 (see this page) provides an excellent example of such a Nostradamian attempt at a description of a technology of a future century.

65

THE ENERGY OF THE ATOM

If we accept that, as was explained on page 65, Nostradamus saw visions of modern aerial combat and found the task of describing it so difficult that he was forced to use terms such as 'pig-like men', we can appreciate that if he had clairvoyant glimpses of even more recent technologies he would have found it even more of an effort to convey in words the nature of what he had seen.

Yet there are a number of quatrains in the *Centuries* in which it seems likely that the prophet was attempting to describe both atomic explosions and space flight.

For instance, Century II Quatrain 6 looks as though it could well have been a prediction of the events that brought about the Japanese surrender in August 1945 – the dropping of atomic bombs upon the cities of Hiroshima and Nagasaki. This quatrain reads:

*Near the harbour and in two cities
Will be two scourges never previously witnessed.
Hunger and plague, those thrown down by the weapon [literally 'iron']
Will cry to Immortal God for succour.*

It is possible, of course, that in this verse the seer was prognosticating twin disasters that still lie in our future – but it has to be admitted that they very aptly fit the events of August 1945. Both cities are contiguous to harbours; their inhabitants were subjected to 'scourges never previously witnessed' – that is, the deliberate release of atomic energy in order to kill human beings; and many of those who survived the immediate effects of the bombs suffered never previously witnessed types of plague and hunger, the plague being radiation sickness and the hunger a consequence of one

A Pershing missile – 'the machine of flying fire'?

of its symptoms – continuous vomiting of such severity that the body of the victim is incapable of absorbing any nourishment.

Nostradamus also seems to have been aware of the possibilities of space travel and to have done his best to describe it. In the first two lines of Century VI Quatrain 34 he probably referred to the military uses of space vehicles when he wrote of 'the machine of flying fire' and the last two lines of Century VI Quatrain 5 are completely meaningless except in the context of a manned space station. They read:

*Samarobin one hundred leagues from the hemisphere [i.e. the earth],
They will live without law, exempt from politics.*

The word 'politics' was probably used here in its primary 16th-century senses – roughly speaking, moderation, balance, reasoned calculation – so Nostradamus was predicting that a group of people would live lawlessly and immoderately one hundred leagues above the earth's surface in some structure he termed 'Samarobin'.

The bombed city of Hiroshima – victim of Nostradamus's 'scourge never previously witnessed'

It seems likely that Nostradamus discerned the nature of some modern epidemics as well as 20th-century technology, for the first three lines of Century IX Quatrain 55 can reasonably be interpreted as a double prediction of the influenza epidemic that swept Europe in 1917-18 (and resulted in even more deaths than World War I itself) and of the current epidemic of AIDS. The relevant lines of this quatrain read:

*The dreadful war which is prepared in
the west,
The following year the pestilence
will come,
So horrible that neither young nor old
[will survive].*

Both of these epidemics were caused by mutated viruses; the influenza outbreak followed upon the slaughters of the Western front in World War I, and the AIDS epidemic, although its

Nostradamus foretold of a time when men would live above the earth's surface

causative virus may have been in existence for centuries, did not really get into its terrible stride until the time when Iraq invaded Iran from the

west and began a war that has been described as more productive of casualties than anything since the great infantry advances of World War I.

67

COMPUTER VIRUSES?

As was explained on pages 46–7 in relation to a quatrain referring to a 'mitred husband', on occasion old, ingenious, but improbable interpretations of a Nostradamian prediction have to be abandoned in the clarifying light of actual historical events.

Another such old interpretation is that of the first two lines of Century I Quatrain 22, which read:

*A thing existing without
any senses
Will cause its own death to happen
through artifice . . .*

Since 1672, when Théophile de Garencières commented on these lines, some Nostradamians have tried to apply them to an event that took place in 1613 – the surgical removal of a petrified embryo from the womb of a woman named Colomba Chantry.

To some, this interpretation has always appeared unlikely – apart from it being a somewhat insignificant event to be the subject of prophecy it has been hard to understand how the embryo could be considered to have caused 'its own death to happen through

artifice'. An up-to-date alternative suggestion is that the thing (or things) which paradoxically exists, is capable of causing its own demise and yet has no senses is a modern computer. A 'senseless savant' of this sort can destroy itself as a result of the artifice being loaded with a program carrying a hidden virus that instructs the machine to progressively eradicate its own memory.

Fantastic? Perhaps – but no more so than some of the accurate predictions that are made elsewhere in the *Centuries*.

Twenty years ago, many Soviet-ologists – supposed experts on the economic, social and political affairs of the Soviet Union and the bloc of allegedly socialist countries which it led – were gloomily or joyfully (depending upon their political orientation) forecasting the decline of the market economies of western capitalism and the 'inevitable' triumph of the socialist bloc. Even five years ago, when the structure of Soviet bureaucracy was already crumbling, there were not only those who talked ceaselessly of 'coming to terms with the Soviet actuality' but some who still clung to the opinion that in some mysterious fashion the Soviet tyranny was morally superior to modern capitalism.

Nostradamus was wiser than all the self-appointed experts. More than four centuries before they were born he was prophesying not only the Russian Bolshevik triumph of 1917 and the persecution of the Orthodox Church which was its consequence, but the eventual downfall of both the Berlin Wall and the empire which had built it.

He predicted the first two of these events in Century VIII Quatrain 80, which reads:

The blood of the innocents, of widow and virgin.
So many evils committed by the Great Red,
Holy icons placed over burning candles,
Terrified by fright every one will be afraid to move.

This was an excellent description, not only of what actually happened during

Karl Marx, founder of communism

the era of Lenin and Stalin but also of the psychological state of fearful immobility that it induced among Russia's Christians.

The eventual downfall of communism in Russia and the other Soviet Republics was predicted in Century III Quatrain 95, which reads:

The Moorish law [way of life] will be seen to fail,
Followed by another that is more attractive:
The Boristhenes will be the first to give way
To another more pleasing [way of life] as a consequence of gifts and tongues.

The verse as a whole made very little sense until quite recently, although some years ago at least one commentator on the quatrain suggested that it prophesied the downfall of Russia as a Marxist state. His interpretation was

based on a piece of Nostradamian wordplay to be discerned in the first line – an ingenious use of the phrase 'Moorish law' to signify something not immediately apparent from its literal meaning. Karl Marx, the theoretician whose writings inspired Lenin, Trotsky, Bukharin and the other leaders of the Russian Revolution, had a nickname which was used only by his family and by such close associates as Friedrich Engels. It was 'the Moor' – and by his use of the term 'the Moorish law' Nostradamus meant 'a society based on the teachings of Karl Marx'.

'The Boristhenes will be the first to give way to another more pleasing [way of life] as a consequence of gifts and tongues,' said Nostradamus in his third and fourth lines. Boristhenes was the classical name for the Dnieper, Russia's great river, while in all probability the phrase 'gifts and tongues' referred to Western influences, the former being smuggled consumer goods, the latter the effect of the siren voices of capitalism heard on Radio Free Europe and other Western radio stations. The quatrain can now be paraphrased:

Lenin inspired the Bolshevik revolution

The Marxist way of life will be seen
to fail
And will be succeeded by one that is
more pleasing.
Russia will be the first [i.e. before
China] to abandon communism
As a consequence of outside influences
upon it.

While, in the last analysis, all these outside influences emanated from the Western world, some of them made their way into Russia as a consequence of the events witnessed by soldiers of the Red Army at the time of the fall of the Berlin Wall – yet another largely unexpected happening which had been foretold by Nostradamus, for he appears to have predicted it in Century V Quatrain 81, which reads:

The Royal bird over the city of the sun,
Will give its nightly augury
[prophecy] for seven months,
Thunder and lightning, the Eastern
wall will fall,
In seven days the enemy directly at
the gates.

The 'Royal bird' is the eagle, a symbol of the old monarchy of Prussia whose capital was Berlin, thought to have been termed 'city of the sun' by the seer for two reasons – the more likely one being that according to at least one 16th-century astrologer, Brandenburg – the state that evolved into Prussia – was 'ruled' by Leo, the sun's own sign.

The events that immediately precipitated the downfall of both the East German state and the wall that it had built with the object of keeping its citizens at home had been preceded

Nostradamus predicted that the Russians would turn away from communism

by roughly seven months of steadily increasing civil unrest; all in all, the quatrain fits in very neatly with what actually happened and can fairly be considered to rank as yet another of Nostradamus's predictive successes.

It is only right to say, however, that in the past the verse in question has been applied to at least two other events – namely the defeats suffered by France in 1870 and 1940. As against this it has to be admitted that as long ago as 1972, almost 20 years before the Wall came down, the Nostradamian commentator Erika Cheetham published her opinion that the quatrain was likely to refer to that possible and much hoped-for event.

69

A submarine-launched Trident missile – modern warfare as foreseen by Nostradamus

In the last line 'the walls' would appear to mean, in the terminology of our own era, 'static defences' – fortified walls were the only important form of stationary defence in the 16th century – and 'its enemies' clearly refer to armed forces trying to break through those defences.

Once again, we have a quatrain that would have been utterly obscure in meaning to someone who read it in, say, the 1840s or even the 1940s. With its wall-threatening fish travelling over land and sea it could be interpreted only by straining its supposed symbolism in a manner hardly convincing to any but the most enthusiastic Nostradamus devotee. In the 1990s, however, it seems probable that, like the 'pig-like half-man', it pertains to the weapon systems of advanced military technology. It could be a reference to an atomic missile being launched from a submarine against an enemy, an event that has not yet taken place. However, to the present writer it sounds much more like a description of the 1991 Gulf War as clairvoyantly seen by a Renaissance psychic and/or practitioner of ceremonial divination (see page 138 and pages 140–1).

If so, the fish travelling over land and sea would be one of the ship-launched Cruise missiles that smashed the command structure of the Iraqi military machine and the supply system which kept it in operation. The 'great wave' that threw it up upon the land would be the sustained roar of the missile's rocket motor, a sound so

As was pointed out earlier, Nostradamus sometimes wrote predictive verses which, until very recently, were seemingly jumbles of confused nonsense but which now make sense in terms of the technology of modern warfare.

A 'nonsense' prophecy of this sort is provided by Century I Quatrain 29, which is now thought likely to refer either to some future nuclear war which will soon be upon us or, more probably and more to be hoped, the Gulf War fought against Iraq and that country's occupation of Kuwait. The quatrain reads:

When the [travelling] earthly and watery fish
Is thrown upon the shore by a great wave,
Its strange form wild and horrifying,
From the sea its enemies soon reach the walls.

unlike any noise known to a man of the 16th century that it would probably be suggestive to him of the sound of large waves breaking upon the shore in a storm.

Finally, the 'enemy from the sea' which was enabled to smash the 'walls' – defensive lines constructed by Iraq's soldiers – as a consequence of the havoc wreaked by the 'fish' (ship-based Cruise missiles) would be the American, British and other allied troops who travelled over the oceans of the world to liberate Kuwait.

As has been remarked earlier, Nostradamus was a man of his own time, one who had to interpret the confusing visions he experienced in terms of what he was familiar with. One can compare his position in this respect with that of the early 19th-century European settlers in Tasmania, who encountered forms of wildlife quite new to them and interpreted what they saw in terms of the fauna of which they did know something. So, for instance, they considered the largest and most ferocious Tasmanian carnivore they encountered to be a tiger – although the 'Tasmanian tiger' was not even a member of the cat family. In the same way, the seer Nostradamus interpreted any streamlined object (such as a missile) he clairvoyantly perceived in terms of the only streamlined creature familiar to him, that is, a fish.

A similar 'fish', in this case a submarine, is referred to in Century II Quatrain 5, which reads:

When iron [i.e. weapons] and letters are enclosed in a fish, From it will come a man who will make war:

His fleet will have journeyed across the sea, To appear near the Latin shore.

Perhaps this is a description of the leader of a band of saboteurs making a surreptitious landing behind the enemy lines during the Gulf War or some other recent conflict – or perhaps, more alarmingly, Nostradamus was making a prediction of a war that is destined to break out in 1996 (see panel below).

CONJUNCTION IN PISCES

Will there be major naval conflict in 1996?

There is an alternative and alarming interpretation of the first line of Century I Quatrain 29 ('When iron [i.e. weapons] and letters are enclosed in a fish') that is derived from the traditional astrological symbolism with which Nostradamus would have been extremely familiar. On this reading of the verse, 'fish' indicates the zodiacal sign of Pisces, 'iron' means the planet Mars, astrological ruler of that metal, war and its weapons, and 'letters' means Mercury, the innermost planet of the solar system and the ruler of all means of communication. The whole line would thus mean something like 'When Mars and Mercury are in conjunction in Pisces', and the quatrain as a whole could be taken as predicting that at the time of such an event there would be war in the Mediterranean – 'near the Latin shore' – involving a fleet which had travelled from afar.

The next conjunction of Mercury and Mars in Pisces is due in the spring of 1996. Will this date be marked by the outbreak of some major conflict that involves the US fleet?

Many vague quatrains have been applied to the Kennedys

In every age there has been an understandable tendency among those who have commented upon the *Centuries* of Nostradamus to seek for references to events that have taken place in their own lifetimes. Thus French Nostradamians of the last two decades of the 19th century sought for quatrains applicable to the Franco-Prussian War; English students of the *Centuries* in the late 1930s believed that they had detected in Century X Quatrain 40 a prognostication of the abdication of Edward VIII; and some contemporary seekers after hidden prophetic knowledge have found – so they assert – an astonishingly large number of quatrains relating to the murdered brothers President John F. Kennedy and Robert Kennedy.

The present writer thinks it likely that many of these Kennedy attributions are mistaken. They are sufficiently vague for it to be impossible to

John F. Kennedy and family

say truthfully of any of them 'this must refer to the Kennedys' in the same way that one can say of, for instance, Century IX Quatrain 20 (see pages 42–3) 'this must refer to the flight of Louis XVI', or of the last two lines of Century VI Quatrain 5 (see page 66) 'this must be descriptive of a manned space station'.

One cannot be sure, for instance, that Century II Quatrain 57 really does apply, as has been claimed, to the Cuban missile crisis and the death of President Kennedy. Certainly it does not read very appositely in translation:

*Before the conflict the great man
will fall,
The lamented great one [will fall] to
sudden death,*

Born imperfect, he will go the greater part of the way,
Near the river of blood the ground is stained.

President Kennedy, although suffering throughout his presidency from a crippling spinal condition and the after-effects of a chronic gonorrhoeal infection, could hardly be said to have been born imperfect, save perhaps in a moral sense. The rest of the quatrain appears to be even less relevant, for while the second line clearly implies an unexpected and probably violent death the murder of the President took place after, not before, the diplomatic conflicts associated with the Cuban missile crisis.

Still vague, but a little more justifiably applicable to John F. Kennedy and Robert Kennedy in that both of these brothers were murdered, are the first three lines of Century X Quatrain 26, which read:

The successor will avenge his handsome brother,
And occupy the realm under the shadow of revenge,
He, killed, the obstacle of the guilty dead, his blood . . .

The problems with accepting, as many have done, that this was even a fairly general Kennedy prophecy are a) that Robert Kennedy neither avenged his brother nor succeeded him as President, either immediately or subsequently, and b) that the last line of the quatrain – 'For a long period Britain will hold with France' – seems to have predicted that whatever the nature of the foretold event or events involving two brothers it was, or they were, destined to be in some way important

Kennedy's ideological enemy, Fidel Castro

in the context of Franco-British relations. This could hardly be said of the Kennedy deaths.

Yet another quatrain that has been applied to the Kennedy family is

Century IX Quatrain 36, the last two lines of which read:

Everlasting captives, a time when the lightning is above,
When three brothers will be mortally wounded.

The present writer is sceptical about the supposed prophetic import of this quatrain. If he is wrong the outlook for the third brother, presumably Edward Kennedy, is poor and the last murder predicted in the final line will take place at some Eastertide – for, according to the quatrain's second line, 'Not far from Easter there will be confusion, a stroke of the knife'.

NUMBERS OF MORTALITY

One reason for doubting the existence of any particular Nostradamian quatrain that can be taken as a definite prediction of the assassination of President John F. Kennedy is that no interpreter of the *Centuries* identified such a verse prior to the event. This is particularly surprising as a number of occultists specializing in numerology – the study of the supposedly mystic attributes of numbers – had, upon Kennedy's election to office in 1960, predicted that he would certainly die in office and would probably do so as the victim of an assassin.

The idea that whoever was to be elected president in 1960 was destined to die in office had been, as it were, 'in the air' ever since President Roosevelt's death in office in the spring of 1944. This was because, as those interested in

numerology had noted at the time of Roosevelt's death, since 1840 every US president who had been elected to office in a year ending with a zero had died in office, and three of them – presidents Lincoln, Garfield and McKinley, first elected to office in, respectively, the years 1860, 1880, and 1900 – had been murdered.

The so-called 'presidential curse of the zeros' was probably no more than an unusual series of coincidences. If it ever really existed it was either limited to a duration of 120 years (in itself a significant period, according to some numerologists) or was, in a sense, lifted by Ronald Reagan, first elected to the presidency in 1980, who managed to survive assassination attempts as well as life-threatening illnesses.

73

The tendency of most of us to wish to be told that our own country (or continent) and its leaders are central to world history is perhaps largely to blame for Nostradamian misinterpretations and dubious predictive attributions of the types described on pages 72–3 in relation to the Kennedy brothers. If, for instance, someone believes both that a) presidents Lincoln and Kennedy were figures of outstanding world importance and b) that Nostradamus was able to clairvoyantly discern the main outlines of history from his own times into the far-distant future, it is difficult to accept the possibility that these men were not mentioned somewhere in the *Centuries.*

Alas, as far as the events that were close to him in time were concerned, Nostradamus appears to have had the thoroughly Eurocentric attitude which, as a 16th-century Frenchman, might well have been expected of him. Apart from some vague references to the 'Hesperides' and their wealth, there are really no Nostradamian predictions that can reasonably be applied to events in American history prior to the present century.

As he looked further into the future, however, the seer's field of vision seems to have enlarged and, as readers of this book will discover, there are a large number of quatrains relating to events that still lie in the future and that are likely to relate, wholly or in part, to the USA. As far as the present century is concerned, there are a number of predictions in the *Centuries* that can be interpreted as pertaining to the USA and some that seem to fit events with a certain exactitude.

As always, the most interesting of the latter are those which not only fit events

Presidents Gorbachev and Reagan

that have actually happened but were interpreted as being predictive of these events before they took place – which invalidates suspicions of interpretive ingenuity based on hindsight. Good examples are those quatrains that were interpreted at a time when the Cold War was at its height as prophecies of a short-lived future friendship between the USA and the Soviet Union.

Such a friendship – of short duration only because of the disintegration of the USSR into its component parts – came into existence in the years of the Reagan/Bush/Gorbachev presidencies and without it the world would have become a very different place. One of the quatrains interpreted as predicting it long before it happened is Century II Quatrain 89, which reads:

America – Hesperides – as it might have been envisaged by a man of Nostradamus's time

One day the two great leaders [leaders
of the superpowers] *will
be friends,
Their great power will be seen to grow:
The New Land* [America] *will be at
the height of its power,
To the man of blood the number
is reported.*

With its mentions of two great leaders
and 'the New Land', a common enough
16th-century term for America, this
quatrain was taken as indicative of future
American-Soviet friendship as long ago
as the 1960s. Commentators, however,
were puzzled by the meaning of the last
line. Was the USA, they asked themselves, to become a virtual ally of a
country ruled by a person whose character was such that the seer referred to
him as 'a man of blood'?

With the presidency of Gorbachev,
however, the meaning of the last line
seemed to become clear – Nostradamus
had been referring to the most obvious
distinguishing mark of the Soviet
leader, the large naevus (a discoloured
area of skin caused by hypertrophied
blood vessels) resembling the appearance of dried blood upon his head.

This seems very clear and apposite,
but some contemporary Nostradamians take an altogether gloomier
viewpoint, identifying the 'man of
blood' with the Antichrist, an evil
ruler whose hour may be close at
hand (see pages 90–1).

The brevity of the endurance of
Soviet-American friendship was predicted by Nostradamus in the first two
lines of Century V Quatrain 78 ('the
two will not remain allied for long
[the Soviet Union] giving way to barbarian satrapies').

BALLOONS, BATTLE, BALONEY

The use of hot air balloons for military purposes was predicted by Nostradamus

One of the oddest attempts at
giving an American slant to a
Nostradamian prediction involved
Century V Quatrain 57, which
reads in partial translation – for
reasons which will be made apparent some words have been left in
their original form – as follows:

*There will go forth from Mont
Gaulfier and the Aventine one
Who through a whole will give
information to the army . . .*

It is generally accepted among
interpreters of the *Centuries* that
these lines refer to the first use of
hot-air balloons for military
observational purposes. This was
at the Battle of Fleurus (1794),
and at the time balloons of this
variety were known as Mont-
golfiers, their name having been
derived from that of the two
Montgolfier brothers who had invented them in 1783.

However, in the 1930s one
determined American, who seems
to have been convinced that
almost any Nostradamian prediction could be twisted to give it
some relevance to the USA,
decided that the phrase Mont
Gaulfier referred to the game of
golf and that the whole verse
prophesied the result of a particular US Open championship. If
one indulges in a single interpretation of this sort one is a
comedian; two or more and the
comedy becomes eccentricity!

In the preceding pages details have been given of some of the astonishing predictive hits contained in the *Centuries* of Nostradamus: of how, for instance, he prophesied the exact years in which the Great Fire of London would take place and World War II would begin; of how he displayed a detailed knowledge of events that took place in the French Revolution, which broke out more than two centuries after his death; and of how he described the guided missiles used in modern high-tech warfare.

In the next section of the book (pages 78–103) Nostradamian predictions which are, as yet, unfulfilled will be examined – those prophecies which relate to the near future of our planet and are likely to affect the lives of each and every one of us. The study of such predictions is an exciting one, for those who engage in it are, in a sense, endeavouring to emulate Nostradamus by tearing apart the very fabric of time. However, excitement must be tempered by a realization that there are two major factors that must always be borne in mind by those Nostradamians who desire to know what the future holds in store both for them and for the world.

The first is this: the exact meanings of Nostradamus's predictions relating to our collective futures are derived from the interpretations made by individual students of the *Centuries* from the crabbed and obscure language often employed by Nostradamus – and some such assessments of the seer's exact meanings may be partially or wholly incorrect. The second is that some prophecies supposedly made by Nostradamus are probably or certainly forgeries. Some of the latter were originated by the Nazi propaganda machine during World War II, others would seem likely to have come into existence as the result of self-delusion or a desire to hoax the gullible.

In this connection the story of a curious event that was reported to have taken place in the early 1970s is relevant. According to this tale, Nostradamus reappeared as 'a living, breathing

According to the American psychic Criswell, Nostradamus predicted a period of sexual licence

human' in a dressing room off a television studio in America. He uttered various new prophecies that were in French but were 'understandable as in English', and gave an exposition of something called the 'Druid Tarot'.

The sole witness to this remarkable event was a well-known American psychic going by the name of 'Criswell', who told of his experience in his book *Criswell's Forbidden Predictions Based on Nostradamus and the Tarot*. Criswell, a man who seems to disdain forenames, was sitting in his dressing room removing his make-up when there was a sharp tap at the door, followed by the entry of a man wearing 16th-century dress. With admirable brevity the unexpected visitor proceeded to introduce himself by saying 'I am Nostradamus.'

Suddenly Criswell found himself whisked away to an enormous grotto furnished with only an oaken table and two chairs. Nostradamus seated himself on one and directed Criswell to the other, whereupon Criswell – clearly a man more able to cope with odd situations than the present writer – calmly listened to his visitor from the 16th century while he made a large number of completely new predictions. Criswell was so impressed by these predictions that he remembered them sufficiently well to be able to include their text in his book.

They were almost all quite startling. And all of them – or rather all of them that pertain to any dates prior to the publication of this book – have in the event proved to be totally and utterly wrong!

GIANT MOTHS AND TOPPLING PYRAMIDS

While the present writer has no confidence in those predictions relating to the years immediately before AD 2000 that were given by Nostradamus to Criswell it seems worth summarizing a few of them as a warning to the unwary.

1 There will be a temporary phase of total sexual licence in which a world orgy will continue until 'even animals are pressed into service'.

2 Bacteria will grow to the size of moths which will then bite people and animals and render them beyond all help. Texas and Mexico will be hardest hit and 'will piteously plead for aid'. Fortunately the bacterial threat will be nullified by the air becoming 'solid with electricity'.

3 An immense occult revival will result in men, women and children casting spells 'on everybody and everything'. Five thousand of

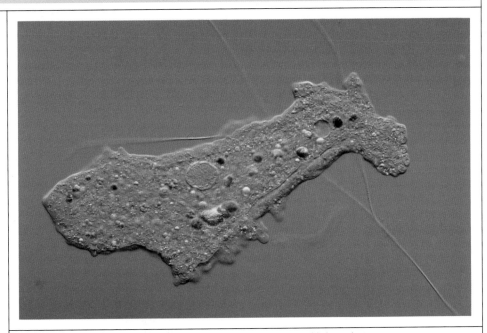

Bacteria will grow to the size of moths – an unlikely prediction

such spell-casters will gather at the Niagara Falls and collectively reverse the flow of the river. Another such group will 'topple the pyramids' while one million psychics will gather at Prairie, South Dakota, in order to hold an enormous seance. At this the spirits of such individuals as Adolf Hitler, Mussolini and Stalin will manifest themselves.

4 All television sets, telephones, typewriters, pens and pencils will be confiscated by the rulers of the world, who will also make a law forbidding three or more people to gather together.

It all sounds very nasty indeed!

THE STRANGE CODED LANGUAGE EMPLOYED BY NOSTRADAMUS IN MANY OF HIS QUATRAINS WAS OF SUCH A NATURE THAT WE CAN BE CONFIDENT THAT HE HAD KNOWLEDGE OF AN ANCIENT MYSTICAL LORE - TO MOST OF US LIVING IN A SCEPTICAL AGE, AN ENIGMA TO WHICH WE ARE UNLIKELY TO FIND THE KEY.

To interpret the predictions of Nostradamus in relation to events that have already happened is not at all easy save, perhaps, for those prophecies in which a specific date such as 1666 or 1792 (see pages 34 and 48) was explicitly or implicitly expressed by the seer. Yet that task is simplicity itself compared with the difficulties of interpreting the exact meanings of prophetic quatrains which have not as yet been fulfilled – those, for example, which seem to pertain to vast social and political upheavals throughout the world, to wars fought with new and terrifying weapons capable of mass destruction, to the emergence of a sinister cult led by one whom Nostradamus identified with the long-prophesied Antichrist (see pages 90–1), and to travel between the stars.

Did Nostradamus predict alien visitors from another planet?

The majority of the quatrains fall into this category of unfulfilled prophecies – that is, their content seems to relate to the future or else they employ terminology that will only become comprehensible in the light of future events. Another possibility is that some refer to secret matters pertaining to mystic arts of which the majority of us know little or nothing. The latter verses, sometimes referred to as 'occult quatrains', are rightly attracting the attention of some present-day Nostradamian researchers.

Nevertheless, it has to be remembered by the Nostradamian interpreter that at least some of the 'occult quatrains' may not – in spite of the mystic language they employ – truly refer to ritual magic, alchemy and other esoteric disciplines. It is possible that in them the seer was using occult symbolism to describe events and concepts which he could not express in the language of his own time because the words needed had not yet been invented.

Even those quatrains relating to the year 2000 and beyond, which are more easily comprehensible than those couched in the language of occultism, are often obscure or capable of more than one interpretation. Consequently, *some* of the interpretations of Nostradamian predictions analysed in the pages that follow are going to be wrong; others are more than likely to be correct.

For more than 400 years there have been those who have sought to find some key which would unlock the (hypothetical) concealed structural framework which they have believed underlies the *Centuries*.

Those who have sought to find this key have been driven by a belief that no seer whose predictions have proved as strikingly accurate as some of those made by Nostradamus could have recorded his visions of things to come in a totally unplanned way; there must, they have felt, have been a hidden inner logic behind the seemingly random order in which the quatrains were written. And, if so, Nostradamus must have intended that those who, like himself, had devoted years of study to the mystic arts of divination should be able to discern the nature of that secret structural logic and, by applying

it, be enabled to read the *Centuries* in a manner which will make complete sense of both their chronology and their content.

As was said on page 79, the *Centuries* contain a number of verses of which the content and terminology is such that they have been labelled 'occult quatrains' – that is, they seem to be concerned with the magical arts. Of course, in the original sense of the word 'occult' – that is to say, 'secret' – there are a substantial number of quatrains in the *Centuries* of which the significance is occult in that they are certainly prophecies but their exact meaning is not likely to become apparent until either they are fulfilled or the long-sought-after predictive key to the *Centuries* is discovered. If indeed that key is ever found it may well be through the

Satan, lord of the necromancers

analysis of quatrains which, according to some, link Nostradamus with cabbalism (see panel opposite), alchemy, numerology, and even the black art of necromancy.

The present writer does not feel competent to make any attempt to discern the innermost secrets of the *Centuries*; but to any readers of this book who may wish to try for themselves he suggests that Century IV Quatrains 28-31 may be of particular significance in this context – for the numbering of these verses may not have been haphazard but have had a numerological import. This is particularly the case with the last two of them, Century IV Quatrains 30 and 31, which read, respectively:

More than eleven times the moon will not want the sun,
All raised and lessened in degree:

The power of the unknown – a present-day magical rite

Put so low that one will sew little gold
After famine and plague the secret will
be discovered.

The moon in the middle of the
high mountain,
The new wise man has discerned it:

By his disciples invited to
become immortal,
Eyes southward, hands on breast,
body aflame.

Whether or not these two quatrains do indeed provide a secret key to the complex structural framework of the

Centuries is a matter of opinion; what they do reveal, however, is that Nostradamus was aware of curious developments of secret cultism which are already in train and may, if some commentators are correct, dominate many aspects of our everyday lives in the near future.

THE SPLENDID LIGHTS

One approach to the finding of a secret key to the interpretation of the *Centuries* which is being pursued by some students of western esotericism at the present day is based upon the virtual certainty that Nostradamus was well acquainted with the outlines of the Christian cabbala.

The cabbala is an ancient Jewish mystical system which by the 16th century also existed in a Christianized form almost inextricably associated with magic and alchemy. That Nostradamus had at one time possessed books on such subjects is made apparent by a passage in a letter he published:

. . . I caution you against the seduction of . . . execrable magic . . . Although many volumes have come before me which have long lain concealed I have felt no desire to divulge their contents . . . after reading them . . . I reduced them to ashes.

It is likely that this passage was written by the seer with the intention of averting suspicion that he practised cabbalistic magic; it is improbable that the scholarly

Nostradamus, an avid book collector, would have deliberately destroyed rare magical texts.

Those present-day students of Christian cabbalism who have endeavoured to use it in order to understand the innermost structure

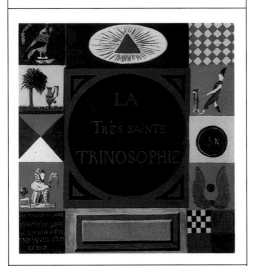

A French initiatory cabbalistic manuscript

of the *Centuries* have been struck by the fact that there are 10 Centuries (not all of them complete) and that cabbalistic theory is based on a system of 10 emanations – the sephiroth or 'splendid lights' – from 'the Unmanifest'. According to the doctrines of contemporary cabbalists, everything in the universe, from

ideas and emotions to material objects, can be classified in terms of the 10 sephiroth. Thus, for example, everything connected with conflict can be taken as mystically corresponding with the fifth of the sephiroth, everything to do with love to the seventh, and everything to do with money to the tenth.

It would be agreeable if the 10 individual Centuries had some obvious correspondences with the 10 sephiroth – if, for instance, Century X was clearly relevant to money, property and so on. Alas, they don't; but it may be that there is a concealed but genuine relationship between the structure of the *Centuries* and the patterns of the sephiroth and that the discovery of the exact nature of this relationship will provide a complete solution to all the problems of Nostradamian interpretation.

A few decades ago the idea would have seemed fantastic beyond belief – but recent historical research has shown that a number of 16th-century books do have a hidden structure derived from cabbalistic teachings, and the *Centuries* may be another of them.

81

A number of dedicated students of the writings of Nostradamus, among them the late James Laver, have been fascinated by the so-called 'prophecy of Saint Malachy' – for they have come to the conclusion that they have discerned a concordance between it and certain of the predictive verses of Nostradamus which pertain to the papacy – for instance, Century V Quatrain 56, which reads:

Because of the death of the very old Pope,
Will be elected a Roman of very good [i.e. young] age,
It will be said of him that he weakens the Seat [i.e. the Throne of Peter],
But he will hold it long with stinging labour.

The meaning of this quatrain is clear enough. Nostradamus was saying that in the course of time a young pope is destined to be elected in succession to an elderly one and to be attacked by some on the grounds that he is weakening the Church. Nevertheless, with great effort ('stinging labour') he will occupy the papal throne for a long time.

This prophecy has clearly not as yet been fulfilled, for the only pope elected at what could reasonably be called a 'young age' between the publication of the *Centuries* and our own times was Gregory XIV who, far from enjoying a long occupation of the papacy, had an unusually short reign.

If, like James Laver and others, one does accept that there is a concordance between the 'prophecy of Saint Malachy' and the *Centuries* it seems likely, for reasons which will be made apparent, that the young pope whose election Nostradamus predicted in Century V Quatrain 56 is fated to be the successor of the present Pontiff, Pope John Paul II.

The 'prophecy of Saint Malachy' has been put in inverted commas here because the general consensus of scholarly opinion is that whoever may in truth have been its author it was not the Irish monastic Saint Malachy (c. 1095–1148). Indeed, there are those who say it is not a genuine prophecy at all but a forgery, probably dating from no earlier than 1590. On the other hand, many pious men and

Saint Bernard of Clairvaux vouchsafed the authenticity of the predictions of Saint Malachy

According to Nostradamus and Malachy, the next pope will be the last to be invested with the papal keys

in the prophecy – so there would seem to be only one more pope to come. Of him Malachy (or whoever wrote what became attributed to him) chillingly said:

In the final persecution of the Holy Roman Church there will reign Peter the Roman, who will feed his flock amongst many tribulations; after which the seven-hilled City will be destroyed and the dreadful Judge will judge the people.

The expression 'dreadful Judge' is usually taken as a reference to the Last Judgment, when the living and the resurrected dead are to be sentenced to either eternal damnation or given the reward of eternal bliss. But it could mean a judgment of a quite different sort – some world-shattering event, or series of events, which destroys the Church. In either case, if Nostradamus and Malachy are in concordance, then the next Pope is going to be the last.

women have believed the attribution of the prophecy to Malachy to be justified: a 19th-century French priest, Father Cucherat, specifically stated that the prophecies were written by Malachy, that the vision or visions on which they were based were experienced in Rome in 1140, and that Malachy wrote down his prophetic mottoes on a parchment which he handed to Pope Innocent II, who deposited it in the Vatican Library – where no one looked at it for the next four centuries or so.

It all sounds a bit improbable – but the office of the Breviary for the Feast of Saint Malachy refers to him as having been blessed with the gift of prophecy and, more importantly, Saint Bernard of Clairvaux stated that Malachy accurately foretold to him the day and the very hour at which he, Malachy, would die.

The prophecy attributed to Malachy is only short. It consists of 108 Latin mottoes, each of which is supposedly appropriate to a particular pope, beginning with Celestine II

(pope 1143–4) and ending with 'Peter the Roman', supposedly fated to be the final Pope. The Latin mottoes are often of only two or three words; for instance, that given to Celestine II was Ex Castro Tiberis ('From a Castle on the Tiber'), an allusion to his family name, Guido de Castello. To the present pope, John Paul II, is attributed the 107th motto contained

THE EX-SWINEHERD

Pope Sixtus V, who occupied the Throne of Peter from 1585 to 1590, was a man of extremely humble origins. In this he was quite unlike the majority of other popes of his time, who tended to be closely related to the great families of Italy.

Born in 1521 as Felice Peretti, the son of a gardener, the future Sixtus V was sent to labour as a swineherd when he was only eight years old. He was, however, an exceptionally intelligent child

and after a year with the pigs was taken away to begin his education in a convent. He was ordained as a priest in 1547, consecrated a bishop in 1566, and made a cardinal four years later.

His eventual elevation to the papacy was foreseen by Nostradamus almost 40 years before that event took place. On a visit to Italy the seer fell on his knees before Peretti, then only a newly ordained priest, and addressed him as 'Your Holiness'.

83

Muslims in worship at the holy city of Mecca

Gordon of Khartoum – victim of a jihad

In recent years, fundamentalist Islam – the belief that the Koran is the inspired word of God, dictated to his messenger Mahomet by an angel, which lays down rules for the conduct of human affairs that are valid for all time – has made more than something of a come-back. For, as has been shown by events that have taken place over the last 15 years in such countries as Iran, Afghanistan and the central Asian republics of the former Soviet Union, the faith of the Prophet Mahomet is once more a considerable force in the world and is likely to play an increasingly important part in international affairs during the first years and decades of the 21st century.

The origins of the current Islamic renaissance can be traced back to at least the 1920s, though the movement really began to gather momentum with the decline of communism in the 1970s. It was then that there began to be a feeling among the peoples of Iran, Afghanistan and Soviet Asia that the solutions to their social and economic problems might be found in a return to Islamic law rather than in the adoption of the materialist atheism of Marxist ideology.

The decline and fall of communism was foretold by Nostradamus in more than one quatrain (see pages 68–9), and one such prediction that appears highly relevant to Islamic resurgence is Century IV Quatrain 32, in which the third and fourth lines refer to 'the old order [Islam] being renewed' and 'Panta chiona philon' (a late classical Greek phrase meaning 'all things in common', i.e. communism) being abandoned.

From the point of view of those who see fundamentalist religion of any variety as being in opposition to the values associated with the dominant western ideologies of both left and right, this Islamic resurgence is an unmitigated evil. Nevertheless, whether the march of Islam be for better or worse we are going to have to learn to live with it – or, at least, such is the case if the predictions of Nostradamus are to be fulfilled in the future as they have been in the past. Live with it and perhaps, for some of us, die with it – for it would appear that Nostradamus predicted that one of the features of the decades close at hand to us would be mighty and enormously destructive wars between Islamic and non-Islamic countries.

The course of these wars, as predicted in the *Centuries*, will include some Islamic set-backs – including the possible capture of a Caliph (see panel below) – but it will also be marked by disasters such as the total destruction of Monte Carlo, some of which are described on pages 86–7.

PROPHETIC OBSCURITIES

One of the problems that faces all commentators upon the *Centuries* is the existence of quatrains of which the content is such that some have termed them 'retroactive predictions' – that is to say, they seem to relate to events which took place before Nostradamus wrote concerning them. Examples of such retroactive predictions are Century VIII Quatrains 51 and 83, the former of which would appear to pertain to events that took place prior to the expulsion of the Moors from Spain in 1492 and the latter to Venetian atrocities at the time of the Fourth Crusade, some 350 years before Nostradamus 'prophesied' them.

Obviously there is something very odd about any seer going to the bother of writing obscurely worded descriptions of events that had taken place long before his own time. Consequently, the seeming existence of such pseudo-predictions in the *Centuries* has always been something of a puzzle to Nostradamian students, and various rationalizations for their appearance have been offered. Among them are ideas connected with alternate realities, worlds which exist in a discrete space time parallel to our own in which history has followed a different course (see pages 132–3), and a suggestion that sometimes the visions of Nostradamus were outside his control and that he clairvoyantly discerned events that had transpired long previously. Both these hypotheses may well be wholly or partially true – but it may equally be the case that some of the 'retroactive' predictions are not retroactive at all, but relate to a future time when an Islamic superpower has come into existence. One such prophecy is made in Century VI Quatrain 78, which reads:

> *To shout aloud the victory of the growing crescent moon,*
> *The Eagle will be proclaimed by the Romans,*
> *Ticcan, Milan and the Genoese will not agree to it,*

> *And the great Basil* [a Nostradamian term derived from Greek and meaning King or Emperor] *will be claimed by them.*

For complex interpretive reasons this quatrain has been generally assumed to describe the capture by Western forces of a Muslim Sultan who also laid claim to the Caliphate, the spiritual leadership of the Islamic world. As the last such Sultan/Caliph ceased to rule when the Ottoman Empire collapsed at the end of World War I the prediction is now held to have been retroactive, probably pertaining to the capture of Sultan Jemm in the 15th century. However, there seems to be no good reason to assume that there will never again be a powerful Caliph who is made prisoner by Westerners whom Nostradamus would, employing the terminology of his own century, describe as 'Romans'. It thus seems likely that Century VI Quatrain 78 pertains to our world or that of our descendants, not to that of our ancestors.

85

Martyrs of a modern jihad – the Iranian holy war

The idea of a jihad – a holy war against those who dwell outside the 'House of Islam' – is one of great antiquity and enormous potency throughout the Muslim world. Between AD 622 and 732, Arabs inspired by the concept conquered almost the whole of North Africa and invaded France; in the 15th century the jihad waged by the Ottoman Turks against Byzantium resulted in the fall of Constantinople, and as late as the 1680s Muslim warriors were unsuccessfully besieging Vienna.

In the 300 years that followed, however, the ideology of the jihad was to lose a good deal of its practical impact, albeit none of its mystical appeal. Such few attempts as were made to use the jihad as a political and diplomatic weapon – by, for instance, the Sultan of Turkey in World War I – were on the whole ineffectual.

For the last 10 years or so there have been signs that this is no longer the case; in Afghanistan the Red Army was defeated by the guerrilla warfare waged against it by devotees of the jihad concept and in Bosnia the idea has inspired some of the most fanatical Muslim fighters against the Orthodox Serbs and the Catholic Croats. If Nostradamus is to be believed, this is only the beginning and we are destined to witness one or more Muslim holy wars.

The seer predicted that the effects of these wars, fought with weapons of mass destruction of such a nature that he was forced to use strange analogies in his attempts to describe them, will be devastating. In Century IV Quatrain 23, which for complex reasons is believed to pertain to a con-

flict between Islam and the West, he prophesied that the use of such weapons would result in the complete destruction of Monte Carlo, today the 'pleasure capital' of the world. This verse reads:

The Legion in the sea fleet
Will burn – lime, magnetic ore,
sulphur and tar:
The long rest in a safe place,
Port Selyn and Hercle will be
consumed by the fire.

The phrase 'sea fleet' (*marine classe* – the latter word, derived from Latin, was invariably used by the seer to mean armada, flotilla or fleet) in line one appeared tautological to Nostradamian students of the last century. It seemed akin to referring to a three-sided triangle or a four-sided square; how could there possibly be any fleet other than a marine one? Today we know the answer to this question – there are also air fleets and, in the not too distant future, there may well be space fleets. So it would seem that by qualifying the word fleet Nostradamus was intending to convey to us that he was aware of humanity's future conquest of the air and outer space.

The second line of the quatrain lists some of the ingredients of the Byzantine incendiary material known as Greek Fire and is presumably a metaphor intended to describe a firestorm – in this context the mention of a 'long rest' in line three is of sinister import – but it is the specific prediction of the fiery fate of 'Port Selyn and Hercle' in line four which

A child of the jihad

A MILLION FRENCH DEAD

At least one contemporary student of the *Centuries* known to the present writer – a member of that small band of Nostradamian interpreters who endeavour to analyse the seer's predictions in the light of the cabbala (see page 81) – contests on numerological as well as other grounds that Nostradamus's prophecy of the total destruction of Monte Carlo contained in Century IV Quatrain 23 is structurally linked with Century I Quatrains 71 and 72, which read respectively:

*Three times the marine tower will
be captured and recaptured,
By the Spaniards, Barbarians
[perhaps Berbers, i.e. North
Africans] and Italians:
Marseilles and Aix, Arles
by Pisans,*

*Laid waste by fire and sword,
Avignon pillaged by the Turinese.*

*The dwellers in Marseilles
changed utterly,
In flight, pursued as far as Lyons,
Narbonne and Toulouse outraged
by Bordeaux,
Dead and imprisoned, almost
a million.*

While the exact meanings of the above quatrains cannot yet be established with certainty, their general import is definite enough. If indeed they were truly intended to be read in conjunction with Century IV Quatrain 23, then the world faces even bloodier battles than those associated with any previous wars in history. As is explained on page 88, there are reasons to believe that these terrifying conflicts may be close to us in time.

is of primary interest. 'Port Selyn' means 'the Port of the Crescent', the crescent being the symbol of Islam, while 'Hercle' is an abbreviation of Herculeis Monacei, a Latin name for Monaco and its capital Monte Carlo. It would appear that in this quatrain Nostradamus was prophesying the simultaneous destruction by fire of a fleet, an important Islamic port and Monte Carlo. Obviously such conflagrations would result in enormous casualties and these would not be confined just to 'Port Selyn' and Monte Carlo – indeed, if one Nostradamian student is correct in his interpretations there would be nearly one million casualties in France alone (see panel right).

Clearly, a world war or perhaps a series of wars is foretold in Century IV Quatrain 23. As is explained on the next two pages, other Nostradamian quatrains seem to predict that this titanic struggle will involve the use of bacteriological and nuclear weapons.

87

Teheran's Fountain of Blood, dedicated to the martyrs of the jihad

For reasons that are explained below and on pages 90–1, it is likely that many of the most dismal predictions to be found in the *Centuries* pertain to times which are very close indeed – particularly to the early decades of the 21st century and possibly to the late 1990s.

One of the most bloodcurdling of these gloomy prognostications is to be found in Century VIII Quatrain 77, which is concerned with a war lasting for no less than 27 years. Its final line reads: 'Red hail, water, blood and corpses cover the earth.' This line is agreed by the majority of present-day Nostradamian students to refer to a coming conflict involving nuclear and/or biological weapons.

Obviously, the use of weapons such as these would have the effect of strewing the earth with corpses. As for the red hail and water discerned by Nostradamus, that would be either an aerosol used deliberately to spread bacterial infections or atmospheric water contaminated by the radioactive fall-out associated with any nuclear explosion (or both). At its worst the latter could even be the product of deliberate radioactive 'dusting' of an entire area by means of an exceptionally dirty weapon – a nuclear device fitted with a cobalt jacket.

That the predicted fall of the red hail of death upon our planet is nigh is suggested by the content of Century I Quatrain 16, which predicts 'plague, famine and death from military hands' at a time when the centuries 'approach their renewal'. This latter phrase is strongly suggestive of a deliberate reference by Nostradamus to esoteric theories concerning astrological and chronological cycles with which he was almost certainly acquainted – notably with the Neo-platonic concept of a 'Great Year' consisting of 12 'months', each of around 2000 years of time as ordinarily measured.

If 'the renewal of the centuries' referred to in Century I Quatrain 16 does apply to the 'Great Year' of the Platonists it is likely that it indicates a date for the fulfilment of the 'plague, famine and death from military hands' prediction coinciding exactly with

The Chernobyl nuclear disaster of 1986 – the shape of things to come?

what some modern occultists term 'the transition from the Age of Pisces to that of Aquarius' – that is, a few years shortly before or after AD 2000, the precise date for that event being a little uncertain as it is dependent upon whichever particular fixed star is taken as the marking point for the beginning of the zodiac. This latter is a technical point, a subject for debate among those who have delved deeply into esoteric theory, but the essence of the matter is quite clear; the fulfilment of Nostradamus's predictions of universal plague and famine is near at hand.

Other quatrains in the *Centuries* would seem to confirm this interpretation – for example, Century I Quatrain 91, which reads:

Technological warfare was foreseen by the seer

The gods will make it apparent to humanity
That they are the devisers of a great war:
Prior to this the heavens were free of espée et lance
The greatest damage will be imposed upon the left.

The words left in their original form in line three would literally imply that the sky would, most improbably, become darkened by swords and spears in the seer's predicted great war. It is therefore likely that the phrase was intended to be taken figuratively by those who read it when the foretold event drew near and that by *espée et lance* the present-day student of prophecy can understand 'weapons and missiles'. The likely significance of the phrase 'the left' used by Nostradamus in line four of the quatrain is examined on pages 102–3; it suffices here to say that it is possible but improbable that the seer used it in its modern political sense, which dates from only the late 18th century.

THE GREAT STAR BURNS

Century II Quatrain 41 is of much interest in relation to Nostradamian predictions of great world conflicts involving the use of nuclear and biological weapons breaking out shortly before or after the end of the present century. This quatrain reads:

The Great Star will boil for seven days,
Its cloud making the sun appear to have a double image:
The great dog will howl throughout the night
When the Pope changes his habitation.

In an attempt to date the time at which the predicted event will take place, the 'Great Star' of line one has been identified with the

Atomic warfare could be the 'great star'

return of Halley's comet. However, as the last two appearances of this comet have been so unspectacular that it has been almost invisible to the naked eye, this interpretation is difficult to believe. It seems far more likely

that the 'star' will be the explosion of an extremely large fusion weapon. Such weapons produce their energy by exactly the same process as that which takes place in the interiors of most stars – the transmutation of hydrogen into helium. In a man-made fusion bomb, however, the actual explosion does not 'boil' for a week, and nor does it produce a double solar image.

Possibly the reference is to a whole series of nuclear attacks, but a more likely explanation is that the boiling metaphor used by Nostradamus implies an enormous dust cloud thrown up by fusion bombs and taking a very long time to fall even partially back to earth.

89

As suggested by the interpretation of the last line of Century VIII Quatrain 77 given on page 88, Nostradamus predicted that the early years of the new millennium would be marked by the strewing of the earth with corpses as a consequence of bacteriological or atomic warfare. But how is the remainder of the same quatrain to be interpreted?

To consider it in its entirety, Century VIII Quatrain 77 reads:

The Antichrist very soon annihilates the three,
Seven and twenty years his war will endure,
The heretics are dead, imprisoned, exiled,
Red hail, water, blood and corpses cover the earth.

The identity of 'the three' whom the Antichrist is described as annihilating is a mystery to all students of the *Centuries*; it has been suggested they are three major world powers or three great world leaders, either spiritual or temporal. But whatever or whoever 'the three' may be, who are the heretics mentioned in line three, and what is the meaning of the word 'Antichrist' as used in the opening line?

It is best to try to answer the last question first. According to traditional Christian beliefs (see panel opposite), the Antichrist is destined to be a false saviour who will serve the great Princes of Hell, wreak havoc in the world, and lead much of humanity into spiritually destructive paths which will, quite literally, result in damnation. While such a belief is of great antiquity it is still held by some at the present day and it is worth remembering that in the comparatively recent past as learned and pious a man as Cardinal Manning (1808-92) delivered a series of lectures concerning the Antichrist and expressed his conviction that some of the stranger events associated with the emergence

The allies of the Antichrist – the Beast 666 and his Bride, the Whore of Babylon

of modern spiritualism might indicate that the infernal Advent – the birth of the Antichrist – was imminent.

Whether or not the Cardinal was right in his beliefs, there seems no doubt that Nostradamus adhered to theological concepts which were, in essence, identical to them. Of central relevance, to be held constantly in mind when endeavouring to interpret those quatrains of the *Centuries* in which Nostradamus mentioned the Antichrist, is that ideas about the coming of the counter-Christ, the 'son of perdition', were as much part of the 'world picture' of Nostradamus as they were of every learned Christian of his time. It must consequently

be assumed that if Nostradamus could see into the future he would interpret his vision of unpleasant persons and events in terms of a concept familiar to him – that is, the advent of the Antichrist, the manifestation of a miracle-working false Saviour whose disciples would be the servants of the Powers and Principalities of Hell.

In other words, just as Nostradamus seems to have endeavoured to describe 20th-century warfare in terms of the material things and the military technology familiar to him (see pages 64–5 in relation to Century I Quatrain 64), so he would have tried to describe those moral attitudes and the actions resulting from them which most of us would characterize as absolutely inhuman and pertaining to the principle of eternal evil in terms of 16th-century eschatology –

Design for the Temple of the Beast

that is, religious beliefs and teachings concerning the end of the world. On the following pages we shall see how such beliefs tie in with what appear to be Nostradamus's predictions concerning the coming of a terrifying 'Supreme Antichrist' at a date shortly after the year 2000.

91

Aleister Crowley, believed to be the Antichrist

THE MESSIAH OF EVIL

Ever since Christianity was in its infancy, the word 'Antichrist' has been used to describe any extraordinarily wicked person. While Nostradamus and other 16th-century Christians employed the word in this sense, for them the Supreme Antichrist would be a Messiah of evil – a prophet of truly hellish wickedness.

The views of Saint Roberto Bellarmine (1542-1651) regarding the origins of the Antichrist were typical of those held by theologians living at much the same time as Nostradamus. Bellarmine believed that the father of the Antichrist would be an incubus – that is, a

demon who has sexual congress with human females – and that his mother would be a practitioner of black magic.

A Dominican friar of the 17th century asserted that the coming Antichrist would not only be fathered by a devil but would be:

. . . as malicious as a madman, with such wickedness as was never seen on earth . . . he will treat Christians as condemned souls are treated in hell. He will have a multitude of Synagogue names, and he will be able to fly when he wishes. Beelzebub will be his father, Lucifer his grandfather.

In the time of Nostradamus, eschatological beliefs (see page 91) concerning world experiences supposedly destined to happen before the Last Judgment were almost inextricably entwined with traditional lore concerning events which it was held would precede and follow the coming of the Antichrist. This means that if Nostradamus clairvoyantly perceived, far in the future, the teachings and the actions of a Hitler, a Stalin, or some absolute ruler who has yet to come to power, he would almost certainly have interpreted them as manifestations of one or more Antichrists.

In this context it is worth taking a look at a particular passage in the Epistle to Henri II which was printed with the first edition of the *Centuries* and which, as described on page 48, gave a specific and completely accurate date for events which took place during the French Revolution. This passage gives a chilling account of the events which would, according to Nostradamus, precede the rule of the one he termed 'the third [i.e. the Supreme] Antichrist'.

Writing of a 'King' (which in this context means an absolute ruler of any sort) who would commit great crimes against the Church, the seer asserted that this man-monster:

> . . . *will have shed the blood of more Churchmen than any could do* [i.e. pour out] *with wine . . . Human blood will flow in the churches and streets, as does water after heavy rain, and will crimson with blood the*

The kingdom of the Antichrist – a 16th-century vision of Hell

> *neighbouring rivers . . . then in the same year and those following there will ensue the most horrible plague, all the more virulent because of the famine that will precede it, and such suffering that there will have been nothing like it since the foundation of Christianity . . . . The great Vicar of the Cope* [the pope] *shall be . . . desolated and abandoned by all . . . . After that Antichrist will be the hellish prince . . . all the . . . world*

> *will be shaken for twenty five years . . . and the wars and battles will be grievous . . . and so many evils will be committed by Satan . . . that nearly all the world will be undone and desolated.*

Save for the mention of the Antichrist as 'the hellish prince' and the reference to the world being desolated as the result of many evils committed by Satan, there is nothing at all in this prose prophecy that could not be taken as a description of a future series of political events. Once it is accepted that there is a genuine possibility that Nostradamus and other seers and prophets could discern the pattern of future events (or perhaps sense what is happening in an alternate reality – see pages 132–3) the passage contains nothing to unduly strain the credulity of its readers. It could well be a prophetic description of some future and monstrously evil dictator – a later and more successful version of Hitler or Pol Pot – who will manage to dominate world events for a period of a quarter of a century. It would not be surprising if a man like Nostradamus, acquainted with only the technology and physics of the 16th century, were to assume that such a dictator, with all the gifts of a perverted science from nuclear weapons to anthrax-loaded bombs at his command, was not a man but a devil – either the Antichrist or a forerunner of the Antichrist.

Some students of prophecy in general, and the writings of Nostradamus in particular, assert – for interpretative reasons that are too complex to be even briefly outlined in these pages – that the advent of the monstrous ruler described by the seer in his Epistle to Henri II is close upon us. Furthermore, they identify this 'King' as the third and great Antichrist. They believe, as did Nostradamus, that this vile creature is destined to pour out 'the blood of more Churchmen than any could do with wine'. His horrible activities, which will result in the outbreak of 'the most horrible plague, all the more virulent because of the famine that will precede it', are held

The children of perdition – the subjects of the Antichrist

to pertain to bacteriological warfare.

The coming third Antichrist, it is argued, is almost certain to be the very same individual who will be responsible for the descent of the King of Terror from the sky in July or perhaps August 1999 (see pages 110–11). If this is indeed the case, the imminent prospects for the future of us all are very grim indeed.

THE SON OF PERDITION

The third Antichrist, the being that Nostradamus prophesied would cause blood to 'flow in the churches and streets as does water after heavy rain', has been identified by many Nostradamian interpreters with a 'son of perdition' referred to in the New Testament as one who would deceive many with 'lying wonders'.

The relevant text is in the thirteenth chapter of the Bible's last book, The Revelation of Saint John the Divine. It describes a 'second Beast', held by traditionalist New

Testament commentators to be the same infernal entity as the Antichrist. The passage reads:

*. . . And I beheld another beast . . .
and he spake as a dragon. And he
. . . causeth the earth and them
which dwell therein to worship the
first beast . . . . And he doeth
great wonders, so that he maketh
fire from heaven on the earth . . . .
And deceiveth them that dwell
on the earth by the means of
those miracles which he had
power to do . . . .*

93

As has been recounted on pages 84–91, Nostradamus foretold that the opening decades of the third millennium, now only six years or so away from us in time, would be characterized by wars, plague, famine, an upsurge of militant Islam and the appearance of a religio-political leader of such malignancy that the seer identified him with the Antichrist.

Inevitably, an epoch foretold by Nostradamus in such doom-laden detail will not leave traditional Christianity unscathed, but that religion will, it is predicted in more than one quatrain of the *Centuries*, retain a capacity to fight back – to be exalted in the sight of some even if it is humbled in that of others. In this context Century I Quatrain 15 is relevant. It reads:

> *Mars threatens us with warlike force,*
> *Seventy times this will cause the*
> *spilling of blood:*
> *The clergy will be both exalted and*
> *dragged down,*
> *By those who wish to learn nothing*
> *from them.*

In other words, following a series of wars there will be a partially successful dragging down of Christianity and its leaders by those who are ideologically opposed to the traditional faith of the West ('who wish to learn nothing') but there will be a reaction in favour of historic Christianity which will exalt, or raise on high, the leadership of the Church Militant.

Nostradamus may have given an interesting clue to the nature of the wars he predicted would bring about such religious conflicts by his use of the phrase 'seventy times this will cause the spilling of blood' in line two. He is unlikely to have been employing the number 70 in a literal sense and, while he may have meant no more than that he was foretelling a very large number

94

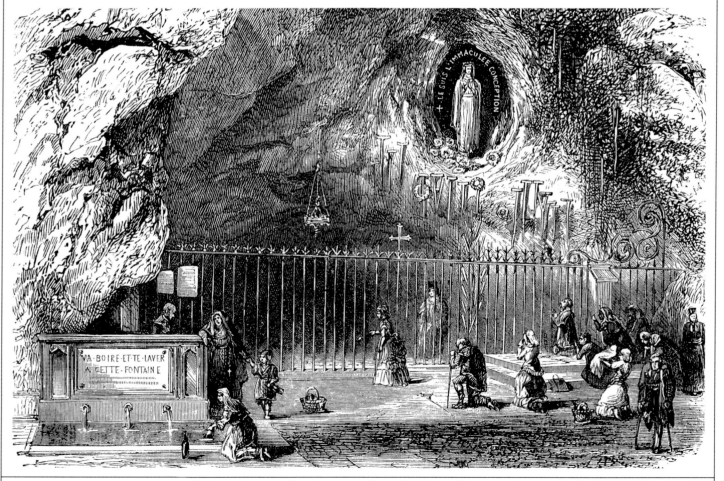

Pilgrims at the grotto at Lourdes – a strong focus of Catholic tradition even today

of conflicts, it may well be that he was making a reference to the significance of 70 in terms of the Christian cabbalistic numerology with which he would have been acquainted.

The number 70 supposedly has a mystical connection with Hebrew and Chaldee words meaning 'night', 'wine' and 'secret'; this suggests the possibility that Nostradamus was implying that those responsible for many of the prognosticated conflicts would be devotees of a faith which taught what Christians would regard as 'dark, nocturnal secrets' and practised rites involving the use of wine and, perhaps, strange drugs.

There is an enigmatic description of one of those destined to lead or

A traditionalist penitent at Seville

inspire the traditionalist resurgence in Century I Quatrain 96, which reads:

*A man will be given the task
of destroying
Temples and sects changed by*

*[strange] fantasies:
He will harm rocks rather than
the living,
By filling ears with eloquence.*

Whether the destructive task prophesied to be given to somebody in lines one and two is predicted to be laid upon him by other human beings or by some supernatural power is unclear. But the nature of the work is apparent – to destroy, wholly or partially, fantastic pseudo-religions which will have deceived many. On this interpretation it is to be presumed that the cult led by the evil one the seer termed the 'third Antichrist' is fated to be the most notable of these 'temples changed by fantasy'.

THE MAN IN THE IRON MASK

It has been suggested to the present writer by one contemporary Nostradamian interpreter (the esoteric numerologist who is referred to on page 87) that apart from mere propinquity there is a hidden link between Century I Quatrain 96 (see above) and Century I Quatrain 95. This link, derived from cabbalistic doctrines concerning a relationship between the letter combinations of the Hebrew alphabet and particular number manipulations of an ancient occult instrument termed 'the cabbala of Nine Chambers', has led this esotericist to suggest that the religious leader forecast in Century I Quatrain 96 to destroy 'temples and sects changed by fantasy' and to 'fill ears with eloquence' must be identified with a mysterious child referred

to by Nostradamus in Century I Quatrain 95, which reads:

*Before a monastery will be found a
twin infant,
Descended from an ancient
monastic bloodline:
His fame and power through sects
and eloquence
Is such that they will say the living
twin is rightly the elect [the
chosen one].*

Most commentators of the last century – and some of the present day also – have based their interpretations of this quatrain on the legend that Louis XIV of France was both the illegitimate son of Cardinal Mazarin and one of a pair of identical twins, and that to avoid any disputes over the succession to the throne his brother

was imprisoned from infancy until his death as the silent, aged and unidentified prisoner known to history as 'the man in the Iron Mask'. However, modern research has shown that this ancient interpretation of Century I Quatrain 95 was erroneous, for while the man in the Iron Mask did indeed exist he was not the twin brother of Louis XIV. Consequently, there is no good reason why the subject of this quatrain should not be the same man as the traditionalist Christian leader of the succeeding verse. If this does in the course of time prove to be the case it is likely that his descent 'from an ancient monastic bloodline' will prove to be a symbolic reference to his beliefs rather than a literal description of his ancestry.

95

THE GREAT CHYREN

In the last century, in a period following the fall of the Empire of Napoleon III in 1870, a number of French Nostradamians were also dedicated Legitimists – advocates of a restoration of the representative of the senior Bourbon line to the throne of France. Their royalism induced them to make an intense study of a number of quatrains in the *Centuries* containing references to a man whom Nostradamus called 'the Great Chyren' and whom these interpreters employed much ingenious argument to identify with the Comte de Chambord, the then Bourbon Pretender of the elder line.

We can be sure that these interpretations were wrong, for the older Bourbon line became extinct in the 1880s – the present Pretender to the French throne is a member of the Orléans branch of the family – but

The pages of French history are spattered with the blood of many battles over who should rule the country

Christianity under threat

there can be no doubt that under the code name of Chyren Nostradamus predicted the advent of a particular Frenchman who would exert an immense influence for good upon both his own country and the entire world. According to some Nostradamians of the present day, this Frenchman may well be the same person as the traditionalist destroyer of false religion (see pages 94–5) and a pope whose future election was predicted in Century V Quatrain 49, which reads:

> *Not from Spain but from*
> *ancient France*
> *Will be chosen* [elected] *one to guide*
> *the shaking ship* [the barque of the*
> *Papacy],*
> *He will make an assurance to*
> *the enemy,*
> *Who will cause a vile pestilence during*
> *his reign.*

There has been no French pope since before the birth of Nostradamus, so we know that this prophecy is not yet fulfilled. The content of the quatrain's first line is very curious, for while it made sense for Nostradamus to give the nationality of the predicted pope there seems to have been no good reason why he should have thought fit to state that he would not be Spanish. The most likely explanation is that the quatrain foretells an imminent schism and that there will shortly be two claimants to the papacy – the one considered legitimate by Nostradamus being of French origin.

The last line, with its suggestion of chemical or biological weapons being used against the true pope's partisans, is disagreeably concordant with another quatrain which prophesies that such weapons will be used by the third Antichrist (see panel opposite).

PROPHETIC OBSCURITIES

Whether or not the man prophesied by Nostradamus in Century I Quatrain 96 (see page 95) to be destined to destroy what the seer, looking far into the future, regarded as being temples dedicated to a false and fantastic faith can be identified with either or both the 'Great Chyren' and the French pope who will guide the shaking ship of the Papacy (see facing page) is a matter for debate amongst students of the *Centuries*. However, unless the seer's many predictions relating to the third Antichrist are completely in error there can be no doubt that the main opponents of the Christian traditionalist 'destroyer' whose advent was foretold in Century I Quatrain 96 will be the threatened Messiah of evil, his disciples, and those who ally themselves with him.

Various Nostradamian verses make it apparent that the seer believed that the third Antichrist would be an Asian by birth and either the site of this event or, alternatively, the place at which the power of the Antichrist will be centred is probably predicted in Century IX Quatrain 62, which for complex numerological reasons is linked to the concept of the Antichrist. It reads:

To the great one of Cheramon agora
Will all the crosses be attached by rank,
The pertinacious [probably meaning 'perpetual in effect']
opium and mandragora,
Rougon will be released on October the third.

This quatrain, as obscurely worded as any in the *Centuries*, has often been interpreted by modern commentators as referring to secret magical techniques involving the use of hallucinogenic drugs ('opium and mandragora') and what the magicians of the ancient world termed 'barbarous words of evocation' – of which Cheramon agora have been claimed to be two.

This interpretation is likely to be in error on two counts. The seer's use of the phrase 'pertinacious opium and mandragora' implies that he was not employing the names of these consciousness-altering drugs in a literal sense; rather was he trying to convey, in words current in his own time, that the subject of the quatrain would use substances productive of frenzy, coma and death as weapons – in other words he would employ exactly the same types of chemical warfare as those associated with the Antichrist in other quatrains. Secondly, Cheramon agora is not an occult 'Word of Power'; it was the classical name for an obscure town in what is now Turkey and the 'crosses' predicted by Nostradamus to be 'attached to it by rank' are likely to be the hierarchy of the sect led by the pseudo-Messiah.

The last line of the quatrain seems to foretell that the third Antichrist will launch an attack by chemical poisons ('Rougon') on a precisely dated 3 October. It is a pity that Nostradamus was not equally precise about the predicted year of the event!

97

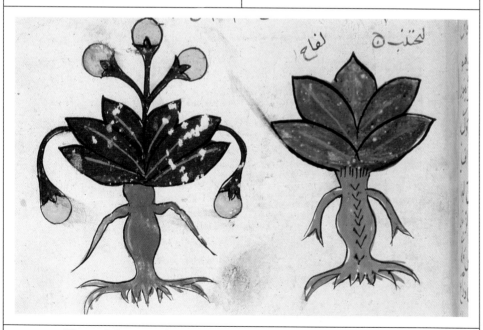

The mandrake, source of 'mandragora', Nostradamus's code word for chemical warfare

Worthless 'scrip' – will all currencies lose their value?

As readers of this book will by now be well aware, from the content of some of his quatrains it seems that Nostradamus prophesied that the years immediately before and/or after AD 2000 will be a time of continued and unprecedented crises. We are doomed, so the seer predicted, to endure an epoch of political and social turmoil, schism and wars – largely religiously motivated – fought with chemical and bacteriological weapons. It is quite certain that if these predicted events do indeed take place they will directly or indirectly result in a disastrous decline in all the world's economies and in misery, starvation, disease and death for hundreds of millions of men and women. Not surprisingly, the seer predicted exactly such happenings – plague, famine, the debauching of currencies and consequent riots and civil disturbance.

It is likely that in every decade of every century since the very beginnings of humanity, people have been starving to death in some part or parts of the earth – and any seer who has made an undated prophecy of future starvation in a particular country must

have been sure that it would eventually be fulfilled. The *Centuries* do, indeed, contain some prophecies of this sort – for instance, an Iranian famine is predicted in Century I Quatrain 70, which reads:

Rain, famine and war will be ceaseless in Persia,
Too great trustfulness will betray the monarch,
The matters begun in Gaul will also end there,
A secret augury for one to be sparing.

Interesting, and possibly connected with future developments in the Islamic Republic of Iran – but its precise significance is much too vague to be even largely, let alone completely, interpreted with a reasonable prospect of success prior to the occurrence of the actual events. On the other hand there is a Nostradamian prediction of a worldwide famine of unique severity which would seem to pertain to the epoch of political, religious and social upheaval which the seer foretold for the years around the turn of the present century. This depressing prophecy is made in Century I Quatrain 67, which reads:

The great famine which I feel approaching
Will often recur [in particular countries] and then become universal:
So great will it be, and so long will it last
That they [the starving] will eat woodland roots and drag children from the breast.

This last line may mean that the starving will drag children from the breast to suckle the milk themselves – or it may be that Nostradamus was prophesying a famine of such severity that cannibalism will be practised on a considerable scale throughout the entire world!

This famine is destined to be accompanied by an equally ubiquitous inflation in which all paper money loses its entire value – or so it would appear from Century VIII Quatrain 28. This verse reads:

The simulacra [images or reproductions] of gold and silver inflated,
Which after the theft [of real value] were chucked into the lake,
At the discovery that all is destroyed by debt.
All bonds and scrip will be cancelled.

As paper money, 'the simulacra of gold and silver', was unknown in Europe at the time when Nostradamus was writing the *Centuries* the first line of the verse is remarkable in itself; if the entire prophecy is destined to prove accurate this approaching inflation will be the most complete and devastating that the world has known, for not only will paper money become worthless but 'all bonds and scrip' – in other words all wealth save real property and other material riches – will be wiped out.

In such a situation it would be likely that there would be a universal desire to get hold of some form of the only easily portable medium of exchange – gold and other precious metals. Such a desire, accompanied by rage against the bankers who would be blamed for the economic situation which had resulted in mass pauperism, could undoubtedly result in civil disturbance, riots and the looting of buildings associated with financial institutions.

Fort Knox – gold reserves destined for looting?

Such an eruption of burning fury from an angry people against a system which they believe has robbed them of everything is apparently predicted in Century X Quatrain 81, which reads:

Treasure is placed in a temple by citizens of the Hesperides [America]
Withdrawn within it to a secret hiding place,
The temple to be thrown open by famished liens [meaning uncertain],
Recaptured, ravished, a terrible prey in the midst [of it?].

Bank vaults and similar modern constructs for the storage of precious metals were, of course, unknown to Nostradamus, who might well have used the word 'temple' in reference to one – in classical times it was quite usual for citizens to store their wealth in temples of the gods. As the 'temple' of this quatrain is in America the whole verse is probably a prophetic description of a violent attack on Fort Knox, the vaults of which contain the bulk of the USA's gold reserves.

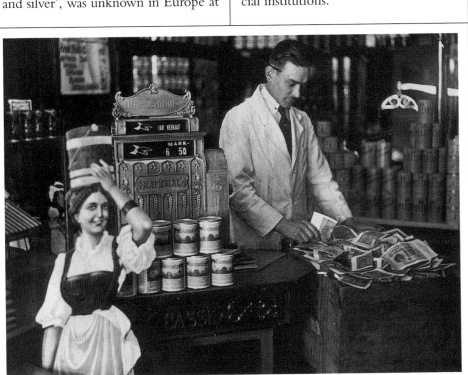
Inflation in Germany – a bin of 6,500,000 Marks to cover a mere 6.50 Mark bill

99

The nuclear accident at Three Mile Island was, according to some, predicted by Nostradamus

There is, and perhaps always has been, a tendency among Nostradamian commentators to fit particular predictions to events which have been in the news in comparatively recent times. While this tendency has been responsible for identifying some remarkable predictive hits, such as the Great Fire of London quatrain (see pages 34–5), it is one which is not without its dangers. First, the interpreter is likely to begin to twist the already convoluted verse of the seer to make it fit events which have taken place in the interpreter's own lifetime. Secondly, it sometimes results in the interpreter abandoning all common sense and coming to the conclusion

that Nostradamus made a large number of prophecies about events that took place hundreds of years after his death which are, except on the shortest of timescales and in the most parochial of perspectives, almost triflingly insignificant.

This tendency has resulted in more than one contemporary student of the *Centuries* hailing Century X Quatrain 49 as a prediction of the American nuclear accident which took place some years ago at the Three Mile Island power station – an accident which was, until the Chernobyl disaster, the most serious to have happened anywhere in the world. The quatrain in question reads:

*Garden of the world near to the
new city,
In the road of the hollow mountains,
It will be seized and run into the tank,
Forced to drink water poisoned
with sulphur.*

Those who have claimed that this prediction relates to the Three Mile Island emergency assert that the 'new city' of line one is New York (which is, in fact, almost certainly the case – see page 103), that the 'hollow mountains' of line two was Nostradamus's way of describing skyscrapers seen by him in vision, and that lines three and four refer to the threat that the accident could have posed to New York's water supply as a consequence of radioactive fall-out.

Perhaps, but even if one accepts the suggestion made by one interpreter that the 'sulphur' of line four is to be taken as meaning the alchemical principle of that name – the essence of the fiery 'element' of destruction, of which uncontrolled radioactivity is a particular manifestation – rather than some compound of the chemical element of sulphur, the prediction can hardly apply to the effects of the Three Mile Island incident. The plain fact of the matter is that while the accidental events which took place at Three Mile Island threatened disaster to a large area of the north-east of the USA they were brought under control in such a way that no catastrophe actually took place and the water supply of neither New York nor anywhere else was poisoned.

Nevertheless, with its mentions of the 'new city' (which, according to general consensus of opinion, was Nostradamus's way of describing New York) the quatrain would seem to be applicable to the (literal) poisoning of the water supply of either New York or some other population centre fairly close to it. Unless the prediction that Nostradamus made in Century X Quatrain 49 was completely in error – and it must be remembered that a few of the seer's prognostications do seem to have been quite erroneous (see pages 142–3) – this event must still lie in the future, for it certainly hasn't happened yet.

The content of this prophecy is not obviously such as to give any indication of the likely date for its fulfilment, but numerological and other considerations seem to link it to a number of other predictive quatrains which pertain to events foretold for the closing years of this century and the opening ones of the next. In other words, this prophecy of New Yorkers or other Americans being in a position where they have no choice save to 'drink water poisoned with sulphur' relates to the epoch of Nostradamian predictions concerning militant Islamic holy wars, the third Antichrist, world conflicts and famines (see pages 84–91).

It is therefore likely that if the poisoned water prophecy is to be fulfilled it will happen a) at some time in the near future, probably between the years 1995 and 2005 and b) as a consequence of a military attack upon the United States. It is also likely, because of the content of the first line of the verse – 'Garden of the world near to the new city' – that the poisoning will make its main impact on New York's neighbour, New Jersey, 'the Garden State', rather than New York itself.

If water purification plants were knocked out by bombing as happened in Baghdad during the Gulf War, water supplies could be polluted in such a way that they were dangerous to drink. However, this could be easily countered by boiling the water before use, so Nostradamus's use of the phrase 'forced to drink' suggests a poisoning of an altogether more serious nature than mere pollution – most likely the use of chemical or nuclear weapons. The former would be the more likely if the seer's use of the word 'sulphur' was intended to be taken literally – there are a number of sulphur compounds of the utmost virulence. If, however, the word was intended to be understood symbolically it is more likely that the prophecy relates to radioactive poisons and a nuclear assault upon the USA. In relation to the possibility of a nuclear assault, the content of Century VI Quatrain 97, examined in detail on the next two pages, is of major and frightening relevance.

101

Nostradamus predicted 'water poisoned with sulphur'

WARPLANES OVER THE AMERICAS

No part of the land area of the continental United States has ever suffered the direct effects of modern warfare – that is to say, of warfare involving the use of airpower and surface-to-surface missiles. While from 1917 to the present day countless American families and whole communities have suffered from the effects of foreign wars – from economic hardships to the grief suffered as a consequence of the deaths of neighbours, friends, and relations – the only damage directly inflicted on the American mainland by foreign military forces since 1814 was the trifling inconveniences inflicted on the West Coast in World War II by shells from Japanese submarines and, even more trifling, incendiary balloon devices launched from the other side of the Pacific.

It is predicted in the *Centuries* that such comparative immunity to the ravages of modern war as they affect the civilian population is not scheduled to last much longer, for Nostradamus prophesied that the series of worldwide conflicts he saw beginning at about the turn of the present century – at some time between 1995 and 2004 if one accepts the Nostradamian chronology that is adhered to by most contemporary students of the *Centuries* – would directly inflict an immense amount of damage upon the Americas and their peoples. Take, for example, the prediction of global conflict contained in Century I Quatrain 91, the whole of which is to be found on page 89. The last line of this quatrain reads: 'The greatest damage will be imposed upon the left'.

The word 'left' is most unlikely to have been used in its modern political sense by the seer – although one cannot completely rule this out, for in some of his fulfilled predictions he

'Fire approaches the great city' – the US would seem to be the target of military attack, according to one of the seer's predictions

seems to have used the word 'Reds' in its modern sense of 'social revolutionaries' instead of one of its more normal sixteenth-century senses, such as 'the Roman Cardinals'. It is also just possible that by 'the left' Nostradamus simply meant the more sinisterly motivated of the antagonists, for the word sinister derives from a Latin word meaning 'left'.

The seer predicted worldwide conflict in our age

It seems most likely, however, that the seer was making a reference to the most common type of map of the world that was used in his own times and indeed still is at the present day. In such essentially Eurocentric productions the northern hemisphere is shown at the top of the map and the western hemisphere – the Americas – on the left. If the prophet was, as seems virtually certain, making a geographical reference of this sort the last line of Century I Quatrain 91 can then be paraphrased, in the context of its first three lines, to mean 'In the predicted World War fought with missiles and other weapons of aerial warfare the greatest damage will be suffered by the Americas'.

Such an interpretation of the meaning of this verse's last line is made more likely by the content of a surprisingly large number of other predictions made in the *Centuries* –

for example, Century VI Quatrain 97, which also contains what is clearly a geographical reference:

The heaven will broil at forty-five degrees,
Fire approaches the great new city,
An enormous, widespread flame leaps high
When they want to have proof
[or evidence] *of the Normans.*

It is often difficult to be sure exactly what is being said in Nostradamian verses relating to our futures, but in the case of this quatrain only the meaning of the last line seems to be in any real doubt (see panel below). The reference to 'forty-five degrees' in line one must relate to the approximate latitude and/or longitude (perhaps extending between 40° and 50°) of some particular area of the earth's surface; it cannot reasonably be taken as an astronomical reference relating to, for instance, elevation or a particular zodiacal degree, as in this case the rest of the quatrain would be meaningless.

As a geographical reference to latitude and/or longitude of between 40° and 50°, 45° could apply to a number of regions, among them oil-producing areas of the Middle East and a huge segment of the continental USA including the whole of New England and New York. It could be that this was one of Nostradamus's double predictions, applying to both these parts of the world, but the mention of the 'great new city' in line two of the quatrain makes it clear that the primary import of the prophecy is to the USA, for every other mention of a 'new city' in the quatrains seems to bear an American interpretation, referring to Washington, San Francisco or, most usually, New York.

It would appear, then, that lines two and three are a prophecy of a widespread nuclear attack on the USA (which may possibly coincide with a similar event in the Middle East), in which New York is damaged – and perhaps utterly destroyed – by the 'approaching flame'.

103

NORMANS AND NORTHMEN

As was explained earlier on this page, Century VI Quatrain 97 would appear to contain a specific prediction of a nuclear attack on New York and other areas of the United States. Only the significance of the quatrain's last line, 'when they want to have proof [or evidence] of the Normans' seems to be a matter for much debate.

Some distinguished Nostradamians, Erika Cheetham among them, have taken the line as a possible reference to the military and diplomatic involvement of France in events associated with the bombing of New York. Possibly – but the word 'Normans' derives from an Old Norse word meaning no more than 'Northmen', so it may well be that the line pertains not to France but to a northern Asian alliance – perhaps one led by Nostradamus's 'third Antichrist'.

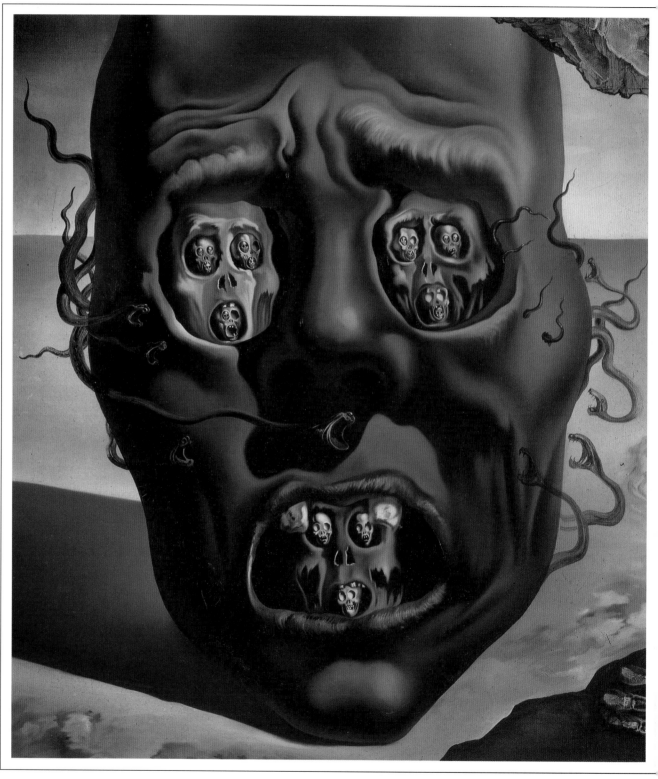

> THE FILM *JURASSIC PARK* TAKES FOR ITS THEME THE RE-CREATION OF ANCIENT MONSTERS EXTINCT FOR MILLIONS OF YEARS. NOSTRADAMUS BELIEVED THAT LONG-DEAD MONSTERS IN HUMAN FORM – SUCH AS GENGHIS KHAN – WOULD RETURN TO STALK THE EARTH IN OUR NEAR FUTURE.

As has been demonstrated in the preceding 25 pages, the prophecies made by Nostradamus which are believed to relate to the approaching decades – from roughly the middle of the 1990s until well into the next century – are grim indeed. We are threatened with worldwide famine of such profundity that many of us will find ourselves eating forest roots and others will practise cannibalism; with wars fought with chemical, bacteriological and nuclear weapons; with the worst inflation that humanity has ever known; and with all the economic and social consequences of fanatical religious excess. In short, an age of monstrous terror and almost unmitigated horror is close upon us.

Such is the dreadful nature of what Nostradamus prophesied for us and our children – or, at least, what the majority of contemporary Nostradamians believe that the seer prophesied for us – that even the most dedicated admirer of the *Centuries* and the track record of its author must hope that as far as the next 10 or 15 years are concerned he was in hopeless error; or, better

Many Nostradamians paint a bleak picture of the near future

still, that interpreters of the obscure language of what seem to be the chronologically relevant quatrains have misunderstood their import or will prove to be several centuries out in their calculations of the timescale appropriate to them. This is all the more to be hoped because of the doom-laden nature of many of the predictions commented upon in the following pages.

Such predictions include: a major disaster, probably involving the use of fusion weapons, taking place at the same time as an imminent Olympic Games; the intervention in the affairs of the world of some horror – which may be either an individual or a material thing – upon which Nostradamus bestowed the enigmatic code name 'King Reb'; sinister religious movements; more wars and famine; and a grim future for Russia.

Not all is quite as dismal as this, for while Nostradamus seems to have predicted many miseries for the years which lie immediately before us he also seems to have believed that one day, long after all this suffering, human beings will live in happiness and will travel amidst the stars.

THE GAMES OF DEATH

Will an Olympic Games of the future herald the arrival of terrible events?

An amazing assertion is made by some present-day students of the strange prophetic quatrains of Nostradamus. They claim that in two of them – Century X Quatrain 74 and Century I Quatrain 50 – the seer predicted that at the time of the Olympic Games in the year 2008 ancient secret cults long thought to be extinct or the preserve of a handful of occult cranks will demonstrate their hidden power to the world. These weird sects are of a pagan nature, pertain to necromancy (the cult of the dead), will be bloody in nature, and by 2008 may be headed by the individual who is destined to be responsible for the coming of the 'King of Terror' (see pages 110–11) in the summer of 1999.

So here, for what it is worth, is a paraphrase of this interpretation of Century X Quatrain 74 and Century I Quatrain 50, from which are drawn the sensational and alarming predictive conclusions outlined on the first page of this section. Century X quatrain 74 reads:

The year of the great seventh
number revolved
It will appear at the time of the games
of the Hecatomb,
Not distant from the great Millennium,
When the dead will leave their graves.

'Not distant from the great Millennium' is taken as meaning 'not far from (i.e. not many years in time from) the year 2000'. This could mean either before or after the millennium year. However, as the exact year intended to be indicated by Nostradamus is after a year date ending with a seven ('The year of the great seventh number revolved', that is, completed) a date subsequent to either 1997 or 2007 is applicable to this prediction. As it is the great seventh number of which Nostradamus wrote it is obviously 2007 rather than 1997 to which he was making reference, so the predicted event, the time

The modern Olympics revived 'the games of Hecatomb' held in ancient Greece

when, metaphorically or literally, the dead will leave their graves, will take place shortly after 2007, probably in the year 2008.

That 2008 is the year strongly indicated for the fulfilment of the prophecy is confirmed by the second line of the quatrain, 'It will appear at the time of the games of the Hecatomb'. A hecatomb – the word is derived from a classical Greek word literally meaning 'a hundred oxen' – is a large public blood sacrifice involving the ritual slaughter of many victims. In early classical Greece such a public blood sacrifice was held at the beginning of the regularly held athletic Games which took place at Corinth and other cities. These Games, of which the best known were those held at Olympus, were far more than mere 'games' in the modern sense of the word; they were solemn pagan festivals frequented by athletes from all over the Greek-speaking areas of the

eastern Mediterranean. The original Olympic Games were connected with the cults of the underworld goddess Demeter (the only women allowed at the Olympics were her priestesses) and of the moon goddess Selene, which probably derived from a primitive fertility cult.

Towards the end of the fourth century AD all the Games, including those held at Olympus, were suppressed by the Emperor Theodosius, who was, like all the emperors of the latter half of that century save Julian the Apostate, a Christian. This was done because of the pagan nature of all the Games and the fact that the convention that athletes taking part in them should compete in the nude was deeply offensive to Christian prudery. This brought an end to all of what were, in name at least, still the 'games of the Hecatomb' although the actual sacrifices would seem to have ceased to be performed many years earlier.

Is there anything at the present day to which Nostradamus's phrase 'the games of the Hecatomb' could apply? Well, there are certainly no public games at which animals are sacrificed to the ancient gods, but the modern Olympics were established in 1896 as a deliberate revival, after 1500 years of near oblivion, of the greatest of all the 'games of the Hecatomb' – those held at Olympus and associated with the cults of Demeter and Selene.

The first of the revived Olympic Games scheduled to take place after the year 2007 – 'the year of the great seventh number' of the first line of Century X Quatrain 74 – will be those due to be held in 2008. It is in that year that 'it' – whatever or whoever that may be – will appear and that, actually and/or symbolically, 'the dead will arise from their graves'. For complex reasons, 'it' is identified as a person referred to in Century I Quatrain 50, which is to be found on pages 108–9.

107

Demeter, patroness of the early Olympics

The three great religious faiths with which Nostradamus and his contemporaries were familiar were Islam, Judaism and Christianity, of which Friday, Saturday and Sunday respectively are the holy days. But in Century I Quatrain 50 Nostradamus refers to someone who is a follower of none of these three faiths, for the quatrain reads:

> *From the Watery Triplicity will*
> *be born,*
> *One who will celebrate Thursday as his*
> *holy day,*
> *His fame, acclamation and power*
> *will grow*
> *On land and sea, causing*
> *Eastern tempests.*

The first line of this strange prophetic verse merely tells us something about the astrological influences fated to be

The birth of the Antichrist, as depicted in a 15th-century woodcut

prominent in the horoscope of the person to whom the prediction pertains (see panel opposite). But what of the second line of the quatrain, describing the person concerned as 'one who will celebrate Thursday as his holy day'? The exact form of paganism to which this individual will adhere is uncertain, but because of the reference in the last line of Century X Quatrain 74 to the dead leaving their graves it is likely that it will involve the revival of an ancient cult of the dead – perhaps, in view of the reference to 'Eastern tempests', some degenerated form of left hand tantrism or a Bon cult.

The interpretations of the two quatrains in relation to both one another and other Nostradamian predictions are apparent and can be summarized thus: by the early years of the new millennium a new and powerful influence will be at work in the world – a malignant political leader who will also be a religious leader or, at any rate, a quasi-religious leader. It is to be presumed that his followers will look upon him as a spiritual genius, and it is quite evident that he will not even claim to be a Christian, a Muslim or a Jew – for he is described as one 'who will celebrate Thursday as his holy day'.

In the year 2008 this ruler will engage in an action, or actions, of a major and unpleasant significance. There is good reason to tentatively identify the 1999 'King of Terror' discussed on pages 110–11 (or, alternatively, the individual who sets whatever reality is symbolized by that phrase into motion) with the one whose fame grows to such an extent that 'Eastern tempests' ensue – unless and until the course of future history

Baphomet, Lord of the Left Hand Path

demonstrates that they relate to two completely different people. However, this seems improbable; it is far more likely that the one who raises 'Eastern tempests' – which in this context must be presumed to be religious, social and political upheavals rather than meteorological turmoils – will prove to be the same person as the one who will be, or be associated with, the 'King of Terror'. It is also very likely that he is identical with the 'Antichrist' referred to as being associated with 'King Reb' in Century X Quatrain 66.

THE WATERY TRIPLICITY

According to traditional astrology, the 12 signs of the zodiac are divided into four triplicities, each made up of three signs. Each triplicity is attributed to one of the 'elements' of ancient esoteric lore – Earth, Air, Fire and Water. The zodiacal signs of the Water triplicity are Cancer, Scorpio and Pisces, so Nostradamus was indicating in the first line of Century I Quatrain 50 that these signs would be significant in his subject's horoscope. Perhaps, for instance, the person concerned would be born with a Scorpio ascendant, with the sun and Mercury in Pisces, and with the moon in Cancer. In other words,

Nostradamus was predicting that a future ruler will have a horoscope dominated by planets and supposedly significant astrological points in zodiacal signs attributed to the Water triplicity.

In certain circumstances such a horoscope could appear very sinister indeed to someone applying to it the astrological rules that were in vogue at the time when Nostradamus was practising what was then still termed 'the celestial science' – widely regarded as second only to theology in its importance.

If, for example, both the sun and the planet Mars were on the ascendant in the Water sign of

Scorpio in an individual's horoscope a competent 16th-century astrologer would have expected its subject to be brutal, bloody, liable to furious rages, highly sexed, clever and deceitful – in the jargon of our own times, a highly intelligent, extremely cunning and abnormally violent sociopath.

This raises an interesting possibility. It may be that Nostradamus did not clairvoyantly discern the horoscope of the individual concerned, but merely got an impression of his or her character and, on the basis of his knowledge of astrological rules, decided that the unpleasant ruler must inevitably have the sort of birth chart indicated.

109

Attila the Hun pillaged Europe

Genghis Khan conquered Asia

Heinrich Himmler wanted to rule the world

CHEMICAL WARFARE

So far humanity has not experienced a war in which enormous numbers of people – either combatants or civilians – have died from the effects of chemical or nuclear warfare. While there were a large number of occasions on which chlorine, phosgene and mustard gas were used in World War I the fatal casualties inflicted by their use were surprisingly small; and while nuclear weapons were used in 1945 against Hiroshima and Nagasaki the number of civilians killed in these two cities was small compared to those who had already died elsewhere in Japan as a consequence of conventional bombing.

This situation is not destined to last – or so it would seem from the content of Century X Quatrain 72, one of that small minority of quatrains in which Nostradamus gave a specific date for a predicted future event. This quatrain reads:

In the year 1999 [and] *seven months,*
From the sky will come a great King
of Terror,
He will resurrect the great King of
Angolmois,
Before and afterwards Mars
rules happily.

As it stands, this Nostradamus quatrain is a great deal easier to interpret than many others. First, in the seventh month of 1999 (that is, July or perhaps early August), the King of Terror will come from the sky and bring back to life the King of Angolmois. Secondly, both before and after the coming of the King of Terror 'Mars rules happily' – a fairly obvious piece of predictive symbolism meaning that in the months before and after the descent of the Terror King the world will be ravaged by armed conflict.

There are still some puzzles, however. Who is the King of Angolmois? And how will he be brought back to life by a King of Terror, and exactly who, or what, is the latter?

'Angolmois' can be read simply as a French province (see page 114–15) or it can be taken as a good example of the sort of wordplay that recurs over and over again in the quatrains – the devising of a meaningless word or name which is either an anagram or, more usually, an imperfect anagram, of the actual word or name the seer had in mind. In this particular case 'Angolmois' can be read as an imperfect anagram of the Old French word Mongolois – Mongolians.

Now the greatest of all Mongolian rulers was Genghis Khan, who was reputed to have been monstrously cruel and destructive. Certainly he conquered a great kingdom for himself, and in so doing was directly or indirectly responsible for the deaths of millions of human beings. In other words, it seems very probable that by the phrase 'the great King of Angolmois' Nostradamus was indicating Genghis Khan. However, it does not seem likely that the seer was predicting that the mysterious King of Terror would literally restore the Mongol ruler to life; he was saying that the King of Terror would be another

Industrial pollution – forerunner of ecological breakdown and chemical warfare

Death in Africa – will poisons or disease destroy a continent?

Genghis Khan in that he would kill as many or more as the Mongol king.

Who or what, then, could be the Terror King whose victims will equal or outnumber the millions killed by Genghis Khan? He could be a living being, quite literally a great ruler who inflicts terror on those subjected to his power. In that case, however, it is difficult to understand how he could come from the sky unless he were an alien being – a conqueror who comes from outer space. At least one student of the *Centuries* is convinced that the latter is the correct interpretation of Century X Quatrain 72 – that in July or August 1999 our planet will be invaded by beings from outer space who will destroy much of humanity and enslave the rest.

Perhaps – but it seems much more likely that Nostradamus was employing the phrase 'King of Terror' in a metaphorical sense pertaining to an inanimate object – much as a copy-writer might refer to a product he or she was writing about as 'the car that is king of the road' or 'the queen of perfumes'. If so the meaning of the

quatrain is clear and, considering the many examples of fulfilled Nostradamus predictions, extremely alarming: in July or August 1999, at a time when a war is in progress, a weapon of mass destruction will come from the sky which will be so powerful that it will be responsible for the deaths of more people than was Genghis Khan.

This immediately suggests the use of a fusion weapon by one of the warring powers; but even the largest of the present-day hydrogen bombs would be unlikely to destroy as many lives as did the Mongolian ruler. Perhaps Nostradamus was using the word 'King' to symbolize a collective reality, tens or hundreds of fusion weapons – in other words, he may have been predicting the outbreak of a war in 1999 in which nuclear weapons would be employed on a very large scale.

Another possibility is that the King of Terror will not be a nuclear weapon of any type: it will instead be a chemical or bacteriological weapon which gets out of control and spreads either chemical poisons or disease spores throughout a continent or even the whole world, killing millions.

For reasons explained on page 112–13, some present-day Nostradamians believe that it is likely to be the continent of Europe that is destined to be the victim of the mass murder of 1999.

111

WAVES OF ALIENS

Since 1947, UFO sightings seem to have come in waves – almost as though we have been 'investigated' by some alien civilization at regular intervals. The biggest wave of sightings was in 1952, when the astronomy consultant on the US government's UFO monitoring project was Professor Allen Hynek of the University of Ohio. After investigating no fewer than 1501 cases, of which 303 remained unexplained, his original scepticism

was thoroughly shaken. Cases where radar confirmation tallied with visual evidence in the vicinity of Washington D. C. were particularly hard to ignore. Sightings by trained airline pilots were also common, and on one occasion military planes played tag with several UFOs while the whole thing was being watched on radar. UFOs seem to have been less frequently sighted recently, but this is not to say they won't come back in force in 1999!

ALCHEMY, MAGIC AND CULTS

As was explained on pages 80–1, the so-called occult quatrains of the *Centuries* have always puzzled commentators. Their attempts to give answers which would provide a solution to the riddle of precisely why the seer thought fit to insert into his prophecies a number of verses which appear to pertain more to the techniques of alchemy and magic than to the future have invariably given rise to more heat than light; they have tended to receive little acceptance or response from others, save for dismissive reference to the oddly worded Century VI Quatrain 100 – to which Nostradamus uniquely gave a title: Legis cantio contra ineptos criticos, 'the Song of the Law Against Unintelligent Critics' (see panel opposite).

Yet it is possible that some of those who have gone beyond attempting to understand the meanings of just the purely predictive quatrains of the *Centuries* have a great deal of information to give concerning the details of what was prophesied by Nostradamus in some of his precise but infuriatingly incomplete prognostications – for example, Century X Quatrain 72, in which he wrote of the King of Terror whom he foresaw as descending from the skies in the summer of 1999 (see page 110–11). These interpreters have attempted to understand the innermost nature of those subjects that are dealt with in the occult quatrains – alchemy, magic and those strange paths to inner knowledge which some have termed 'cults of the shadow' –

A kit for practising the black arts

and, by applying them to the *Centuries*, have endeavoured to learn more of the nature of particular aspects of 'future history'.

Such interpreters risk attracting derision and making foolish mistakes, but they are probably following the path which Nostradamus referred to as being that of 'priests of the rite' (see panel). One such experimenter, a person who in Nostradamian terms could be called 'a priestess of the rite' – that is, a woman who possesses a detailed theoretical and practical knowledge of both ceremonial divination (see pages 138–9) and of those

ancient techniques of consciousness-alteration which supposedly enable those who practise them to obtain a glimpse of the pattern of the future – has supplied the present writer with the result of an experiment which was aimed at re-experiencing the 'King of Terror' vision which Nostradamus recorded in Century X Quatrain 72. The techniques that were used to carry out this experiment are described on pages 150–1; here it suffices to summarize the content of the psychic vision which was the outcome of their employment.

According to this experimental psychic vision, by the beginning of 1999 the ruler of an expansionist central

Paracelsus, master of occult medicine and magic

Asian state which was formerly a constituent republic of the Soviet Union will have within its control some sort of orbiting space vehicle. By this time, the whole of what was formerly the USSR will be riven by a turmoil of ethnic and religious foreign and civil wars. As a means of deterring both actual and potential enemies, this orbiting space vehicle will be equipped with some means of launching bacteriological and chemical weapons. As a consequence of what will be subsequently claimed an accident, these terrible weapons will be launched, hitting the southern part of France but spreading death and devastation over the entire European land mass.

If this modern prediction proves to be correct, Europe will have been subjected to a murderous attack from one of the states of the former USSR and World War III will have been unleashed in all its terror.

An early 15th-century practitioner of alchemy at work

113

THE SEER'S SONG

Century VI Quatrain 100, the only quatrain to which Nostradamus gave a title (see facing page), is possessed of another singularity: it was printed (except for one word) in Latin, instead of the usual convoluted language of French, anagrams and neologisms to be found in other quatrains. The verse reads:

Let those who read this verse ponder its meaning,
Let the common crowd and the unlearned leave it alone:

All of them – Idiot Astrologers and Barbarians – keep off,
He who does the other thing, let him be a priest for [or to] the rite.

In this quatrain the seer was clearly indicating that the content of this verse was intended neither for the generality of men and women ('barbarians') nor even for 'idiot astrologers' – mere fortunetellers as distinct from those who at the present day might be termed 'initiated diviners' – but for 'priests of the rite'.

However, the seer obviously intended to communicate more than this and it is likely he was saying one or both of two things: first, that there is – as some students of his writings assert – a hidden structure to the *Centuries*. Secondly, that those who were 'priests of the rite' – that is, those who were skilled in the predictive arts and not mere fortune tellers – should be able not only to interpret the quatrains but to expand and elucidate their meanings by the use of ritual divination.

WORLD WAR III

Famine will be the inevitable consequence of the third world war predicted by Nostradamus

Nostradamus makes what can be interpreted as a prediction of World War III in at least 12 quatrains. The most famous, Century X Quatrain 72, has already been discussed (see pages 110–11), but it can be interpreted in another way which yields a bit more detail. Instead of interpreting Angolmois as an imperfect anagram of Mongolois (Mongolians) it could be taken to mean the French city of Angoulême. A recent French leader who comes from near here is François Mitterand, who was born in Charente. The quatrain now suggests that after the 'King of Terror' comes from the sky, Mitterand will be politically resurrected and brought back to power temporarily to deal with the situation. Mars could then either refer to war generally or a French leader whose horoscope is strongly martial, and whose rule is interrupted by the temporary reappointment of President Mitterand – or perhaps some other French leader from the same region.

In Century I Quatrain 16, Nostradamus uses astrological symbolism to date the impending war:

A scythe joined with a pond in Sagittarius
At its highest ascendant.
Plague, famine, death from military hands,
The century approaches its renewal.

The scythe in this astrological context represents the planet Saturn, while 'joined with a pond' refers to a watery zodiacal sign or planet. One commentator has translated 'pond' as Aquarius, and has interpreted the passage as 'when Saturn and Aquarius are in conjunction with Sagittarius'. However, it is not possible for two zodiacal signs to be in conjunction and it is more correct to talk of two planets in conjunction rather than a planet (Saturn) joined to a sign (Aquarius). Obviously, the 'pond' may represent the Moon in conjunction with Saturn in Sagittarius. The fourth line strongly suggests that the events occur at the end of a century. The most recent time in which Saturn was in Sagittarius was 1988; from now until the end of this century, Saturn, being a very slow-moving planet, only passes through Aquarius, Pisces, Aries and Taurus. This suggests that the arrival of this particular plague, famine and death is not scheduled until well into the 21st century.

Century II Quatrain 46 gives us further insight into the possible advent of a third world war:

After great misery for mankind an even greater one approaches
When the great cycle of the centuries is renewed
It will rain blood, milk, famine, war and diseases
In the sky will be seen a fire, dragging a tail of sparks.

Again the time frame is specified as 'when the great cycle of the centuries is renewed'. Unlike Century II Quatrain 41 (see page 89), which talks of a Great Star boiling or burning, this quatrain specifies 'a fire, dragging a tail of sparks'. This would seem to be an even more likely reference to some great comet. As Halley's comet came and went in 1986 with very little visibility or astrological disturbance, Nostradamus's 'fire' is likely to be an unexpected meteorological phenomenon, perhaps the impact of a meteor on earth.

Whatever the exact timing, the phrase 'when the great cycle of the centuries is renewed' does suggest the end of this millennium. The war will bring with it a rain of blood, milk, famine, and disease. The odd word out is 'milk', so perhaps the original French word 'laict' would be better interpreted as laicité, meaning an outbreak of secularity or anti-religious feeling.

Nostradamus refers to the advent of the comet yet again in Century II Quatrain 62:

Mabus will soon die and there will happen
A dreadful destruction of people and animals:
Suddenly, vengeance will appear,
A hundred hands, thirst and hunger,
when the comet shall pass.

The key to the timing is the identity of Mabus – perhaps someone who has not yet come to prominence. In view of the reference to animals dying as well, the cause of this dreadful

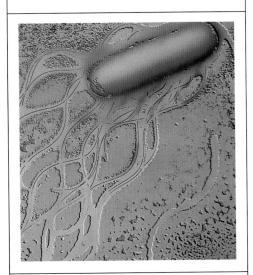

Bacteria – another deadly threat to humanity

destruction is probably some kind of indiscriminate nuclear device. Erika Cheetham suggests that 'a hundred hands' refers to the many refugee camps springing up all over the world where there are wars or famine. The passing of a comet might, however, be Nostradamus's vision of a missile rather than a natural comet.

Another quatrain which is specifically relevant to the 20th century is Century I, Quatrain 63 where, amazingly, Nostradamus says very clearly that:

Pestilence is past, the world becomes smaller,
For a long time the lands will be inhabited peacefully.
People will travel safely through the sky [over] land and seas:
Then wars will start up again.

The world becoming smaller is a 20th-century phrase – it seems as if Nostradamus had even overheard a snippet of 20th-century conversation. He certainly would not have 'seen' the physical world shrink. It is an interesting aside on how Nostradamus received the quatrains, almost as if he had time-travelled at random (or so it appears from his ordering of the quatrains) and then both viewed and overheard events. Some of his visions are of things like the fighter pilots (see page 65) for which he could have had no frame of reference, so he describes them in terms of objects of his own time, often quite ingeniously.

The last line suggests that wars will start up after a period of peace. This phrase might refer to the world wars that have already taken place, or suggest a third erupting after an interval of 50 years of relative peace. From the end of World War II, an interval of 50 years brings us to 1995.

As the first two world wars of this century both started in the Balkans, that confused and ethnically very divided area which was until recently called Yugoslavia, it is very tempting to point to the present troubles in the Balkans as the potential touchpaper for the third world war which Nostradamus predicts.

115

THE FUTURE OF RUSSIA

The country of Russia existed for many centuries before the Revolution of 1917 which was to herald the formation of the Soviet Union – now, after 72 years, again broken down into its constituent parts. The alliance between the old Soviet Union and the US in early 1990 is predicted by Century VI Quatrain 21, where these countries are identified in the first line:

When those of the Northern Pole are united together,
In the East will be great fear and dread:
A new man elected supported by the great one . . .

The failure of the 'Moorish law' – Marxism – has revived the fortunes of the Orthodox Church

The second line may refer to the reaction of China, now left alone as the only large Communist country. The 'new man elected' is obviously Boris Yeltsin, who, despite some clashes, was supported by the 'great one' who brought it all about, Mikhael Gorbachev.

The break-up of the Soviet Union into its constituent republics, no longer governed by Moscow, has left a legacy of squabbling between these new countries who are trying to forge a Commonwealth of Independent States. Nostradamus has something to say about two of them – the Ukraine and Belorussia – in Century III, Quatrain 95:

The Moorish law will be seen to fail,
Followed by another that is more attractive:
The Boristhenes will be the first to give way,
To another more pleasing as a consequence of gifts and tongues.

The 'Moorish law' was actually a pun meaning the teachings of Marx and hence communism (see pages 68–9), which has been seen to have failed. The reference to the river Boristhenes (or Dneiper) clearly identifies the two states as the Ukraine and Belorussia (White Russia, as it used to be called), through which it flows. It is clear that

Boris Yeltsin – the first Christian leader Russia has had since 1917

the upsurge of Islamic fundamentalism in some of the previous republics of the Soviet Union will fail in these two states. The form of government which will finally take over in these countries is seen by Nostradamus as more pleasing than Islamic fundamentalism or even communism.

As these former Soviet satellites are the 'first to give way' to Western propaganda and perhaps bribery or the lure of consumer goods (gifts and tongues), the thought occurs that they will at some stage be involved in a conflict, presumably with their neighbour, Russia.

Further elaboration is to be had in Century IV Quatrain 95, where Nostradamus writes:

The rule left to two, they will hold it a very short time,
Three years and seven months having passed they will go to war.
The two vestals will rebel against them;
The victor then born on American soil.

The 'rule left to two' suggests two world powers, the old Soviet Union (now Russia) and the US. The dating of this event would seem to be very accurate – three years and seven months after the break-up of the Soviet Union, some time in 1994 or early 1995. At this time there will be a war, not between Russia and America but between Russia allied with the US and the two 'vestal' (virginal) or new states. The new states might well be the newly independent states Belorussia and the Ukraine, which used to form part of the old Soviet Union.

The war will be won by assistance from America, or by a commander or

diplomat born there. Despite this help from America, the alliance between the two world powers will last no more than 13 years, according to Century V, Quatrain 78:

The two will not remain allied for long.
Within thirteen years they give into barbarian power.
There will be such a loss on both sides,
That one will bless the Barque and its leader.

The date when this alliance gives in to a barbarian power is some time early in the new millennium, about 2003. The only major non-Christian power likely to qualify is China, whose sheer population size dwarfs the two world powers combined.

The 'barque' is usually interpreted as the papacy or its leader the pope – if you believe Malachy and other references made by Nostradamus, the last of the line of popes. The quatrain may refer to the rapid rise of Christianity in the northern republics whose believers were so thoroughly repressed by communism and its doctrines over the period of its 72-year rule, or alternatively it may suggest the intervention of a Catholic president in the US.

Other quatrains suggest a growing Islamification of the southern ex-Soviet republics contrasting with Russia's newly revived Christianity, thereby causing friction amongst the southern republics.

THE PROPHECIES OF RASPUTIN

117

Rasputin, Russian healer, sage and prophet

One of the most influential men in Russia before the Revolution broke out was the monk Grigory Rasputin, who was intimately connected with the Russian royal family. Before his violent death at the hands of

Prince Yusupov, he wrote a letter to the Tsarina in which he made the prediction that he would die before the first day of 1917, the year of the Revolution. He added that if he was killed by a peasant then Russia would remain a prosperous monarchy for hundreds of years, but if he was killed by an aristocrat the Tsar and his family would die within two years, and no nobles would be left in Russia after 25 years.

All his predictions came true after he was murdered by an aristocrat on 29 December 1916. The Russian Revolution broke out the following year, and a year later Rasputin's second prediction came to pass with the murder of the royal family.

Nostradamus prophesied that Iris, the rainbow, will not be seen for 40 years

One of the most unequivocal quatrains is Century I Quatrain 17. It states in very plain French that for 40 years Iris will not be seen. Iris means 'rainbow' in Greek, and from this statement the quatrain appears to mean that for 40 years there will be no rain, a drought even longer than those experienced in the very dry central parts of Australia.

The next line of this quatrain states that for 40 years Iris will be seen every day. This sounds like rain of deluge proportions, followed by flooding, but with at least the sun showing through long enough to create a rainbow. To confirm this interpretation, the quatrain continues:

The dry earth will grow more parched,
And there will be great floods when it
is seen.

Although the Bible records a flood of 40 days and 40 nights, the world has not seen either a flood or a drought of these proportions, so the quatrain must refer to the future. The increasing occurrence of the 'greenhouse effect' and its alteration of the climatic patterns of the globe, including the spread of desert and semi-desert conditions into parts of Africa which were previously fertile, might be a beginning of the fulfilment of this terrible prophecy.

If we try to look beyond the fairly obvious literal meaning of the quatrain our only clue is Iris, who in Greek mythology was the daughter of Electra and the sister of the Harpies. In Homer's *Iliad* she is referred to as the messenger of the gods (particularly Hera and Zeus, the most senior Olympian gods of ancient Greece), so perhaps the drought and floods are to be construed as a serious warning of an ecological nature from the gods. Iris is also the wife of Zephyrus, the drying west wind and the cause of drought; by contrast, in her hand she holds a pitcher of water that symbolizes rain.

Drought brings famine, and in Century III Quatrain 42 Nostradamus speaks of famine in Tuscie, or Tuscany in Italy:

The child will be born with two teeth
in his throat,
Stones will fall like rain in Tuscany.
A few years later there will be neither
wheat nor barley,
To satisfy those who will weaken
from hunger.

The reference to the person born with two teeth in his throat occurs again in Century II Quatrain 7, also in conjunction with famine:

Among many people deported to
the islands
Will be a man born with two teeth in
his throat.
They will die of hunger having stripped
the trees.

'People deported to the islands' was a common French method of dealing with criminals, who were sent to penal colonies such as the Ile du Diable in French Guiana. The key to both of these quatrains is the child born with two teeth in its throat.

The clearest reference to a great famine is made in Century I Quatrain 67, which is quoted on pages 98–9. The emphasis is upon local famines becoming worldwide, possibly as a response to the greenhouse effect and the consequent alteration of climatic conditions. The African famines are just a forerunner of a much more widespread global famine.

The timing of this great famine is expressly indicated in Century IV, Quatrain 67:

In the year that Saturn and Mars are
equally fiery,
The air is very dry [from a]
long passage
From the hidden fires a great place
burns with heat.
Little rain, a hot wind, wars and raids.

The next dates when Saturn and Mars occur in the same fiery sign, Aries, are from 8 April to 2 May 1996, and from 5 March to 13 April 1998.

Nostradamus' prediction of widespread famine in this century is most likely to come true in these two key date ranges. These two planets are also both in fire signs from 10 September to 30 October 1996 and again from 29 September to 9 November 1997. These dates will probably see an increased climatic hardship in African countries, for Nostradamus indicates that the drought will escalate at the time of the proximity of these two 'malefic planets', as they used to be known. Because of the excess heat and very drying air, this may well be the worst famine of the century, and the famine will be more widespread than just Somalia or Ethiopia.

A very specific reference that Nostradamus made in Century V Quatrain 90 to famine in Greece confirms that the famine will not be limited to Africa:

In the Cyclades, in Perinthus
and Larissa,
In Sparta and all of the Pelopennese:
A very great famine, plague through
false dust.
It will last nine months throughout the
whole peninsula.

The 'false dust' may be either an agricultural spray, radioactive fall-out, or possibly some kind of southwards-drifting chemical weapon from wars in the Balkans.

119

The famines of the past, such as that at La Rochelle in the 18th century, will be eclipsed by those of the 21st century

Space exploration has only been a fact of life for the last three decades, yet Nostradamus appears to have foreseen even events occurring within this context – though, in an age when even basic flight had only been hinted at by Leonardo da Vinci (1452-1519), the idea of leaving the surface of the earth like a bird would have been beyond the imagination of the average man. The clearest reference to flight is in Century II, Quatrain 29:

The Eastern man shall come forth from
his seat
Passing the Apennine mountains
to France:
He will cross through the sky, the seas
and the snow,
And he will strike everyone with
his rod.

The third line clearly indicates Nostradamus's vision of air travel over both seas and the snowy mountain peaks of the Italian Apennines on the Eastern man's way to France, suggesting a Middle Eastern origin. One can only speculate if he 'saw' the shape of aeroplanes to come. Probably he did: Century I Quatrain 64 refers to 'battle fought in the skies' where the early flying helmets seem to have been 'visible' to him. The same theme is picked up in Century II, Quatrain 45 where 'human blood is spilt near to heaven' – a very unambiguous image of human warfare in the heavens. The next quatrain describes a missile (or possibly a comet): 'in the sky will be seen a fire, dragging a tail of sparks'. A less

120

Man's travels in space will soon take him to the stars

ambiguous reference is supplied by Century IV, Quatrain 43, which clearly states that 'weapons will be heard fighting in the skies'.

It is but a short conceptual step from here to manned space flight. The key quatrain is Century IX Quatrain 65, which reads:

He will be taken to the corner of Luna,
Where he will be placed on
foreign land.

If Luna is taken to be the physical moon, rather than some symbolic allusion, then this describes the landing of astronaut Neil Armstrong on lunar soil in a ship placed on the moon's surface by the controllers at

Saturn, stepping stone to the stars

NASA headquarters. Here he claimed the 'foreign land' for the US and made his giant step for mankind in 1969, more than 400 years after an astrologer in a small town in Provence gazed up at the moon and foretold this extraordinary event.

THE CHALLENGER DISASTER

The third and fourth lines of Century IX Quatrain 65 touch upon the events of 28 January 1986 when, 71 seconds after lift-off, the space shuttle Challenger exploded, killing its crew of seven:

The unripe fruit will be the subject
of great scandal.
Great blame, to the others
great praise.

The 'unripe fruit' is the malfunctioning space shuttle, whose explosion set back the whole US space programme by perhaps a decade. Great blame indeed, and unthinkable that such an expensive and complex operation could have gone so wrong before it even escaped the earth's atmosphere. Nostradamus's great praise goes instead to Neil Armstrong's team. At the same time the USSR space programme had been very successful in establishing the MIR orbiting space station, which is still in use.

Nostradamus refers to the Challenger disaster yet again in Century I, Quatrain 81, where he gives some intriguing clues:

Nine will be set apart from the
human race,
Separated from judgement
and advice:
Their fate is to be divided as
they depart,
Kappa, Theta, Lambda, banished
and scattered.

The Challenger is torn apart in the sky

'Their fate to be divided as they depart' is an image of the crew being torn asunder in the explosion as the Challenger departed – beyond all help, without even the time to make a decision ('separated from judgement'). However, Nostradamus got the number of astronauts wrong, for he says nine rather than seven. The Greek letters, banished and scattered, sound like American fraternity letters, and may have corresponded to the fraternity allegiances of some of the crew, or alternatively spelt their initials, or even the code name for this particular launch. These are details which probably only NASA can confirm or deny.

Many of Nostradamus's prophecies were of unpleasant events rather than joyful ones. Cynics have remarked that it is always wise for those who wish to gain a reputation for being able to see into the future to forecast plenty of disaster, doom and gloom – for catastrophe, like death and taxes, is always with us. The clairvoyant who tells us to expect calamities, will, so it is said, inevitably be admired for his or her psychic powers, for calamities there will surely be.

So many of Nostradamus's prophecies were negative that in 1562 no fewer than 20 English printers were fined for selling the *Prognostications of Nostradamus*. These fines are entered in the Stationer's Register for that year, alongside the titles and authors' names of a number of almanacs of the period. Political predictions were taken very seriously by the English government of the day and they made such an impact upon the citizens that, according to a pamphlet dating from 1561, 'the whole realm was so troubled and so moved with blind enigmatical and devilish prophecies of that heaven-gazer Nostradamus . . . that even those which in their hearts could have wished the glory of God and his Word most flourishing to be established were brought into such an extreme coldness of faith that they doubted God'.

The Delphic Sibyl

Such publications were big business, and perhaps the establishment was loath to see what may have been considered pro-French prognostications distributed in England. This gives us some idea of how popular Nostradamus's publications were even in England, as well as an insight into the official disapproval they provoked.

There has always been an ambiguous relationship between prophets and their rulers. No ruler likes to feel that his or her decisions will be brought to nought by a prophecy of failure, and besides it is bad for morale. Perhaps the most universally disliked and persecuted prophet was the Hebrew prophet Jeremiah: his first book of prophecies was first cut to pieces and then burnt. He was often imprisoned under very unpleasant conditions for his apparently unpatriotic prophecies, and had to ally himself with the Babylonian governor for safety before fleeing to Egypt, where he was finally stoned to death for his lugubrious insights.

Amongst the earliest of the Greek prophets were the Sibyls. Like the priestesses of Branchus, whose techniques of prophecy Nostradamus copied, they were also priestesses of Apollo. The most famous of the Sibyls was the Cumaean Sybil, who is reputed to have guided Aeneas to the underworld as reported in Virgil's *Aeneid Book VI*. This Sibyl, whose talents were obviously not appreciated, offered nine books of her prophecies to King Tarquin. When he refused to pay the apparently exorbitant price for these prophecies she threw three books into the flames of a brazier and then demanded the same price for the remaining six books. He refused and she repeated the same performance, burning a further three books. He finally gave

Jeremiah, like Nostradamus, made many predictions of calamity

in and paid the price asked for the whole nine books just for the remaining three. These books were preserved in the temple of Jupiter on the Capitol in Rome until it was burnt down in 83 BC.

Apart from books containing actual oracular pronouncements, many books which were not originally compiled for such interpretation were used for oracular purposes; they were literary or religious works which had come to be held in such veneration that they were looked upon as being endowed with a supernatural virtue. In both ancient Rome and Renaissance Europe, for example, Homer's *Odyssey* and Virgil's *Aeneid* were regarded with such respect that copies of the books were used in this manner.

The process of using the oracle was referred to as 'casting the lots'. The inquirer would carefully formulate the question and then open the book three times at random, each time letting a finger fall upon the page. A note would be made of the three lines upon which the seeker's finger had fallen, and an attempt would be made to apply these lines to the situation about which the question had been asked.

From the latter decades of the Roman Empire onwards, both the Old and New Testaments were quite often employed in the same manner, the process being referred to as sortes Sanctorum, 'the lots of the Saints'. Even though the use of the Bible in this manner was specifically forbidden by many local ecclesiastical councils, the casting of the sortes Sanctorum was widespread.

In the *History of the Franks*, Saint Gregory of Tours (538-594) recorded

A hen revealing Greek words with oracular meanings by pecking at grains of wheat

that when the Frankish prince Merovechus was in terror of the wrath of the bellicose Queen Fredegond he cast the sortes Sanctorum in the Basilica of Saint Martin of Tours. The oracles he derived from these books were of a gloomy nature, especially one that read: 'The Lord our God has betrayed you into the hands of your enemies.' The oracle was to prove accurate enough, for Merovechus was eventually killed by henchmen of Queen Fredegond.

Such an accurate prediction would seem to have been by no means unique. It is small wonder, then, that prophets were often seen as doomsters and consequently persecuted.

123

SIBYLLINE ORACLES

The early Christian Sibylline oracles proclaimed the Emperor Constantine as a messianic king. For them, of course, a Roman emperor who was also a Christian was a real godsend. One of these oracles (Tiburtina) spoke of the Emperor of the Last Days who fought against the Antichrist, for in those times the early Christian converts fully expected that the end of the world would follow closely upon the crucifixion of Christ. This Emperor of the Last Days was a wish-fulfilment figure for the early Christians, as he was expected to convert the pagans, destroy the temples of the false gods and baptize the converted, particularly the Jews. The prophecy concluded that when his work was finally done he would lay down his sword and retire to Golgotha, the hill upon which Christ was crucified.

The widely predicted Great Fire that destroyed much of London in 1666

124

The Fire of London and Nostradamus's uncanny pinpointing of the year 1666 with his 'three times twenty and six' in Century II Quatrain 51 is discussed on pages 34-5. The famous diarist Samuel Pepys was aware of Nostradamus's prophecy, which had been reprinted in *Booker's Almanack* before the fire.

A number of other prophets seem to have come to the same conclusions about this seminal event. The astrologer William Lilly (1602-81), who was born just over a century after Nostradamus, published a pamphlet called 'Monarchy or no Monarchy' 14 years before the Great Fire of London. In it were 19 'heirogliphics' (sic) or enigmatic pictures designed to depict the future of the 'English Nation and Commonwealth for many hundreds of years yet to come'. Besides a number of plates that depict scenes which may be yet to come – for example, a strange animal like a weasel attacking a crown and Parliament lounging idly by while an invasion of England takes place – there are two particularly striking pictures printed on the same page.

The first shows bundles of corpses lying on the bare ground and two men busily digging graves for two coffins, while over a church in the background fly four birds of ill omen. This disturbing vision of the plague that preceded the Fire is linked by proximity with the picture of a city in flames by a large river – a city which is almost certain to be London. Nearby some men are pouring water on to a flaming bonfire, into which falls a pair of twins. The twins are symbolic of the zodiacal sign of Gemini, the sign most usually associated with London.

Although plague and fire were common hazards of the time, the striking aptness of these pictures was reinforced by a pamphlet that Lilly wrote in 1648, in which he pointed a further astrological indication of what was to come. 'In the year 1665 . . . when the absis . . . of Mars shall appear in Virgo who shall expect less than a strange catastrophe of human affairs in the . . . kingdom of England.' He goes on to say that 'it will be ominous to London, unto her merchants at sea, to her traffique on land, to her poor, to all sorts of people . . . by reason of sundry fires and a consuming plague'. The description of this twofold tragedy could hardly be more clearly expressed, seven years before its occurrence.

Lilly was astoundingly accurate, for in the aftermath of the Fire of London there was no lack of theories as to its cause, and the citizens of London were more than happy to pin the blame on any individual or conspiracy. Lilly noted in his diary that several persons including Colonel John Rathbone 'were then tried for their lives' for plotting to burn the City as a way of killing the King and overthrowing the government of the day. The conspirators had even used *Lilly's Almanack* to calculate a lucky day (3 September) for their evil deed. In the event, fate forestalled them and the Fire broke out one day before their planned attempt. Nevertheless, they were still hanged.

Lilly was duly summoned to the Speaker's Chamber in order to be cross-examined about his prediction. In some apprehension, he asked his friend the well-known antiquary

Elias Ashmole to accompany him. Ashmole had been made a herald at Windsor by the King, and by his presence helped to protect the prophet from undue victimization. The Committee may have even suspected Lilly of setting fire to the city in order to vindicate his prophecy, but the presence of Ashmole helped to keep the discussion away from conjecture and firmly on the provable, and Lilly walked away a free man. He gave Ashmole a parcel of rare books by way of thanks for his aid. Such is the danger involved in making prophecies that turn out to be true during one's own lifetime!

Nostradamus must too have been worried when he was summoned to Paris in 1556 by the French Queen Catherine de' Medici . As a result of this meeting the Queen believed implicitly in Nostradamus's predictions for the rest of her life, but the meeting could so easily have gone the other way – especially as Nostradamus was charged with the delicate and difficult task of drawing up the horoscopes of the seven Valois children, whose tragic fates he had already revealed in the *Centuries*. It is no wonder that for his own safety Nostradamus deliberately obscured the dates and names in his quatrains.

THE FIRE FORESEEN

Francis Bernard, a physician and astrologer, attempted to establish a general astrological theory which would enable him to chart the course of all future fires that a city was likely to fall heir to by the astrological process of 'rectification'. This is a practice whereby the horoscope of a city (or, more usually, a person) is adjusted by reference to known events in the life of that person or city.

Others thought that in the Fire of London they recognized one of the many prophecies of Mother Shipton, the seer born in 1488 at Knaresborough, Yorkshire, who was reputed to have lived in a cave. This was first mooted in 1641, 21 years before the Fire, but as each successive edition of her prophecies seemed to contain new predictions that were suited to the season, little

William Lilly, astrologer and seer

credence can be placed upon this.

It seems almost as if the gravity of the Fire of London was sufficient to stir a number of prophets to make the same prediction. Or was it that the Fire became inevitable after so many seers saw it?

125

In 1985 Dr Ravi Batra published a book called *The Great Depression of 1990* in which he accurately predicted the onset of a terrible recession or depression in 1989, with a great increase in unemployment, a decrease in inflation, a rapid fall in property prices, a great increase in business failures, and a number of other economic events which have come very true in the western world. He even suggested that real estate investments should be sold at the end of 1989, and business indebtedness reduced — perfect timing, as it turns out. Yet he never claimed to be a prophet, merely a close observer of economic cycles.

By implying that 1990 paralleled the events of 1930, and by extrapolation that 1996 will herald the real end of this current recession, he has provided us with a prediction and unconsciously underlined two interesting key ideas. First, the period between events of the 1930s and those of the 1990s chosen by Dr Batra is exactly 60 years. This is exactly the time specified by the ancient Chinese

Will this typical scene from the Depression of the 1930s be repeated in the 1990s?

to complete one 'Great Year', during which all possible combinations of events as described by the interaction of the 10 Celestial Stems and 12 Earthly Branches of Chinese metaphysics are supposed to happen. After 60 years, everyone comes back to exactly the same Chinese year combination of Branch and Stem as the year they were born in. Perhaps the Chinese Great Year has other implications which are relevant to prophecy and not obvious to the world at large: perhaps the very choice of the words 'Branch' and 'Stem' which echo the structure of the 'time tree' discussed on page 148–9 is not a coincidence.

Secondly, the use by Nostradamus of astrological dating of the quatrains suggests that a particular prediction

may 'actualize' at any one of the times when a certain astrological conjunction occurs. This means that as the planets cycle at different rates round the sun, certain configurations come up very frequently, and others at long intervals. Those occurring at very long intervals — say every couple of centuries — can be seen as almost uniquely dated events, fated to happen once. Others that come round several times a century may happen at one or other of these conjuctions, or even in one form or another at several of these conjunctions. Likewise, the revolution of the earth around the sun enables calendar-makers to 'predict' the seasons.

Perhaps these astrological configurations mark points when the twigs of

A sign of the times

the 'time tree' brush against each other in some cosmic wind. Maybe they are points where events 'grow together' again, and a divergent twig is reunited with the main branch. An examination of the cyclical aspects caused by the revolution of the planets round the sun over unequal periods of time might reveal some of the patterns of futurity, for after all it is by the revolution of only one of these planets, the earth, around the sun that all human time is measured. An understanding of the workings of the whole cosmic clock might reveal the structure behind the sequence of events we call history, be they national or personal. In fact it is these very aspects in the natal horoscope of an individual which may predict some of the events in his or her life.

Perhaps Nostradamus was in reality a much greater astrologer than has

The spectre of mass unemployment worldwide has appeared once more

ever been appreciated, but in a different way to that which is normally understood by the term. It may be that he comprehended some workings of the cosmic clock that enabled him to gain a vision of other times, not just those that are governed by the revolution of one planet – the earth – round the sun. For further details and some examples of Nostradamus's more precisely dated astrological quatrains, see pages 128–9.

127

SIXTY-YEAR CYCLICAL PREDICTIONS

Ravi Batra draws a number of 60-year parallels:

1920 & 1980 Both years of high unemployment, high inflation and high interest rates, which is a very rare combination.

1921 & 1981 A large tax cut favouring the upper end of the pay scale, with unemployment rising sharply.

1922 & 1982 Both years see a sharp fall in inflation and interest rates, with a sharp rise in the UK stockmarket.

1923 & 1983 A strange parallel is that banks offered interest on cheque accounts for the first time

Sixty-year cycle marked by the Chinese zodiac signs

in history in 1923 and reintroduced it after a long break in 1983. In both years there was a very sharp fall in unemployment (the largest in three decades in the latter year).

1924 & 1984 Inflation is lower and the UK stockmarket continues to rise.

1925 & 1985 A sharp rise in bank failures, with 120 failing worldwide in 1985 alone.

1926 & 1986 The UK stockmarket reaches record highs in both these years, while unemployment falls sharply. Energy prices fall steeply in both years.

With all forms of prediction, the trickiest part for the seer is to get an exact date, a precise fix in the interconnected web of the various possible futures. The seer might 'see' an event with all sorts of detail but have trouble in identifying the exact date of an era into which he or she has arrived almost by accident, while with forms of divination like the *I Ching*, geomancy and the Tarot, there is virtually no way of getting an accurate date fix. Consequently, it is extraordinary that Nostradamus was able to pinpoint exact years and sometimes even exact months.

Despite the fact that Nostradamus claimed in a letter to César, his son, to know the dates of all his prophecies, he only actually specified precise dates in just a few of his quatrains. These include:

Century II Quatrain 51, which gives the Fire of London's date as 'three times twenty and six' or 1666.

Century III Quatrain 77, where he accurately predicts the peace between the Turks and the Persians in 1727.

Century X, Quatrain 72 is the gloomy prediction of the coming of the King of Terror in July 1999 – a prophecy yet to be confirmed.

In addition to specific dates, Nostradamus gives a number of astrological indications from which a range of possible dates can be derived. Century I Quatrain 52, for example, depicts the time of its fulfilment as a conjunction of Jupiter and Saturn in the zodiacal sign of Aries (the head of the zodiac):

Saturn – depicted here as both god and planet – moves very slowly through the heavens

*The head of Aries, Jupiter and Saturn,
Eternal God what changes?
Then after a long century the bad times will return,
Great upheavals in France and Italy.*

This conjunction took place in December 1702 during the War of the Spanish Succession, with the events 'after a long century' being the French campaign in Italy in 1803 and the declaration of Napoleon as President of the Italian Republic. It is not a future prediction as asserted by several commentators, and this conjunction does not again take place between now and the end of this century.

Another astrologically indicated dating occurs in Century I Quatrain 16. The interpretation of the astrological references in this quatrain has confused several commentators, one of

The Orrery marks out the paths and conjunctions of the planets

whom even says 'this description is so general it could fit the 20th century as well as any other'. Not true – the key line is 'A scythe joined with a pond in Sagittarius'. The scythe is a symbol for the planet Saturn conjunct with only one possible planet, the Moon, both in the zodiacal sign of Sagittarius. This conjunction happens for a period of

The sign of Virgo

2½ years every 29½ years, because Saturn is a very slow-moving planet. One such occurrence of this conjunction is in 1999 – a highly significant Nostradamian year. Nostradamus could not date events solely by using the fast-moving planets such as Mercury because these would have provided a very large and confusing range of dates to choose from.

Another astrological dating occurs in Century II Quatrain 48, which states that:

The great army will pass over mountains
When Saturn is in Sagittarius and
Mars moving into Pisces.

This conjunction has occurred three times in this century, the last time in late November 1986. However, an appropriate event corresponding to it does not appear to have yet transpired, so it seems it is a future prediction for the next century.

Century VI Quatrain 24 is another clear astrological dating:

Mars and the Sceptre will be
in conjunction,
A calamitous war under Cancer:
A short time afterwards a new king will
be anointed,
Who will bring peace to the earth for a
long time.

Clearly a ruler will be appointed after a war that may take place between 22 June and 23 July (under the sign of Cancer). The year will be determined by a conjunction between Mars and Jupiter (the sceptre) in Cancer. This conjunction has occurred six times since 1812, and will happen next on 21 June 2002. This is a possible time for this war, but not a certainty.

There is a specific dating in Century V Quatrain 91, in which Greece is threatened by attack from Albania:

At the great market called that of
the liars
All of Torrent and the field of Athens:
They will be surprised by the light
armed horses,
By the Albanois [when] *Mars* [is in]
Leo, and Saturn [is] *in Aquarius.*

The last occurrence of this conjunction this century was from 28 April until 3 June 1993. Consequently, this prophecy will not be fulfilled until the next millenium.

Apart from these quatrains, most dating is recognizable only in retrospect. It is a pity that Nostradamus, if he did know the exact dates as he claimed to his son, chose to obfuscate them in most quatrains. It is, however, more likely he was unable to put precise dates to many of his predictions.

129

THE AMAZING ACCURACY OF MANY FULFILLED PREDICTIONS OF NOSTRADAMUS, SUCH AS THOSE IN WHICH HE GAVE ACTUAL DATES FOR SPECIFIC OCCURRENCES, MAKES HIS MISTAKES - FOR INSTANCE, THE "PREDICTIVE MISS" – ALL THE MORE PUZZLING. IS IT POSSIBLE TO RECONCILE THEM?

The amazing accuracy of many of Nostradamus's predictions raises several important questions. Firstly, was he a natural clairvoyant – that is to say, a person born with an innate ability to see in vision events taking place far away in both time and space? And did he employ any methods other than astrology in order to help him prophesy? If so, what was the nature of these methods and were any of them connected with ritual magic or other techniques regarded by some as pertaining to 'forbidden knowledge'? And if Nostradamus truly saw events that did not take place until long after his death, does that mean that the idea of free will is illusory, that all of us are, in a sense, robots, biological machines destined to live out our lives to a predestined end?

The future can branch in different directions, like cars leaving a freeway

In the pages that follow, an attempt is made to provide tentative answers to all these questions in relation to the prophecies of Nostradamus, both fulfilled and as yet unfulfilled – as well as those few which were unquestionably erroneous or, very oddly, would appear to have been fulfilled before they were made (see page 85).

In this respect readers will have to consider what is meant by the word 'time', for some theories concerning prophecies in general and those of Nostradamus in particular involve looking at time in quite a different way from that in which we almost all tend to view it. We think of it as being like a great river, running from its source to its end. The 'Big Bang' – or the divine act of creation – is seen as the source of the river of time, the extinction of the universe – or the Last Judgment – as its end. Our own lives are, metaphorically speaking, short journeys along that river which are always downstream.

There are, however, many other hypotheses concerning the nature of time. One of them, looked upon with favour by some reputable physicists, regards the structure of time as suggestive not of a river but the above-ground form of an enormous forest tree, 'our time', which embraces the entire universe of matter and energy as we know it, being no more than a twig upon one of the branches of the tree. In this section, this idea and others will be considered in relationship to the *Centuries*.

An acceptance of what seems to be the overwhelming evidence that Nostradamus knew the nature of events that were to take place hundreds of years after his death in 1566 has some very unpleasant implications for all of us – for it suggests that the future is fixed by forces utterly outside our control, that when we believe we are making any choice, however trivial it may be, we are in truth making no choice at all. Rather we are simply following the dictates of Fate, whose playthings we are.

Another way of regarding our future is to posit an 'alternate realities' hypothesis – the theory which, metaphorically speaking, looks upon time as a tree rather than as a river (see pages 148–9). From the base of this 'time tree' grows a trunk from which sprout numberless branches, each of them an alternate reality, a 'parallel universe', of which only one is our own.

The beginning of all time is the base of the metaphorical tree's trunk, while the earliest alternate realities (formed after time had begun) are the huge branches which extend from the trunk. Later alternate realities are the smaller branches which sprout from the great main boughs of the time tree – and from these extend a countless number of twigs.

Our reality – which virtually all of us assume is the sole reality that exists – is viewed as just one of the twigs sprouting from a small branch of the time tree. Our history is only unique back to that point at which the

According to the theory of alternate reality, time is like a tree with many branches and twigs

twig – the alternate world in which we live – budded from its branch. Before that, we share our history with other twigs that sprouted at the same time as our own.

What caused our particular twig, and other twigs – each a reality in its own right and with all its intelligent inhabitants convinced that they live in the only reality – to sprout off from

the small branch on which they grow? And what caused all the small branches to sprout from the greater branches which grew from the main trunk millions or hundreds of millions of years ago?

According to some theorists – who include not only writers of highly imaginative science fiction but also mathematical physicists – the time tree shoots forth a new twiglet on each occasion that a conscious being makes a choice between two or more possible courses of action. In the words of the noted science-fiction writer Harry Harrison, that means that 'there must be an infinite number of futures . . . . If, on the way to work in the morning, we decide to take the bus and are killed . . . if time is ever-branching then there are two futures – one in which we die . . . and another where we live on, having taken the tube'.

Some mathematical physicists – whose work is concerned with an area where physics, philosophy and mystical concepts seem to blend into one – take the possibility of the existence of alternate realities very seriously indeed. Take, for instance, the following passage from a paper that was published by the mathematical physicist Dr Martin Clutton-

Brock in the journal *Astrophysics and Space Science* vol. 47 (1977): 'Imagine the universe branching into many worlds, only one of which we experience. There are closed worlds and open worlds; initially uniform worlds and initially chaotic worlds; high entropy worlds and low entropy worlds. In most worlds, life never evolves; in some worlds life evolves but is scarce; and in relatively few worlds, life is abundant.'

From a comparison of these two quotations it is apparent that there is a resemblance between the fantasies of science-fiction writers who have concerned themselves with alternate realities and the hypotheses of some astrophysicists and mathematicians.

If one accepts some variant of the alternative realities hypothesis as it is outlined by Harry Harrison and Dr Martin Clutton-Brock there is no great difficulty in reconciling the

fulfilled predictions of Nostradamus with a belief in free will – nor in explaining a string of prophecies by one and the same person which prove to be a curious mixture of the completely accurate, the almost completely accurate, and the utterly wrong. For if Nostradamus and other prophets were not, in fact, genuinely seeing into the future of our world in its own separate reality but into parallel universes of which the time lines differ from our own, there is no reason at all why our alternate reality should not be a decade, a century or a millennium in advance of, or behind, any particular parallel universe. In other words, it is possible that sometimes the 'future' that Nostradamus predicted was, in fact, the present of another reality in which the course of history followed a different path from that which it was to do in our own world.

133

FANTASY AND REALITY

Sir Fred Hoyle, who occupied the Plumian Chair of Astronomy and Experimental Philosophy at Cambridge University, combines the astrophysicist and the writer of imaginative science fiction in one person, and has handled the theory of time in his book *October the First Is Too Late*. In the preface Sir Fred made it quite clear that while he had written it as imaginative fiction, the discussions of the significance of time and the meaning of consciousness were intended to be quite serious.

Sir Fred Hoyle, distinguished astrophysicist

In the course of *October the First Is Too Late*, a variant of the alternate realities hypothesis is advanced in which the entire history of our planet, past and future, consists of a four-dimensional spiral moving around the sun. Everything that has taken place in the past and everything that will happen in the future is in reality happening in the present – in other words, past, present and future are all one and it is only the limitations of human consciousness that lead us into dividing the past from the future.

Is there an explanation of the fact that many natural prophets such as Nostradamus can be so very right in some of their predictions and so very wrong in others? The sceptic would say that such alleged prophets have never in fact been anything but lucky guessers. However, convinced believers in the existence of psychic 'wild talents' – which are natural human abilities, albeit exercised by very few – would maintain that a seer's prophetic abilities and power to accurately decode messages from the future wax and wane like the transmission of an ill-tuned radio.

A belief that there are authentic prophets amongst us at the present day is supported by a good deal of strong evidence that such men and women have existed in even the recent past. Towards the end of 1891 a 25-year-old palmist and clairvoyant, a man who called himself 'Cheiro' and 'Count Louis Hamon', made an extremely unlikely prediction about the future of the second son of the future King Edward VII, the then Prince of Wales. In the course of time, he said, the second son, Prince George, would inherit the throne of the United Kingdom. At the time most people would have considered such an eventuality not in the least probable for, although Prince George was second in line to the throne, his elder brother 'Eddie', the Duke of Clarence, was generally thought to be in excellent health, had just become engaged to be married to Princess May of Teck, and was virtually certain

Cheiro, controversial seer and palmist

to have sons and daughters of his own in a few years' time.

In reality, the health of the Duke of Clarence was not as good as was generally assumed – there is some evidence to suggest that at the time of the Duke's engagement he had long been suffering from incurable syphilis. In January 1892 he died from pneumonia – or, at any rate, so it was said in an official announcement from Buckingham Palace. After a discreet interval Prince George became first engaged, and then married, to Princess May of Teck and eventually succeeded to the throne as King George V.

It would seem that a very specific prediction of what was an improbable event – the early death of the Duke of Clarence and the eventual succession to the throne of the Duke's younger brother – had been proved correct by the course of history. Cheiro appeared

to have triumphantly established his possession of a 'wild talent' which enabled him to discern the shape of things to come. Alas, there is no independent written evidence of his prediction, so sceptics might totally disregard it. However, it can be proved beyond any doubt that towards the end of his life Cheiro made even more surprising, and absolutely accurate, predictions about both the eldest son of King George V and the former's brother, the then Duke of York.

In a forecast of the future which was in print before the year 1930, Cheiro wrote: 'The portents are not favourable for the prosperity of England or for the royal family, with the exception of the Duke of York. In his case it is remarkable that the regal sign of Jupiter increases in power as the years advance, which . . . was also the case of his royal father before

The ill-fated Duke of Clarence

there was any likelihood of his coming to the throne.' Cheiro also made a further statement with regard to the royal family. Writing of the Duke's elder brother, the then Prince of Wales, he first of all referred to 'changes likely to take place greatly affecting the throne of England' and then predicted a royal crisis: 'Owing to the peculiar planetary influences to which he [the Prince of Wales] is subjected, he will fall a victim to a devastating love affair. If he does, I predict that the Prince will give up everything, even the chance of being crowned, rather than lose the object of his affection.'

That is exactly what happened. On the death of his father in 1936 the Prince of Wales came to the throne as Edward VIII but was never crowned, the planned Coronation being cancelled because he abdicated rather than give up the twice-divorced Mrs Wallis Simpson. At the time Cheiro published this prediction the Prince of Wales was

Cheiro predicted that Edward VIII would 'give up everything' for Wallis Simpson

King George V

135

not involved with Mrs Simpson in any way – indeed, it seems likely that he had not even met her.

Cheiro also prophesied the creation of the State of Israel, and, writing in 1930, a world war within 10 years or so: 'Italy and Germany [an unlikely alliance at the time Cheiro was writing] will be at war with France . . . . The United States will be at war with Japan and not take part until later in the European carnage.' These predictions were correct, although Cheiro's prophecy that during the world war he foresaw there would be a renewed Irish civil war was not fulfilled.

Beside being a palmist and an astrologer, Cheiro seems also to have been a 'natural prophet'. One of the most puzzling things about such natural prophets as Cheiro and Nostradamus is that even those of them who have made startlingly accurate predictions have also made forecasts which have proved to be partially or even wholly incorrect. Maybe they are not seeing into the future of our world, but into parallel universes whose time lines differ slightly from our own; it is possible that the 'future' they predict is the present of another reality in which the course of history followed a different path from that which it was to do in our own world. This might explain why their 'wild talents' enable them to perceive something that did not happen with the same clarity as something that actually did transpire.

DRUGS, MAGIC AND THE SEER

Some commentators on the *Centuries* have described Nostradamus as the greatest astrologer of all time. They are almost certainly wrong, misled by an assumption that all the accurate predictions outlined in the *Centuries* and the other writings of the seer were derived from his observations of the ever-changing positions of the sun, moon and planets in relation to both one another and the signs of the zodiac. Nostradamus certainly used astrology as a shorthand method of expressing dates (see pages 128–9), but not to derive the prognostications themselves.

Hashish enjoyed modern-style

Nostradamus could not possibly have relied upon astrology alone when he made his predictions. This is proved beyond doubt by one simple fact pointed out by the 19th-century Nostradamian commentator Charles Ward – that the seer 'mentions the birth of persons who were born after his death . . . judicial astrology could give no help in such cases, since to commence casting a nativity presupposes birth'.

In other words, while Nostradamus was undoubtedly an astrologer – after all, he was the compiler of a number of almanacs – and while at least some of his successful predictions may have been partly made on the basis of astrology, he must also have been a talented clairvoyant. Indeed, suggestions have been made that he used

It has been suggested that Nostradamus used hashish, which is traditionally smoked through a hookah

psychedelic drugs to induce trances in which his clairvoyant capacities could operate more freely (see panel below).

However, the most controversial question as far as the clairvoyant faculties of Nostradamus are concerned is not whether or not these faculties were heightened by drugs; it is whether they were supplemented by the use of methods which pertained to ceremonial magic, ritual divination and other secret and forbidden arts.

The possibility of Nostradamus having been a participant in magical rites, perhaps of a pagan nature, has been indignantly rejected by some of those who have devoted years of intense study to the life and writings of the seer of Salon. This has particularly been the case amongst those authors who have inclined to the ultramontane Catholicism which has been associated with French royalism

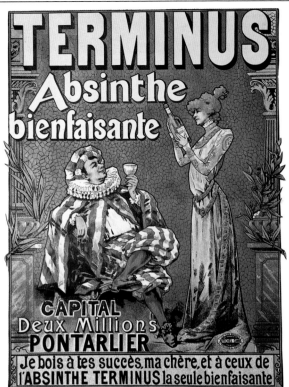

Alcohol is another drug which alters consciousness

since 1870. Yet there have also long been those who have considered it possible that Nostradamus was in fact an adept magician, a man who, like the writer Eliphas Levi (1810-75), engaged in mental gymnastics which

enabled him to combine a qualified loyalty to the Church with the employment of certain techniques derived from ancient secret traditions.

It seems likely that even in the seer's own lifetime there were those who suspected as much, for in a passage Nostradamus printed in the preface to the first edition of the *Centuries* he seems to have been attempting to avert any suspicion that he dabbled in dubious occult arts. In this passage he solemnly warns his son against the dangers of 'execrable magic' and purports to give an account of how he himself had actually destroyed printed or manuscript treatises devoted to ritual magic and, by implication, alchemy. However, as will be demonstrated on the next pages, there are good reasons to suspect that Nostradamus's denunciation of 'execrable magic' was more than somewhat insincere.

137

DRUGS, SUFIS AND BIOELECTRICAL ENERGY

A number of modern students of the writings of Nostradamus have claimed that the seer owed his remarkable clairvoyant abilities to his use of hallucinogenic drugs. However, there appears to be no real evidence, even of the most tenuous variety, of the truth of this assertion and it is perhaps significant that some of those writers who have disseminated it have made other statements about the life of the seer

which are inherently improbable.

For example, the author of one recent book has not only stated that Nostradamus resorted to drugs in order to heighten his clairvoyant abilities but that while in Sicily he made contact with Sufi mystics, and when engaged in prophesying was accustomed to sit on a brass tripod with legs 'angled at the same degree as the pyramids of Egypt in order to create a similar bioelectric force

which it was believed would sharpen psychic powers'.

As historians are convinced that all Muslims, Sufi or otherwise, had been expelled from Sicily long before Nostradamus was born, and that the angles of the pyramids were not properly measured until over 300 years after the burial of the seer, it is a great pity that the sources of this fascinating and novel information have not been given to the world!

It seems likely that some of the strange occult quatrains to be found in the *Centuries* provide coded details of ancient, secret and forbidden predictive techniques used by Nostradamus in order to look far into the future. The most easily understood and significant of these quatrains are the first two verses of the *Centuries* – Century I Quatrains 1 and 2. In these, Nostradamus described himself – in language that would have been understood by all who had some acquaintance with late classical mysticism – as carrying out 'workings' pertaining to white magic. Cleverly, he couched his descriptions in terms which would have been quite meaningless to the general reader. The quatrains read:

Sitting alone at night in secret study,
Rested on a brazen tripod,
An exiguous flame comes from
the solitude,
Making successful that worthy
of belief.

The handheld wand is placed in the
midst of the BRANCHES,
He moistens with water his foot and
garment's hem,
Fear and a Voice make him quake in
his sleeves,
Divine splendour, the divine sits nigh.

Croesus tests the Oracle at Delphi with a little cookery

The Oracle receives prophetic vapours

Throughout these two quatrains Nostradamus was describing a variant of a divinatory magical rite of great antiquity, but the third line in each quatrain is of major significance. By wording these lines as he did the seer was doing two things: first, he was making it apparent to students of occult philosophy that he was acquainted with the Chaldean Oracles, a collection of ancient Hermetic lore, by echoing a passage referring to a 'Formless Fire' from which comes a 'divine Voice of Fire' to which the sojourner with the gods must listen. Secondly, he was hinting that the 'exiguous flame' of which he wrote was of heavenly origin, an emanation from the solitude, which in this context could have meant 'Oneness'.

The two quatrains also contain several clues as to the nature of the divinatory rituals employed by Nostradamus. One of them is the use of the word 'branches'. It was rendered in capital letters in the original printing of the *Centuries*; a clear hint, of the sort given recurrently by Nostradamus, that it was intended to be understood in more than one way, or that some punning or allusive word play was involved.

In this particular case Nostradamus was almost certainly using the word in

Numa, King of Rome, consults the Oracle

The tripod and serpents of Apollo's Oracle

This passage, which describes a divinatory rite involving the wetting of a foot and the hem of a garment, was clearly being referred to by Nostradamus in the second line of the second quatrain of Century I. Another passage in the same ancient text mentions the use of a bronze tripodic stool in a rite of prophecy.

The work from which the above quotation has been taken was originally written in Greek; in the 15th century it was translated into Latin as *De Mysteriis Aegyptorum* – 'Of the Mysteries of the Egyptians'. It is very likely that Nostradamus became acquainted with this work early in his life, for there is reason to believe that copies of Italian printings of the Latin translation were circulating among French students of Neoplatonic mysticism as early as 1500. In any event, it is certain that *De Mysteriis Aegyptorum* was published in France in the 1540s, and it may be

three senses, all pertaining to prophetic inspiration. The most important one was as a word resembling the name of the Greek demigod Branchus, the son of the sun god Apollo. According to Greek legend, when he was a youth Branchus had been given the gift of prophecy and the capability of endowing others with that same gift. As a consequence of this he was the centre of a cult which flourished until the triumph of Christianity. The cult was focused on revelations about the future received through the mediumship of inspired priestesses, and the techniques employed to obtain them were described by Iamblichus of Chalcis, who died about AD 335: 'The prophetess of Branchus either sits upon a pillar, or holds in her hand a rod bestowed by some deity, or moistens her feet or the hem of her garment with water . . . and by these means . . . she prophesies. By these practices she adapts herself to the god, whom she receives from without.'

highly significant that Nostradamus began to issue his almanacs not long after that event. Certainly it can be inferred from these two quatrains that the seer employed similar methods to those described in Iamblichus's text as one way of obtaining his knowledge of the future.

139

THE PYTHIA

In ancient Greece, the women who acted as oracles were called Pythia, after the python reputedly slain by Apollo, to whom all oracles were sacred. The Pythia were always natives of the town of Delphi, and once they had entered the service of the god they were never allowed to leave it, nor were they allowed to marry. In early times they were always selected from the town's young girls but, after one of them was seduced by Eucrates the Thessalian, the people of Delphi

altered the law to the effect that no one younger than 50 should be elected to the position of prophetess. However, the dress of the Pythia remained that of maidens rather than matrons.

When the oracle was flourishing there were always three Pythia ready to take their seat on the tripod. The effect of the smoke rising from below the tripod was so great that sometimes a prophetess would topple from the tripod in her prophetic delirium, fall into convulsions or even die.

There is evidence to be found in the curious forty-second quatrain of Century I that makes it seem quite certain that Nostradamus had some knowledge of both the darker aspects of the occult arts and of modes of divination involving the use of basins. The quatrain reads:

*The tenth day of the Gothic Calends
of April
Is resuscitated by a wicked race,
The fire is extinguished and the
Diabolical Assembly
Seek the bones of the Demon of
[and?] Psellus.*

When read in conjunction with Nostradamus' reference to a divinatory rite involving water (see page 138) this verse indicates the nature of one of the white magical techniques that were used by the seer of Salon to supplement his clairvoyant abilities and his astrological expertise.

That technique was described by the Neoplatonic philosopher Psellus as follows: 'There is a type of predictive power in the use of the basin, known and practised by the Assyrians . . . Those about to prophesy take a basin of water, which attracts the spirits of the depths. The basin then seems to breathe as with sounds . . . The water in the basin . . . excels . . . because of a power imparted to it by incantations which have rendered it capable of being imbued with the energies of spirits of prophecy . . . a thin voice begins to utter predictions. A spirit of this sort journeys where it wills, and always speaks with a low voice.'

Tibetan divinatory techniques in the wheel of life

That it was this passage from Psellus to which Nostradamus was referring when he made his allusions to a divinatory rite involving water seems clear beyond any shadow of a doubt.

In the light of this we are now in a position to understand Century I Quatrain 42 – which, when it is examined in conjunction with Century I Quatrains 1 and 2, is the most important of all the verses of Nostradamus in relation to both his life and his probable involvement in ritual divination and other varieties of white magic.

On a Good Friday – in the words of Psellus, 'the time when we commemorate the

redemptive Passion of Our Lord' and, according to him, the annual ecclesiastical festival on which 'Messalian' sorcerers (see panel opposite) were accustomed to hold an incestuous orgy which was a prelude to murder and cannibalism – Nostradamus began to make serious use of a mode of ritual divination in which a bowl of water was employed. It would seem likely that his technique had a general resemblance to that described, in what seems to have been a slightly muddled way, by Psellus – although there is no need to believe that the water actually spoke to him in a 'thin voice'. However, in the words of the late James Laver, writing of Psellus in 1942, while there is 'something slightly comic in the notion of a basin of water composing verses . . . we seem to be on the track of a mode of divination approaching Nostradamus's own methods [of predicting the

The Oracle prophesies while seated on a tripod

future] well known in antiquity and . . . still practised among primitive people. The fakirs of India are said to be able to make water boil and bubble beneath their gaze. Is it all any more than a technique for going into a trance?'

In the opinion of the present writer, the use of a bowl of water can be (although by no means always is)

something 'more than a technique for going into a trance'. However, it does seem likely that Nostradamus used a bowl of water as a focus when he wished to induce the sort of dissociation of consciousness which is an essential preliminary to authentic scrying (see pages 150–1). In other words, Nostradamus sought the predictive 'demon of Psellus'.

Among the first things discerned by him in his Good Friday vision was a 'Diabolical Assembly' engaged in a black magical rite, which may have taken place anywhere and at almost any time. This blasphemous ceremony seemed to Nostradamus to be a re-enactment of the one conducted by that 'wicked race' of supposed Messalians (see panel below).

MURDEROUS ORGIES

The connection that Nostradamus discerned between his vision of a black magical rite conducted by a 'Diabolical Assembly' and black magic as described by the writer Psellus was based upon an account given by the latter of a heretical rite conducted by people he termed 'Messalians': 'In the evening . . . at the time when we commemorate the redemptive Passion of Our Lord, they bring together . . . young girls whom they have initiated into their rites. Then they extinguish the candles . . . and throw themselves lasciviously upon the girls . . . each one on whomsoever falls into his hands . . . . They believe that they are doing something greatly pleasing to the demons by transgressing God's laws forbidding incest . . . . After waiting nine months, when the time has come for the unnatural fruit of the unnatural unions to be born, they reassemble . . . . On the third day after the birth, they . . . cut [the babies'] tender flesh with sharp knives and catch the spurting blood in bowls.

The concept of ritual cannibalism is of great antiquity

They throw the babes . . . upon a fire and burn their bodies to ashes. After which they mix these ashes with the blood in the bowls and in this way make an abominable drink . . . They partake together of these foodstuffs.'

Whether such a rite was actually celebrated at the time Psellus wrote his description of it is uncertain. Certainly, however, if it was so celebrated in any part of the Byzantine Empire at any date

during the lifetime of Michael Psellus it was not done so by Messalians, for that sect was already long extinct by then. This does not mean to say that murderous orgies of this sort never took place at all; there is some resemblance between the rite described by Psellus and well-authenticated accounts of sinister ceremonies conducted by the initiates of unorthodox death-oriented tantric cults.

141

While most of the predictions to which Nostradamus attached specific dates have been verified by the course of history, this is not true of all of them. The seer of Salon made a few notable prophetic misses as well as many hits. For instance, in Century I Quatrain 49 he made a prediction specifically related to the year 1700:

A long time before these events,
The peoples of the East, by lunar influence,
In the year 1700 will cause many to be carried away,
And will almost subdue the northern corner [area].

The events referred to in the first line of this quatrain are obviously those described in the preceding verse, Century I Quatrain 48, which seems to refer to a cycle of time beginning about AD 3000 – but what of the remaining three lines of the quatrain, with the exact dating of 'many being carried away'?

Alas, there is no real trace of any event taking place in or around the year 1700 which really fits this prediction – although some Nostradamian devotees, anxious to find the right happening to fit the prophecy, have attempted to apply it to such things as the occupation of Iceland by the forces of Charles XII of Sweden and a

The shape of things to come, as seen in 1936

Did Nostradamus prophesy Charles XII of Sweden's occupation of Iceland?

campaign in northern India undertaken by one of the commanders of the armies of the 'Great Mughal', the Emperor Aurungzeb. However, most sensible students of Nostradamus – that is, those whose enthusiasm and credulity are not unbounded – admit that in this particular instance the seer was mistaken.

There is strong evidence that all the psychic abilities of any particular individual – whether those abilities be innate or acquired through the use of arcane training and disciplines – are subject to a periodic waxing and waning. It is as if what could be termed 'psychic athletes' can, like their physical equivalents, go completely off form for no easily perceptible reason. Thus, for instance, mediums who have in the past produced amazing phenomena become so psychically enervated that they lose their authentic abilities and resort to childish trickery that would deceive no one possessed of the most elementary powers of observation.

There is no reason to believe that Nostradamus was immune from the tendency of lesser psychics to have their off days – times when psychic energy is low and clairvoyant vision is distorted or, much worse, entirely absent and replaced by self-deception.

It is therefore perfectly possible that when Nostradamus made his seemingly quite mistaken prediction that the year 1700 would be marked by some outstanding event his psychic abilities were at a low point of their cyclic waxing and waning. If so, however, it seems surprising both that the prediction was so very specific in its dating and that such an experienced

clairvoyant as Nostradamus did not realize that his abilities were so diminished that the prophecy should be suppressed as doubtful.

Perhaps a more plausible suggestion is that on the occasion that this prediction was made – as perhaps on many other occasions – Nostradamus was not looking into the future of our own reality but was seeing, as it were, what was then the present of an alternate reality (see pages 132–3) in which some major world event took place in the year 1700.

KENNEDY AND THE SHAH

Nostradamus was only one of many psychics who have had a remarkable run of predictive successes but have then made prognostications which time has proved to be partially or wholly incorrect. Take, for example, prophecies made by Jeane Dixon, the best known of all the clairvoyants who have practised their art in 20th-century America.

Some were truly remarkable. She forecast the 1963 assassination of President Kennedy as early as 1956, when *Parade* magazine published an interview with her in which she described a vision she had experienced some four years earlier: 'A voice came out of nowhere, telling me softly that this young man, a Democrat, to be elected as President in 1960, would be assassinated while in office.'

In the early 1970s she correctly predicted that the Shah of Iran would be overthrown by a popular uprising. So far, so good; but she forecast that the event would take place in 1977, two years earlier than was actually to be the case. Furthermore, she stated that after living in secluded exile the Shah would again 'stride into the

The Shah of Iran

143

world spotlight'. In reality he died in exile of cancer.

Ms Dixon's Iranian predictions were at least partially correct; those she made in the 1970s in relation to Britain were utterly wrong. For example, she said that the Labour MP Eric Varley would 'leap into the spotlight'; he is largely forgotten. She also tipped Sir Geoffrey Howe as the next Conservative Prime Minister. He never held that office and, at the time of writing, is remembered chiefly for the speech he made following his resignation as Foreign Secretary.

Alternate reality as explored in the film Time After Time

144

indication of the presence of Union troops. The Confederate troops retreat in panic. This causes the Southern triumph that the time traveller has come to see to be transformed into a Southern defeat. The Confederacy loses the war and the future from which the time traveller has come vanishes in an instant! He finds himself trapped in an utterly alien alternate world – our own, the one in which the North won the Civil War.

Ideas similar to these were also given literary expression in the late Philip K. Dick's *The Man in the High Castle* (1962), set in an alternate reality in which the decision that caused that particular twig of the time tree to branch off was a collective rather than an individual one – that of the voters in the USA election of November 1931 thinking fit to elect to office someone other than Franklin

Another explanation of how Nostradamus was able to obtain glimpses of the future – and perhaps the most interesting – is concerned with the existence of alternate realities, as explained on pages 132–3. The idea that we live in, and are conscious of the existence of, only one of a number of realities was first expressed in an easily graspable form by a number of science-fiction writers. It is none the less believable for that, for it is worth remembering that the early science-fiction writers were writing stories concerning the exploitation of nuclear energy at a time when almost all physicists were convinced that such things were simply not possible.

The whole concept of alternate realities, each branching off from another time line as a consequence of some seemingly insignificant decision – and sometimes destroying the original reality in the process of branching off – has been a favourite of science-fiction and fantasy writers since the 1930s. One example of such destruction occurs in *Bring the Jubilee* (1976). The author, Ward Moore, depicts a time-travelling historian from the future of a world in which the Confederacy won the American Civil War journeying into the past and visiting the scene of one of the Confederacy's most significant victories. His activities at the scene are mistakenly interpreted by a Southern advance guard as an

Time travel has been a recurring theme

Delano Roosevelt. This resulted in the creation of a time line in which Germany and Japan won World War II and the North America of the early 1960s was divided into three separate political entities: the eastern States of the Union, under brutal Nazi domination; the western area, a virtual colony of Japan, which adopted a much more beneficent approach to its American subjects than did the Nazis in their American domain; and finally, all that remained of the once great United States – the economically backward central mountain states.

There are many complexities in the plot of *The Man in the High Castle*.

For instance, the central character, the man in the 'High Castle' – this being a fortified retreat in which he has taken refuge from Nazi murder gangs – is in some way in subliminal contact with an alternate reality, or time line, in which Japan and Germany lost the war. However, it is not our own world of which he is aware – the other reality which he senses is yet another twig of the time tree, one in which no ships of the US Fleet suffered any damage as a consequence of the Japanese aerial attack on Pearl Harbor because they had all been sent out to sea by a wise and wary US President.

Other alternate reality novels which are relevant reading in the same context are Keith Roberts's *Pavane* (1968) and Kingsley Amis's *The Alteration* (1976). Both are set in an alternate world in which the 16th-century Protestant Reformation was crushed and a triumphalist Catholic Church dominates every aspect of European life and culture. Amis's book, which features two notably unpleasant heresy hunters named Foot and Redgrave, is readable and funny – but *Pavane*, set in an alternate Dorset in an England in which Queen Elizabeth I was assassinated in 1588, is certainly the more original of the two.

145

What would have happened if the Confederacy had won the American Civil War?

ANCIENT WISDOM, MODERN SCIENCE

The magician has always been able to see into realms beyond the physical. His world-view assumes that by insights into other worlds, planes or realities he is able to bring about surprising changes on the physical plane – 'surprising' because, without a knowledge of the elaborate and serpentine connections between the different realities, the effects caused by the magician are as surprising as the workings of radio would be to a Stone Age hunter. The theory of how a radio works is well understood today, but even so nobody can point to the radio waves in the air actually carrying the sound. So it is with magic; unless the theory of other realities, such as the astral plane, is understood then the effects of magic cannot be understood.

Magicians have always been given to explaining the universe in terms of complex cosmologies, and do in fact often employ the tree motif as a metaphor. A traditional example of this is the use for more than 1000 years of the tree of life by Jewish Cabbalists, and later by generations of European magicians who appropriated this complex diagram as their guide to the universe.

The image of the tree of life parallels the idea of time as an infinitely branching tree. Each branch and twig contains a reality that is different, albeit maybe only slightly, from that of its neighbour. This vision of alternate realities could explain the non-fulfilment of the prophecy by the clairvoyant Cheiro of a war in Palestine in which Russian troops were

to be directly involved; it may well have happened in an alternate reality, though it did not happen in ours. Fantastic? Perhaps – but the alternate realities hypothesis would also explain some varieties of psychic phenomena that have puzzled researchers for more than a century.

The psychic phenomena in question are those associated with almost right, but not quite right, premonitions, precognitive dreams, and even actual visions of the future that are, and have been, reported as being sometimes experienced by quite ordinary people – men and women who make no claim to the possession of seership or supernormal abilities of any sort whatsoever.

By comparison, modern science is moving away from the solid building blocks of matter, the elements, and moving towards a universe where force (energy) and form (matter) convert one into the other. Stephen Hawking, in his classic book *A Brief History of Time*, takes the modern reader through the various stages of modern scientific thought from the Greek philosopher Aristotle through Newton and Einstein to the latest theories of space and time. At each point in the evolution of scientific thinking, more apparent 'certainty' is thrown away. Ptolemy, for example, was certain that the Earth was the centre of the universe, and that both the sun and the planets revolved around it. In 1514, Nicholas Copernicus observed the changing shape of the moon, and theorized that the planets instead revolve round the sun, although

Science can only detect one of many realities

this was not generally recognized until Galileo Galilei used a telescope to confirm this in 1609, almost a century later. The Earth had moved from the centre of the universe to being just another planet.

In 1687 Newton published his findings which defined gravity – an invisible force, not directly measurable, which appeared to cause all bodies in the universe to be attracted to every other body, as if by magic! Man became less important, and even the Earth became dependent (upon every other body in the universe). It took almost 130 years before someone started to think about the relationship between gravity and light. Even that certainty, light, might now be 'bent' by gravity.

In this century, Einstein extended science further to embrace the concept that matter and energy might be interchangeable, finally reaching the

magician's point of view that the universe is generated from the interplay of force and form. It still seemed that time must be 'eternal' – but then Hawking revealed that 'the theory of relativity put an end to the idea of absolute time! . . . Each observer must have his own measure of time, as recorded by a clock carried with him, and identical clocks carried by different observers would not necessarily agree.' If different observers have different times because of their different points of view, a really different point of view could have you observing a

time that was decades or centuries different from our own. Nostradamus had found the secret of this different point of observation.

Hawking gradually kicks away each successive scientific theory designed to explain the deficiencies in the last, until the scientific explanation of the universe looks much more mystical than the most complex magician's cosmology and time looks as mutable as anything else in the universe. We are definitely not travelling along a simple time river – we are living in something infinitely more complex.

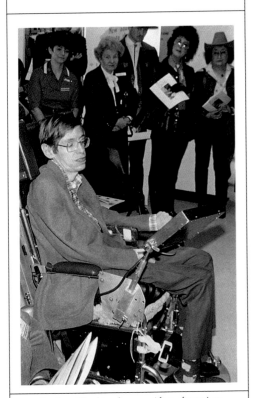

Stephen Hawking has new ideas about time

THE TREE OF LIFE

The Tree of Life is a mystical diagram of the universe of great antiquity, much older than the diagram of the paths of the planets round the sun. It is also a map of the mystical make-up of man, because the mystical 'anatomy' of both the universe and man was supposed to be similar.

The Tree of Life consists of 10 circles or spheres (Sephiroth) which are interconnected by 22 Paths (marked with the 22 letters of the Hebrew alphabet). Each of the spheres is symbolically (but not physically) associated with one of the planets or the sun or the moon. The total of 32 spheres and paths is thought of as being duplicated throughout four 'Worlds' of varying degrees of solidity, making a total of 128 paths and spheres.

Of all these different spheres, only one actually corresponds to

the physical world around us as we know it. The rest of the diagram enables the cabbalist or magician to describe the secret and mystical parts of the Universe: the source of dreams, the treasure-house of the archetypal images of the subconscious mind, the abode of angels and of demons, and a million other things from which our late-20th-century consciousness has cut us off, but which are real nevertheless.

These depths of description and delineation address many more concerns than just those of light, gravity and relativity, although no doubt the worlds of the cosmologist and the magician are but metaphors for the terrifying reality of the Universe itself – a reality we understand about as well as a newborn babe is able to understand the content of a set of encyclopedias.

147

OUR DESTINIES ARE FAN-SHAPED

The problem we are confronted with in dealing with Nostradamus and the *Centuries* is that we simply don't have a wide enough perspective on his predictions. We can only see a window of history from before his time to the present day, while he was able to range forward and backwards along the various branches taken by events. In Century 1 Quatrain 2 he speaks of 'au milieu des BRANCHES', a reference to the prophetess of Branchus (see pages 138–9), as well as to the branching paths of fate which have been written about by the Argentinian writer Jorge Luis Borges.

There is an implication in this quatrain that the events of history are not one long continuous line, a concept dear to the heart of the modern

Jorge Luis Borges

historian, but a subtle interweaving of events and people which might allow the time traveller to pop up in very disparate places and times, and view events which are separated by many decades or centuries but which appear to be almost side by side.

This approach to the work of Nostradamus goes some way to explaining why his quatrains apparently jump backwards or forwards in time without any apparent pattern. Perhaps the seer simply wrote what he saw in the order in which he saw it, and this order is in fact a reflection of the way the past and present intertwine rather than a cunning 'blind' deliberately inserted to make the task of decipherment more difficult. In fact, it may be that it was impossible for Nostradamus to disentangle the skeins of time without the benefit of hindsight which is partially granted to us. Perhaps here we have not a deliberate obscurantism but a real key to the structure of the 'branches of time'.

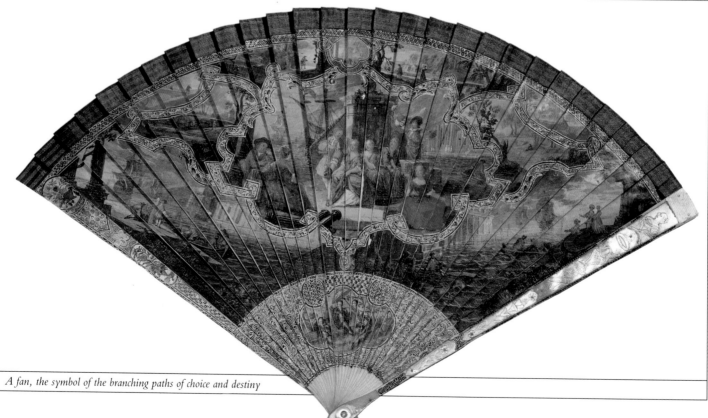

A fan, the symbol of the branching paths of choice and destiny

Finally, in many theories of time, or even in ordinary wish-fulfilment, it is recognized that if the earlier action had been different, the course of events precipitated would also have been very different. In fact, once a different fork in the garden of branching paths has been taken, the course of events will never be able to return to the original route. Time, events and the people involved have branched off in a different direction.

At every major (or even minor) decision point in one's life there are a certain number of choices and each decision takes you along a particular branch of each fan of options. Our destinies are like a succession of fan-shaped decisions, or a garden of branching paths. Perhaps the true nature of our collective destiny, history, is likewise fan-shaped – in which case it is no wonder that there have been only a few seers who, like Nostradamus, found their way through this garden of branching paths centuries before the decisions charting this route had been taken. Perhaps this explains why some quatrains don't quite fit – they are visions of an alternate reality at the end of a path which was not finally taken.

This seems to provide us with some solid conclusions. First, time is not linear but infinitely branching, constantly splitting like a living, growing tree. Secondly, some prophets, through a 'wild talent' or a knowledge of certain traditional techniques, can assume a viewpoint which allows them to see into alternate realities. Thirdly, these alternate realities may well be 'ahead' of our own reality, so the prophet can see what is for us a

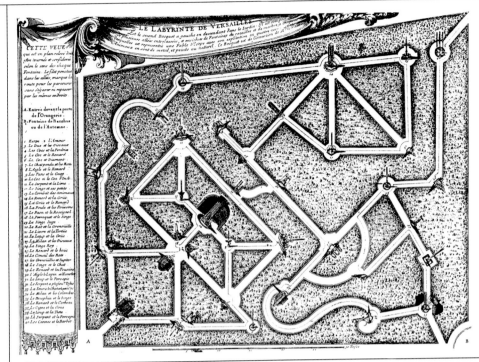

Like a maze, time presents many different choices

future event, but for that reality is the present. Fourthly, we do have the free will to make decisions which can alter the flow, and some alternate realities that have been glimpsed by otherwise very talented prophets will not ever happen in our reality.

The following pages look closely at certain techniques of prophecy which you, the reader, can try out for yourself.

THE ALEPH

The Argentinian writer, poet and scholar Jorge Luis Borges (1899–1986) wrote many apparent fictions about the relationship of time to space and how events relate to one another. In his book *The Aleph*, he describes a vision that was brought on by his concentrating on a single luminous spot he calls the Aleph, which acts in the manner of a crystal ball. It was 'a small iridescent sphere, of almost intolerable

The Aleph

brilliance. At first I thought it rotary; then I understood that this movement was an illusion produced by the vertiginous sights it enclosed'. Staring into it, Borges could see other times, other spaces and infinite objects – a heavy-laden sea, a paving tile he had seen 30 years before at the entrance to a house, horses on a beach by the Caspian Sea and convex equatorial deserts and every grain of sand in them.

Did the angels predict to Edward Kelley the destruction of the Spanish Armada?

There is no reason why Nostradamus, Cheiro and a handful of other seers should be the only ones who can traverse the time tree; the techniques used to peep into either the personal or collective future are not just the preserve of a few gifted people.

Oracles used to form part of the ongoing religious life of ancient Greece; the worship of Apollo included the establishment and maintenance of places of prophecy by means of which the gods could communicate with mankind. The practice at Delphi was for the prophetess to seat herself upon a brass tripod placed over a vent in the floor of a cavern

John Dee, mathematician and geographer

from which emanated narcotic fumes. This is a very close parallel to the description of Nostradamus's own method in Century I, Quatrain 1 (see pages 138–9).

We cannot easily replicate these methods, but we can look forward less than a century from Nostradamus's time to a method of divination that we can use. In Elizabethan times Dr John Dee, mathematician and court adviser to Queen Elizabeth I, wanted to see into the future, not by consulting professional oracles, but by 'scrying' – having visions in a crystal or 'glass'. Dee went even further in his efforts to obtain divine knowledge: he attempted to converse with the angels through the crystal. His techniques, if not his angels, are available to us still.

The technique of scrying requires only a quiet, darkened room and a non-reflective surface upon which is laid the crystal, sometimes in a dark wooden frame; a beryl is a suitable stone to use. After suitable preparation to clear the mind of distracting thoughts, the seer gazes into the stone, which is normally a spherical lump of polished natural crystal – usually some variety of quartz. There should be no distracting reflections on the surface of the crystal.

The purpose of staring intently into the stone is to bore, as it were, the part of the mind which is concerned with everyday consciousness so that it is switched off and the vision is freed to explore other times or places, or sometimes other planes. The seer may be lucky within minutes or may have to wait several hours, depending upon conditions and natural aptitude. When you are attempting the technique, try not to look at the surface of the stone, but about halfway into it. Once the extrasensory perceptive processes are fully in operation the crystal gazer 'sees', as though with a psychic analogue of physical vision, things far off in time and/or space. In the case of certain advanced forms of crystal-gazing involving what are known as out of body experiences, the scryer actually has the sensation of being physically present at the scene of the vision (see pages 160–1).

Scrying is often found to be an effective dissociative technique by those who wish to look into the future and bring their psychic abilities into play. Only a minority of scryers employ real crystal balls as they tend to be very costly, and an imitation made of moulded glass is more easily available, much cheaper and usually productive of equally satisfactory or unsatisfactory results. In fact, almost anything can serve as such a focus – a glass of water, a pool of ink or a semi-translucent stone.

The fact that a number of accurate scrying visions have been experienced in the past cannot reasonably be doubted by any person who looks at the evidence dispassionately. Some scryers are possessed of a 'wild talent' which is sometimes innate, sometimes deliberately cultivated by the use of such psychic exercises as are described on pages 160–1.

THE FALL OF A QUEEN

One scryer in Elizabethan times accurately foretold the execution of Mary Queen of Scots and the sailing of the Spanish Armada on the basis of visions seen in a polished piece of hard 'cannel cole' – which in a 16th-century context probably means anthracite or jet.

The scryer in question, Edward Kelley (1555-95), was one of those talented but amoral people who were a combination of authentic seer and petty criminal. Dr John Dee employed Kelley to scry in his experiments with 'angelic revelations'. The vision that was interpreted at the time as a forecast of the execution of Mary and an attempt at a seaborne invasion of England was recorded in Dee's diaries on 5 May 1583. Through the mediumship of Kelley, Dee asked 'the angel Uriel': 'As concerning the vision wch [sic] yesterday was presented to the sight of E[dward] K[elley] as he sat at supper with me in my hall – I mean the appearing of the very great sea and many ships thereon and the cutting off the head of a woman by a tall, black man, what

Edward Kelley, seer and alchemist

are we to imagine thereof?' To which Uriel replied: 'Provision of foreign powers against the welfare of this land: which they shall shortly put into practice. The other, the death of the Queen of Scots: it is not long unto it.'

So it transpired. In 1587 Mary Queen of Scots was executed for treason, and the next year the Armada sailed against England. Dee had already informed Elizabeth I of this prophecy, and Drake had more than enough time to prepare; Kelley's was a prophecy which may have changed history.

151

Precise instructions for using classical methods of oracular prophecy such as were employed by Nostradamus are nowhere recorded in any detail, and scrying requires a certain amount of natural ability. However, there are a number of other tried and tested methods of divination that will, with a bit of application, allow anyone to explore the time tree and see into the future. Of these divinatory methods, the traditional European Tarot pack is considered in detail on pages 156–7, and the even more

ancient oracle books and sortes are covered on pages 122–3.

For one of the most reliable of all methods for obtaining answers to specific questions we have to look to the *I Ching* or 'Book of Changes', the world's most ancient and best-known oracle book. This classic Chinese text is attributed to King Wen and his son the Duke of Chou, who, in the 12th century BC, arranged the book 'in order to release the wise administrator from dependence on unstable priestly types for interpreting the oracle', a

clear indication that this oracle is for everyday use.

The technique involves the generation of one or two of 64 distinct hexagrams, each made up of its own unique combination of six whole or broken lines called Yang (whole and male) or Yin (broken and female) lines. This is followed by consultation of the text. In addition to this, the numerous commentaries the *I Ching* gives on the hexagrams should be referred to. The hexagram is derived by either manipulating 50 special yarrow stalks or, more recently, by tossing coins, which by their pattern of fall will accurately predict the conditions of the moment and hence the outcome of the question being asked.

To perform a divination, first still the mind and perhaps burn a little incense to invoke the right mood. Then formulate the question as unambiguously and carefully as possible, and write it down. Take three coins (ideally but not necessarily Chinese ones) with holes in the middle. Each side represents Yang (usually heads) or Yin (usually tails). The coins are to be thrown in the air six times, with each throw indicating the type of line. If the coins fall with two Yang (heads) and one Yin (tails) side, the line indicated is Yang. Likewise, if two Yin sides and one Yang side appear, the line is Yin. If all three sides are Yang then the line is considered to be a 'moving' Yang line – that is, Yang but with a tendency to convert to Yin in the future. Three Yin sides give a 'moving' Yin line.

A ceremonial consultation of the I Ching *using yarrow sticks*

A consultation of the I Ching *in a Chinese temple*

Let us take a sample question and answer to illustrate the technique. Suppose the question is, 'What will be the outcome for me of this court case?' The three coins are thrown six times, giving the following six lines:

1 2 Yang + 1 Yin sides = YANG
2 1 Yang + 2 Yin sides = YIN
3 3 Yang sides = moving YANG
4 1 Yang + 2 Yin sides = YIN
5 1 Yang + 2 Yin sides = YIN
6 2 Yang + 1 Yin sides = YANG

When you have constructed the hexagram of six lines as above you need to look up the meaning in the *I Ching*, which gives an interpretation of the outcome of the question. In this case the hexagram is number 21, called Shi Ho, of which the text reads: 'Success in legal proceedings. You are not to blame for the present trouble. Separateness.'

This is a very unambiguous answer to the question, but its interpretation can be taken one step further by taking the so-called 'moving' line and changing it to its opposite, in this case from Yang to Yin. The resultant hexagram is number 27, called I, of which the text is 'Consistent effort brings good success.' This confirms the reading.

Practice makes perfect and the use of the *I Ching* on a regular basis leads to a greater facility. Although the *I Ching* is not very good on dating its predictions, it sometimes offers advice

The eight trigrams that form hexagrams

where appropriate. If just dipped into it reads almost as abstrusely as Nostradamus's quatrains, but when it is used properly the particular text chosen by the oracle is often blindingly clear and apposite to the question being asked.

Dreams may open the gates to other realities

Carl Gustav Jung, one of the greatest psychologists of the 20th century and originally one of Freud's students, was very interested in the way in which the human mind related to the world, 'reality' and time. From 1920 onwards Jung frequently consulted the oracle of the *I Ching* (see pages 152–3), fascinated by its uncanny predictions. Uncertain how to reconcile its consistent accuracy with its apparently random and unscientific method, he evolved a theory of 'synchronicity' to help explain how internal events or thoughts sometimes appear to be related to, or even cause, apparently unrelated actions in the world around us (see panel opposite). He also hoped to account for parallels between dreams and actual events, or dream prophecy.

Given that there is a connection between the subjective mind and the external universe, it is only a short step to the conclusion that if internal events can precipitate external events then perhaps some wild-talented individuals can, by inward concentration and the application of the right techniques, actually foresee external events that have not yet happened. In his book *Dreams*, Jung writes, 'In the superstitions of all times and races the dream has been regarded as a truth-telling oracle . . . . The occurrence of prospective dreams cannot be denied'. Examples of synchronicity appear to happen at random; to be able to

precipitate them at will would be an almost magical ability.

John William Dunne, an aeronautical engineer and the author of *An Experiment with Time* (1927) noticed that stray images that had entered his mind in reflective moments or during dreams later became part of experiences which he could not have foreseen. In an effort to discover if this type of precognition was common, he got 22 people to write down the content of their dreams immediately upon waking and then report if any of these dream images became part of reality within a short period of time. He was amazed to find 'how many persons there are who, while willing to concede that we habitually observe events before they occur, suppose that such prevision may be treated as a minor logical difficulty'.

In 1916 Dunne dreamt of an explosion in a London bomb factory. This explosion actually occurred in January 1917, when 73 workers were killed and more than 1000 were injured. Dunne felt that this and similar experiences provided proof that segments of experience can and do get displaced from their proper position in time.

Take the case of the Hon. John Godley, later Lord Kilbracken. On the night of 12 March 1946 he had the first of several precognitive dreams. In it he was reading the following Saturday's newspaper and on waking he could remember the horse-racing results and the names of two winners, Bindal and Juladin, both with starting prices of 7-1. The dream impressed

Princess Anne (horse number 2) loses a race at Epsom. Did she win in an alternate reality?

him enough for him not only to tell several friends of it but to consult the morning paper on Saturday. Bindal and Juladin were both running. He backed Bindal to win. The horse did so and Godley then put his entire winnings on Juladin, which also won. Godley's precognitive dream was exactly in accordance with reality except for the starting prices of the two winners, respectively 5-4 and 5-2.

A month or so later Godley had another dream in which he was once again reading the racing results. The only name of a dream winner he could remember was Tubermore. No horse of that name was listed as a runner in any race meeting, but a horse called Tuberose was running at Aintree on the following Saturday. He backed it and Tuberose obliged him by coming home first.

The next time his dream consisted of making a telephone call to a book-maker. 'Monumentor at five to four', said the dream bookie. No horse of that name was listed as a runner at any forthcoming meeting, but remembering the Tubermore/Tuberose success

Godley backed Mentores, which duly romped home at a starting price of 6-4.

We see here a slow divergence from the early, precise predictions, as

if the alternate reality which he had tapped into was 'growing away' from this reality: soon some of his dream tips were not coming home at all.

Nine years later Godley had another precognitive dream, this time of a horse named What Man? winning the 1958 Grand National at Aintree. There was no such horse, so the lucky dreamer backed Mr What, who duly won this gruelling and extremely uncertain race.

This is an interesting illustration of how Nostradamus's predictions often included names that were not quite correct but were similar in meaning or were anagrams. The difficulty for the seer was sometimes having to render words he may never have seen.

JUNG AND SYNCHRONICITY

155

Jung defines synchronicity as a meaningful coincidence, but there is also a strong flavour of some hidden connection between an inner and outer event. One example that Jung quotes concerns a young female analysand with whom he was having considerable difficulty because she always 'knew better about everything'. One day she was telling Jung about a particularly vivid dream of a scarab beetle of a type common in Egypt but not in Europe. As she spoke there was a tapping on the window which grew more and more insistent. Jung finally opened the window and in flew a gold-green scarab beetle of the rose-chafer variety. Jung caught it and handed it to his

Dr Carl Jung, who defined synchronicity

patient, saying, 'Here is your scarab.' This broke the ice of her rationalism and resistance, and her analysis was rapidly and success-fully completed.

The Tarot is an ancient set of cards used for games of chance, divination and esoteric exposition. It consists of 78 cards, of which 22 are picture cards called the Major Arcana. These have played a very important part in Western esoteric thinking in recent years. Since the early 1960s, when only a few Tarot card packs were easily available, there has been a huge increase in the number of packs to the point where even catalogues of the packs that are currently obtainable fill large volumes.

In addition to the Major Arcana, there are a further 56 cards divided into four different suits: Cups, Wands, Pentacles and Swords. These are similar to ordinary playing cards, being numbered one to 10 with four Court cards per suit – the Page, Prince, Queen and King. The numbered cards range in complexity from designs simply carrying the numerical 'pips' in the appropriate suit through to fairly elaborate picture cards, according to the taste of the artist. Here we are primarily concerned with the picture cards of the Major Arcana. These archetypal symbols are drawn from the images that were current in Europe in the centuries prior to Nostradamus's lifetime.

Although it used to be popular to ascribe the creation of the Tarot to the ancient Egyptians, the images are very much of a European mould, although the gypsies (often mistaken for Egyptians in that era) certainly would have played a part in their spread throughout Europe. The earliest

Cards from both the Major and the Minor Arcana of an Italian Tarot pack

unambiguous reference to the Tarot in Europe occurs in Berne in 1367, fixing their origin as probably medieval and European.

The Tarot soon appeared both in cheaply printed forms in taverns and in splendidly executed versions used by the rich. Even King Charles VI of France had three personal packs painted for him in 1392 by the artist Gringonneur, who used vellum, lapis lazuli and gold to produce them very lavishly. They were variously seen as the devil's picture book, as pagan relics, as a leisure diversion, or sometimes as keys to the future. Certainly Nostradamus must have handled a pack at some time in his life.

To use the Tarot for divination, it is necessary first for you to become familiar with each of the main cards by spending at least half an hour meditating on its meaning before reading the interpretation of that card given by one of the standard books on the subject. In this way you will have formed your own instinctive relationship with the card before having someone else's views overlaid on the image.

When you have worked through each of the Major Arcana, and read a little about the basic meaning of the Minor Arcana, then you are ready to start your own voyage of discovery into what the cards can tell you. First try a simple question that will later be easy to verify, but one that has not got a highly emotional content: it's too

soon to ask the 'big' questions. You may find that in the beginning it is easier to read the cards for someone else rather than yourself.

The simplest divination you can use involves first formulating the question and then writing it down. With your mind as free from specific thoughts as you can make it, carefully shuffle the pack several times and then lay the top three cards face down on the table. Turn these up one at a time and verbalize what comes into your head. (Sometimes the answer will be given to the question that was in the enquirer's mind, rather than the one that was actually put.) The first card will show the past conditions, the second the present situation and the

last card the future as it relates to that particular question.

If the cards are the Major Arcana a story should naturally form itself in your head. If you are using a full pack it is permissible to look up the meanings of the numbered or court cards, or indeed the meanings of the Major Arcana if nothing intuitive comes to you. Remember that the meaning of a card differs according to whether it is the right way up or inverted.

A more comprehensive method of divination is the 'Celtic Cross', which uses 10 cards dealt from the pack in a specific order, and which gives considerably more information about the question. Further details will be found in any book on the Tarot.

THE MAJOR ARCANA

157

Three cards from the Major Arcana

The 22 traditional images used on the Major Arcana fall into several distinct categories:
1 Personages: the Fool, the Magician, the High Priestess, the Empress, the Emperor, the Pope, the Lovers, the Hermit, the Chariot (or Prince), the Hanged Man.
2 Virtues: Temperance, Justice, Strength (Fortitude).

3 Astrological: the Sun, the Moon, the Star.
4 Allegorical: the Wheel of Fortune, Death, the Devil, the Tower (of Babel), Judgment, the World.

These cards can be seen to be an incomplete series – a number of the virtues such as Faith, Hope and Charity are missing, for example, as are five of the planets that are to be found in the traditional Tarot pack. Some early packs called 'naibi' and 'minchiate' included these extra cards, plus the full set of 12 zodiacal images. However, the above set of 22 cards is the form in which the Tarot has evolved into an unsurpassed divinatory tool over the last 600 years.

Another of the methods of divination which Nostradamus would have encountered is geomancy. This is a particularly useful technique for answering specific questions about the future which relate particularly to material affairs, that is, matters concerning business, finance, agriculture and property. There is much evidence that geomancy's reputation for predictive accuracy in these fields is well-justified.

Many detailed records of both successes and geomantic failures exist. Among the most interesting are those kept by an Elizabethan doctor, Simon Forman (1552-1611), who used this method for everything from medical diagnosis to political prediction. There is no reason why the same geomantic predictive techniques employed by Forman and many others should not work just as well for you. Geomancy is, however, best confined to material matters and not employed where subtler considerations, such as those relating to human emotions, are in question.

The technique of geomancy consists of interpreting a series of dots made in the earth or sand, or by pencil upon a piece of paper. Whichever medium is chosen, the question must first be carefully and accurately framed to allow for no ambiguity in the answer. Let us assume that the question is, 'Will my new venture bring me financial gain?' The diviner must then make 16 lines of dashes or dots with whatever instrument he or she has chosen, while requesting the aid of the earth spirits.

The dots on each line are then counted. The first row of dots is totalled and, depending on whether the resultant number is odd or even, one dot or two dots respectively are marked on the first line of a fresh piece of paper. The same observation is made for each of the subsequent 15 lines. The resultant page has 16 lines,

Gnomes, the elementals behind geomancy

each containing either one or two dots. These are broken vertically into four groups of four. The first group of four lines might look like this:

odd number of dots	●
even number of dots	● ●
odd number of dots	●
even number of dots	● ●

This is one geomantic figure, the first so-called 'Mother' figure. The subsequent Mother figures are derived in the same way from the remaining lines and the results placed beside the first figure. For example:

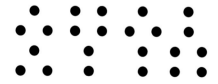

It can be seen that what is being generated is a set of four four-line binary figures and that there are 16 possible combinations of such figures. These 16 figures are usually referred to by their Latin names. The four shown above are called Amissio (meaning loss), Fortuna Major (great fortune), Puella (girl), and Fortuna Minor (lesser fortune).

Immediately you have a very rough answer to your question: there will be a major loss of fortune, but luck may come through a girl or woman connected with the proposed venture. The next step is to use a form of binary arithmetic to combine the four Mother figures into four Daughter figures, and from these are derived four Nephew figures, who in turn produce two Witness figures. The combination of these last two geomantic figures produces the Judge figure, by means of which you may judge the outcome of the question. Without going through all these steps, which can be looked up in any of the books on the subject of geomancy, the result of these manipulations is:

This is Albus, usually a good sign, but in this case it simply confirms that the venture will be mercurial and unstable, one best not embarked on. Although you should not ask the same question more than once, this divination was performed a second time. It came up with almost the same Mother figures but the Judge was Caput Draconis – an emphatic warning that does not bode well for the new venture, which, if embarked upon, will almost certainly lose money.

It seems that geomancy first became popular as 'raml' in the ninth century in the Arab world, probably in North Africa. From there it travelled south across the Sahara to Nigeria, Dahomey and Ghana, where it was practised under the name of Ifa divination and was subsequently exported to the New World as part of the divinatory techniques of the practitioners of Voodoo. Before that, however, it migrated with the Moors into Spain and hence into Southern France, where Nostradamus would have known it as Geomantiae. It is certain that the seer would have read writers such as Ramon Lull (1235-1315) who were experts in this form of divination.

The alchemist in a Tarot pack

THE GEOMANTIC FIGURES

Geomantic Figure	Meaning	Ruler
Puer	Boy, yellow, beardless, rash and inconsiderate, is rather good than bad.	Bartzabel
Amissio	Loss, comprehended without, that which is taken away, a bad figure.	Kedemel
Albus	White, fair, wisdom, sagacity, clear thought, is a good figure.	Taphthartharath
Populus	People, congregation, an indifferent figure.	Chashmodai
Fortuna Major	Greater fortune, greater aid, safeguard entering, success, interior aid and protection, a very good sign.	Sorath
Conjunctio	Conjunction, assembling, union or coming together, rather good than bad.	Taphthartharath
Puella	A girl, beautiful, pretty face, pleasant, but not very fortunate.	Kedemel
Rubeus	Red, reddish, redhead, passion, vice, fiery temper, a bad figure.	Bartzabel
Acquisitio	Obtaining, comprehending without, success, absorbing, receiving, a good figure.	Hismael
Carcer	A prison, bound, is good or bad according to the nature of the question.	Zazel
Tristitia	Sadness, damned, cross, sorrow, grief, perversion, condemnation, is a bad figure.	Zazel
Laetitia	Joy, laughing, healthy, bearded, is a good figure.	Hismael
Cauda Draconis	The threshold lower, or going out, dragon's tail, exit, lower kingdom, is a bad figure.	Zazel & Bartzabel
Caput Draconis	The head, the threshold entering, the upper threshold, dragon's head, entrance, upper kingdom, is a good figure.	Hismael & Kedemel
Fortuna Minor	Lesser fortune, lesser aid, safeguard going out, external aid and protection, is not a very good figure.	Sorath
Via	Way, street, journey, neither good nor bad.	Chashmodai

159

To derive answers to specific questions you can use any of the techniques outlined in the previous chapters: scrying, the Tarot cards, divinatory sortes, the *I Ching* or geomancy – each in its own way will provide answers.

But what if you want to be there, see the future, feel the future, or the past, and record direct impressions as did Nostradamus? There is a way to penetrate the curtain of time. The idea that each human being has an 'astral body' capable of separating itself from the physical body and engaging in 'astral journeying' is very old. The Neoplatonic philosophers of the early Christian era referred to Plato's doctrines when they called this 'dream body' after the Latin word for star, 'astrum'. Centuries later, Cornelius Agrippa confirmed the possibility of leaving the body consciously in dream as 'vacation of the body, when the spirit is enabled to transcend its bounds'.

Creative dreaming or astral projection is, after scrying, probably the most direct form of perception of other places or other times, but it does take considerable perseverance to accomplish. Although astral projection does not lead directly to prophecy or predictive powers, once it has been achieved the scope for first-hand experience of other times or other realities is considerable.

The purpose of the technique of astral projection is to do with your conscious mind what is carried out by your unconscious mind after you go

Projection of the astral body during sleep

to sleep. There is nothing at all unnatural in that, except that you will be consciously aware of your 'dream', and be able to direct it, just as Nostradamus could.

The body has many unconscious functions, such as breathing. Most of the time it conducts these operations without any disturbance from the conscious mind, but you can take over with the conscious mind the function of, for example, breathing. If you had to do this all the time it would be a bore, but breathing is a function which can be controlled by either the conscious or the unconscious mind. Dreaming is another such function. There are some well-known positive benefits in regularly taking over and deepening the breathing cycle. Likewise, there are definite benefits in taking over and consciously directing your 'dreaming'.

There are a number of techniques designed to project the astral body, These all share several basic prerequisites, the most important of which is confidence in what you are doing, and a lack of fear. If for a moment you begin to succeed with a projection, even the slightest touch of fear will instantly drive you firmly back to your body. Fear is a natural response to new sensations which in this particular case needs to be curbed, just as the breathing response needs to be overcome while you are diving underwater.

The second is concentration. If your will or visualization slackens, either your mind will wander, in the everyday meaning of that expression, or you will go to sleep – not a bad thing in itself, but inimical to success with this practice.

The steps involved in projecting the astral body are:

1 Make sure there is no possibility of disturbance by the phone (take it off the hook) or any impending callers. Remove any metal objects touching your skin. Sit in a very comfortable and fully supporting chair, or stretch out on a bed in a north-south orientation, head to the north. (Although the latter is not always desirable as it does encourage sleep.) Concentrate on each part of your body in turn, starting with your feet. Tense the muscles and then relax them, working up to the top of your head. Then mentally check each part of your body again to see it is fully relaxed.

Close your eyes and attempt to hold for a few minutes that delicious feeling of verging on sleep, while staying very much alert.

2 Take a few deep breaths. Try to imagine yourself lying or sitting 15cm (6 inches) to the left of where you actually are. When you have successfully convinced yourself of this, try visualizing a new position 15cm (6 inches) to the right of your actual position. When you are sure of this, try for 15cm (6 inches) above your present position. When this slightly more difficult position has been convincingly established, try sinking into the bed, through the mattress, and coming to rest in your imagination 15cm (6 inches) below it. At this point the temptation simply to go to sleep should be fought. Repeat these exercises every night for a week.

3 When these visualizations are successful, but not before, visualize yourself in your original position but slowly raising yourself into a sitting

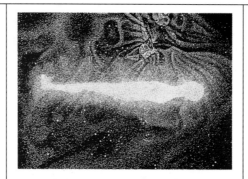

The aura as conceived by occultists

position. Then, without even attempting to open your eyes, try to see what is in front of you. Repeat these exercises every night for a second week.

4 Spend every night of the next week repeating the above exercises, but adding a further practice. Try imagining yourself slowly swinging side to side from one position to the other, like a pendulum. Get to feel perfectly comfortable with this, then try moving backwards as if someone were pulling you out through your own head and shoulders. Move this newly visualized position further back from your body each time you try it. With some luck the time will come when you suddenly

find yourself apparently able to stand up and move away from your body.

5 If this does not work, add an additional exercise. This involves sitting in front of a mirror, closing your eyes, then attempting to reverse the situation, so that instead of looking at your reflection you may be able for a few seconds to feel you are looking out of the mirror at yourself. Add this to the previous exercises for another week, trying the whole cycle of exercises.

Eventually the time will come when you will get a jerk-back feeling, as if you had just pulled back from falling: try to encourage this but let yourself go. Keep persisting until suddenly you will find yourself apparently standing in your room, slightly disorientated, having successfully transferred your consciousness outside your body. Then the interesting experiments which are outside the scope of this book begin. Suffice it to say that there is much to explore before you need to go looking for other times.

161

SEEING THE ASTRAL BODY

The astral body is a concept that is found in most civilizations and is even indirectly mentioned in the Bible. The Theosophists, a worldwide movement founded by H. P. Blavatsky, went to great lengths to try to 'see' the astral body clairvoyantly and books were produced with coloured paintings of different auras, which were considered to be an extension of the astral body.

A depiction of the astral body

In the early 1960s a type of goggle called the Kilner goggle was produced which enabled even people who were not psychic to see the flow of the aura round living human beings. In the 1970s, claims were made that a form of photography called Kirlian photography could actually photograph the aura. More recently, direct photography of the whole astral body has been attempted.

What of Nostradamus's prophesies for the 1990s? He predicted in Century VI Quatrain 21 that there would be a US/USSR alliance in 1990 (see page 117). Certainly the closeness that originated between Reagan and Gorbachev in the late 1980s has now reached the point (unthinkable just 10 years ago) where President Clinton of the US has offered aid to Russia. In Century II Quatrain 89 the same prediction is rephrased:

One day the two great leaders will
be friends,
Their great power will be seen to grow:
The New Land will be at the height of
its power,
To the man of blood the number
is reported.

The man with the blood mark (on his head) is obviously Gorbachev, who subsequently loses his power. Even at the time of his friendship with Reagan his number was almost up. The New Land is the New World or the US, probably at the height of its powers before succumbing to the current recession.

Nostradamus predicted a Middle Eastern war in 1991 in Century VIII Quatrain 70 with amazing detail:

He will enter, wicked, unpleasant,
infamous
Tyrannizing over Mesopotamia.
All friends made by the adulterous
woman.
The land dreadful and black of aspect.

Saddam Hussein certainly entered Kuwait in a wicked and infamously underhand manner. He still tyrannizes Mesopotamia, the ancient Greek name for Iraq. The 'adulterous woman' might be a 20th-century friend and ally of Hussein, but this is more likely to be a reference to the Biblical whore of Babylon. Babylon's position as capital of the region has been taken over by Baghdad, Saddam Hussein's capital. The last line is a perfect description of the huge black clouds hanging over Kuwait after Saddam Hussein set fire to the oil wells.

In Century VI Quatrain 59 Nostradamus speaks of another drama which hit the headlines in 1991:

The lady, furious in an adulterous rage,
Will conspire against her Prince, but
not speak to him.
But the culprit will soon be known,
So that seventeen will be martyred.

The Duchess of York was upset by the newspaper reports of her alleged adultery with a Texan (the culprit who was soon discovered). She left on a trip to Indonesia without Prince Andrew, not speaking to him. It remains to be seen who the 17 persons are who will suffer.

By early 1991, Margaret Thatcher had been pushed from power, and later that year Princess Diana was rejected by Prince Charles. It is possible that one or other of those events is reflected in Century VI Quatrain 74:

She who was cast out will return
to reign,
Her enemies found among conspirators.
More than ever will her reign be
triumphant.
At three and seventy death is very sure.

Whoever is the main protagonist, it looks like a welcomed return, ended by death predicted very precisely at the age of 73.

Nostradamus predicted war in the Middle East in 1991

In 1991 civil war broke out in the former Yugoslavia, and has been rumbling along ever since. Here is an interesting resurgence of the old quarrel between Muslim and Christian groups which has fuelled feuds in Eastern Europe since the Turkish occupation from the middle of the 15th century until the end of the 17th. Nostradamus obviously points to the current unrest in this area and in Romania in Century IV Quatrain 82:

A mass [of men] *from Slavonia will draw near,*
The Destroyer will ruin the old city:
He will see his Romania quite deserted.
Then will not know how to extinguish the great flame.

Certainly there has been much destruction of the old city of Dubrovnik, and it is doubtful if the UN knows how to extinguish the flames of religious and civil hatred. Romania, meanwhile, has been reduced to a shadow of its former self by its last Communist dictator.

The year of 1994 is designated by Nostradamus for the beginning of the drought of 40 years followed by floods of the same duration (see pages 118–19). Despite the use of the French word 'ans', perhaps this should be interpreted as months, as a 40-year drought is inconceivable in terms of the world's current climate.

In 1995 an unloved pope is predicted to be chosen from French or Spanish candidates – the penultimate pope, according to Malachy. This year will also see friction in Albania with a probable attack by this country on Greece (see also page 129).

Is the Whore of Babylon manifest in modern-day Baghdad?

In 1996 environmental disasters (see pages 118–19) not entirely unconnected with the depletion of the ozone layer are predicted in Century IV Quatrain 67.

Late in the decade will come two Islamic expansionist invasions, one from Algeria and the other from Iran (Persia), according to Century VI, Quatrain 80, resulting in the burning of a city and many deaths by the sword. This may be a holy war, or jihad, with Muslim armies converging from North Africa and Iran against Christian Europe, just like the Muslim invasion of Spain 700 years ago:

From Fez the [Islamic] *kingdom will stretch out to Europe,*
The city blazes, and the sword will slash:
The great man of Asia with a great troop by land and sea,
So that the blues, Persians, cross, to death is driven.

The concluding events of the 1990s and the millennium itself are discussed in the next few pages.

DESCENT INTO DESPAIR

The overwhelming quantity of catastrophic prophecies in the quatrains make the future look very bleak indeed. In this Nostradamus is not alone: the Revelation of St John the Divine, with which he would have been familiar, predicts the arrival of the four Horsemen of the Apocalypse (Plague, Famine, War and Death) which will herald the rise of the Antichrist, the millennium, and the end of the world. Century X Quatrain 72 (see pages 110–11) warns of the arrival from the skies of the King of Terror, five months before the year 2000. Variously interpreted as a giant nuclear bomb, or even a full-scale alien invasion from outer space, whatever it turns out to be will be very unpleasant indeed. As if to confirm this prophecy, Professor Hideo Itakawa, who pioneered Japan's rocket technology, predicts the end of the world one month later in August 1999. He suggests this will be due to a very rare astrological Grand Cross of the planets which forms in this month.

This Grand Cross is formed by an opposition of Venus (in Scorpio) to Saturn and Jupiter (in Taurus), square (at right angles) to Neptune and Uranus (in Aquarius) opposed to the Sun, Moon and Mercury (in Leo). The four zodiacal signs – Taurus the bull, Leo the lion, Scorpio the eagle and Aquarius the man – are the signs of the four beasts of the Apocalypse which are also shown on the very last Tarot card in the pack, the World.

Scientists are beginning to associate the incidence of sunspot, earthquake

The City of London after a bomb attack – are such scenes to become commonplace?

and volcanic activity more with planetary positions than with solely geological causes. Consequently, as a result of this configuration there may be a much higher incidence of natural disasters at this time than one would normally expect. By way of confirmation, the American seer Edgar Cayce has prophesied that a shift in the polar axis of the earth will cause many natural catastrophes, earthquakes and tidal waves, resulting in the destruction of much of mankind.

This is also the time of Armageddon, predicted by Biblical prophets as the 'battle of the great day of God', when the last fight will take place between the powers of good and evil. Its name is indubitably taken from the famous battlefield mentioned in Judges V 19 in the plain of Esdraelon, where the Israelites fought their major battles. Unfortunately, it is not scheduled to be quite as localized as these battles.

Others who are in complete agreement about late 1999 being the end of the world are the Jehovah's Witnesses and the Seventh Day Adventists. Obviously a lot of people will be holding their breath over the last five months of 1999, just as they did with equal justification in 999.

In his Preface to his son César, Nostradamus speaks more plainly of the events to come before the last conflagration: 'the worldwide conflagration which is to bring so many catastrophes and such revolutions that scarcely any lands will not be covered by water, and this will last until all has perished save history and geography themselves.' Before this occurs, Nostradamus avers that 'This is why, before and after these revolutions in various countries, the rains will be so diminished and such abundance of fire and fiery missiles shall fall from heaven that nothing shall escape the holocaust . . . . For before war ends the century and in its final stages it will hold the century under its sway'.

A grim vision indeed, and one that may come to pass within a very few years. Nostradamus predicts in Century V Quatrain 25 that as we reach the year 2000 a new Arab Empire, probably made up of the more extreme Arab countries which are geographically located around Israel, will attack Iran (Persia), Egypt and Turkey (Byzantium). This empire will be supported by ruthlessly anti-Christian and venomously anti-Western fanatics in Algeria, Tunisia, and possibly 'Greater Syria', which will include parts of the Lebanon:

The Arab Prince, Mars, the Sun,
Venus, [in] Leo,
The rule of the Church will succumb
to the sea.
Towards Persia very nearly a
million [men]
The true serpent will invade Egypt and
Byzantium.

The precise conjunctions as described here occur on 21–23 August 1998 and 2–6 August 2000. As the Church is referred to by Nostradamus as a ship, its succumbing to the sea means the end of the Church, or at the very least the papacy. The standard of the attacking force will be the sign of the serpent or in some way related to it.

Two years later, in June 2002, Century VI Quatrain 24 predicts a dreadful war that will be followed by the anointment and reign of a new king. This will 'bring peace to the earth for a long time', of that Nostradamus is in no doubt. (See page 129 for the reasons for the exact dating of this prophecy.)

If we survive all these terrible events, Nostradamus clearly states that we may then look forward to 1000 years of much greater peace.

MODERN PROPHETS

One present-day seer predicts that on 1 January 2000 the centre of London will be almost completely destroyed by a cosmic catastrophe – a direct hit from a meteorite, containing large amounts of uranium, thorium and other radioactive elements, of a size even greater than the meteor which is now known to have devastated a vast area of largely uninhabited Siberian forest in 1908. According to Dr David Hughes of Sheffield University, there are perhaps 100,000 'small' asteroids in the solar system that we cannot currently detect. By small, Dr Hughes means less than 6km (3½ miles) across – ample 'ammunition' to devastate London.

Many of these prophecies relating to the year 2000 indicate major climatic variations, which will render large areas of the earth virtually uninhabitable. Also predicted are earthquakes which will devastate densely populated areas as far apart as California and Portugal and atmospheric pollution of such intensity in New York, Los Angeles, Tokyo, and a major Australian city that those who can afford to do so will move to the suburbs and countryside.

165

A pale foretaste of things to come?

NEW HOPE FOR HUMANITY

The hope of the future – Nostradamus's vision extends beyond the traumatic millennium

Nostradamus appears to give us two possible but incompatible scenarios for the world from 1999 onwards. The first scenario of horror and war was explained on pages 164–5. Now we look at the reverse side of the coin, where a golden age of enlightenment takes us into the third millennium AD, or the seventh millennium counting from Nostradamus's dating for the beginning of the world. Maybe both futures exist already on the time tree and it is our reactions to the very crucial last years of this millennium that will determine which of these worlds or realities we shall in fact enter.

Jewish scholars view the year 2000 as the end of a Shemitah and the beginning of a period when Utopian peace will reign. The Shemitah cyclical theory of time is based upon the almost universal reverence for the number seven; in a time context this is recognized in the number of days in a week, in the importance of 50 (seven times seven plus one) to the Hebrew calendar makers, and the academic and agricultural habits of a sabbatical rest year. The Jubilee year is the fiftieth year after every cycle of seven times seven years, and the larger Jubilee cycle is of 7000 years. After the present Shemitah ends in AD 2000 the Torah will no longer contain prohibitions, evil will be curbed, and

Utopia will be realized: the return to Israel of modern Judaism is in preparation for this transmission to the next Shemitah. Nostradamus was born into Judaism, even if his family later converted, and these time cycles would have been part of his upbringing.

Many thinkers and prophets point to the end of this millennium as also the end of the Age of Pisces and the beginning of the Age of Aquarius (see panel). The present writer's view is that with the ending of the Cold War threat and with an increasing desire worldwide to treat our planet in a more kindly and thoughtful fashion, the branch has already been made and we are currently on course for the second of the two alternate realities – that of a new and more civilized age. However, it will not be by any means an easy journey, as it will be marred by flashes of ethnic and religious rivalry and other squabbles. This journey will lead eventually to Nostradamus's final date of 3797. Who knows what will happen then?

KEY MILLENNIUM DATES

The year 2000 approximately marks the beginning of the Age of Aquarius – a time of fundamental change for all humanity. It is measured by the precession of the equinoxes, and as the millennium closes we are moving from the Age of Pisces (which is frequently associated with Christianity because of that religion's early use of the symbol of the fish) into the Age of Aquarius after about 2160 years. A complete circuit of all the 12 signs takes 25,290 years.

Because each zodiacal sign is not exactly 30 degrees in extent there is some controversy about the exact date that marks the transition. Here are a few of the more interesting from the many possible dates:

1904 The 20th-century magician Aleister Crowley's Aeon of Horus was for him the point of entry to the Aquarian Age, an era of the Crowned and Conquering Child of Horus. The latter half of this century has certainly been an age of the child, particularly in the year of 1964, when Flower Power raised its head.

1962 The American clairvoyant Jeane Dixon had a vision of the birth of the Antichrist in Jerusalem, an event whose significance was not lost on the makers of the Omen series of films. On the previous day there had been a solar eclipse with all seven traditional planets in the sign of Aquarius.

2000 Many prophets agree that this magic number will be the start of the Age of Aquarius, including Nostradamus, Edgar Cayce (the American 'sleeping' prophet), Saint Malachy (who forecast each of the popes until the end of the Catholic Church in this year), Garabandal and the astrologer Margaret Hone.

2001 Some writers, for example Barbarin, and the Seventh Day Adventists see the first year of the new millennium as the key date. Of course there is an argument for saying that the 'zero year' (like the 'zero year' of a baby before he turns one year old), is the first year of the Aeon. If these predictions come about then the answer to this arithmetical puzzle will be quite important.

2010 Peter Lemesurier, author of *The Gospel of the Stars*, suggests this is the correct year, quoting as his authority the French Institut Geographique National.

2012 Basing his conclusions on cycles in the ancient Mayan calendar, Jose Arguelles, author of *The Mayan Factor*, suggests this date for the collapse of global civilization and a regeneration of the earth.

2020 Basing his theory on the first conjunction of Jupiter and Saturn in Aquarius since 1404, Adrian Duncan, author of *Doing Time on Planet Earth*, proposes 21 December 2020 for the astrological transition.

2160 A date of exactly 2160 years since the birth of Christ forms another religious (but not astrological) entry point for the New Age.

167

Nostradamus's writings give a number of key dates which help us understand his quatrains. He published his first predictions in 1547 – a date which was quite significant in France, for it was the year when French instead of Latin was declared the official language of the French authorities. It is not therefore surprising to find the Curé de Louvicamp stating in 1710 that 'when France's oracle [Nostradamus] made his Gallic prophecies, he hardly ever departed from the Latins' usage, often writing Latin under the pretext of writing French . . . . Often he even employed a Latinate French, drawing attention and alluding to the Latin phraseology in word order and . . . syntax'. Latin would of course still have been the main language for scholarly interchange in Europe, and Nostradamus often thought in Latin even if he wrote in French. It is precisely for this reason that some of his quatrains so zealously guard the secret of their meaning, unless they are approached with both the Latin and French languages in mind.

In his letter to his son César, Nostradamus confirmed that his Centuries comprise 'prophecies from today [1 March 1555] to the year 3797'. This date is either the limit of Nostradamus's exploration of the time tree, or a definite date for the end of the world as we know it, 'when all has perished save history and geography themselves', at least in one of the alternate realities which make up the time tree. Even Nostradamus thought this far-distant date 'may perturb some, when they see such a long timespan'. As the events come to pass more of Nostradamus's predictions become understandable, but it is perhaps not until this far-distant date that all of them will become clear.

Looked at from a wider perspective, why should the end of the world be exactly 2000 years from the birth of Christ, an event whose dating could be incorrect by anything up to a decade anyway?

At the time that Nostradamus was writing the accepted calendar was the Julian calendar, so called because it was first adopted by Julius Caesar in 46 BC. Interestingly, the Julian cycle consisted of 7980 years, commencing on 1 January 4713 BC. Archbishop James Ussher (1581–1665), who lived shortly after Nostradamus, calculated from Biblical chronology that the world began in 4004 BC, a date which has since been referred to as Anno Mundi. To understand Nostradamus's chronology we could use Anno Mundi as a base date, but as Nostradamus's family were originally Sephardic Jews it is reasonable to look also to the Jewish tradition of dating to discover the significance of the year AD 3797.

The Jewish calendar commences from Creation in 3760 BC. The year of Christ's birth, according to the Jewish calendar, is therefore 3760. As Christ's birth is now thought by scholars to have actually been 4 BC, we add four years to this date to give 3764 Anno Mundi. As Christ is reputed to have lived 33 years, the date of his crucifixion becomes 3797 Anno Mundi.

Will the world regain the lost innocence of Eden?

Suddenly it all makes sense: Nostradamus has placed the Crucifixion as the central point of the history of the world, with the Creation and the end of the world at an equal timespan on either side. It seems, therefore, that the Jewish calendar is a far more accurate guide to time in a Nostradamian context than either the Julian calendar (current in his day), Archbishop Ussher or the Gregorian calendar (current in our own time).

The validity of the above calculation may be questioned, but this (or a very similar course of reasoning) is likely to have been used by Nostradamus to generate the date AD 3797 – with the implication that, for Nostradamus, time (embraced by the Creation and the end of the world) pivoted around the death of Christ. Beyond this timespan was eternity. By this reasoning, the total span of time between Creation and the end of the world was just over seven and a half millennium.

Nostradamus did not believe, as many prophets do now, that the end of the world would happen in AD 2000. On the contrary, he seemed fairly sure that AD 2002 was to be the beginning of a new and peaceful golden age.

At the very least, we should rejoice that the year 2000 is only a step upon the way. We should not see that year as the end, as did those farmers who in the year AD 999 left their crops unharvested because they were encouraged by the Church to feel that they would not live beyond the end of the first millennium to see the fruits of their labours. Nostradamus reassures us that there will be at least another 1797 years of human history beyond the year 2000!

For the very reason that Nostradamus could, like other prophets, see another reality which did not always take place, so we have the collective free will to guide events in order that the year 2000 brings us to that twig on the time tree which embodies a new age of relative peace, rather than fulfilling the prophecies of millennial terror, war and doom. We have that choice – though it is doubtful if we know how to make it. The future is predictable but it is not fixed!

THE PROPHECIES OF CHRIST

Christianity foresees a Last Judgment – was this what Nostradamus saw?

Although many wars and famines are predicted by Nostradamus, there is nothing new in these cycles of nature and history. Even Christ made similar predictions (Matthew 24, verses 6-8): 'And ye shall hear of wars and rumours of wars; see that ye be not troubled: for all these things must come to pass, but the end is not yet. For nation shall rise against nation, and kingdom against kingdom; and there shall be famines, and pestilences, and earthquakes, in divers places'.

On the other hand, in line with the theory of alternate realities, even Christ's prophecies seem to have failed on occasion. He correctly predicted the Fall of the Temple of Jerusalem in AD 70, when the Romans sacked it. However, he also predicted incorrectly that the end of the world would come shortly after the destruction of the Temple.

169

Antichrist St John the Divine predicted in the Book of Revelation that a false Messiah – the Antichrist – will appear shortly before the end of the world. Some commentators maintain that Nostradamus predicted three Antichrists, of which Napoleon and Hitler were the first two, but the traditional view is that there is only one Antichrist, yet to come. The Antichrist is also mentioned in the Epistles of St John.

The reign of the Antichrist

Apocalypse A revelation concerned with the state of the end of the world, usually applied to the last book of the New Testament, the Revelation of St John the Divine.

Ascendant The exact zodiacal degrees of the horizon at any particular time, most usually the time of a birth.

Astral projection The ability of projecting consciousness out of the body to a distant place or time, or another plane of reality.

Astrology The art or science of charting the position of the planets, zodiac and other heavenly bodies at a specific time and place, often a specific birth, and drawing conclusions therefrom.

Branchus The Oracle of Apollo at Didyma in ancient Greece. Branchus was a son of Apollo, and his oracle can be traced back to the seventh century BC. It is upon the methods of this oracle that Nostradamus based his methods as explained in Century I, Quatrain 2.

Cabbala Ancient Jewish metaphysical system used by modern-day European magicians as a 'map' of the other planes and worlds of the universe.

Capet Name of an earlier French dynasty than the Bourbon family of which Louis XVI was the head. However, the word was often used in a looser sense by Nostradamus to mean any French ruler, or indeed any reigning king.

Caput and Cauda Draconis Ancient Latin phrases meaning 'the Dragon's Head' and 'the Dragon's Tail' – the highest and lowest points of the moon's 'wobble' on its orbit around our planet.

Century By this Nostradamus meant a group of 100 quatrains rather than a period of a hundred years. He did not complete every Century.

Henry Howard consults Agrippa

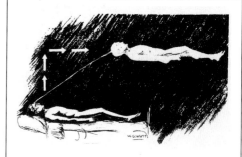

The astral body projecting

Cosmology Theoretical account of the nature of the universe, particularly with reference to space-time relationships.

Divination The art of obtaining the knowledge of future events through specific techniques – not necessarily divinely inspired, as prophecy is supposed to be.

Elementals The spirits of the four classical elements Fire, Air, Water and Earth.

Feng-shui The Chinese art of selecting the best positioning for houses or tombs in order to maximize the owner's luck. Feng-shui is not directly related to European geomancy.

Geomancy A technique of divination which uses 16 four-line figures generated from dots made at random on paper or the earth, which are often related to gnomes, or the elemental spirits of the earth. (Not to be confused with Feng-shui or Chinese geomancy.)

Gregorian Calendar The Calendar that replaced the Julian Calendar and corrected the calculation of leap years.

Hieroglyph A form of symbolic writing practised by the ancient Egyptians. In the 16th century the word applied simply to any symbolic picture or sign.

I Ching Chinese book of divination based on 64 hexagrams or figures made

170

up of six lines, one on top of the other, either broken (Yin) or whole (Yang).

Ifa An African form of divination which is based on Arabic geomancy.

Judicial astrology Astrology that is largely concerned with the judgment of the horoscope of a particular individual in order to diagnose that same individual's character and to predict his or her destiny.

Julian Calendar The calendar first adopted by Julius Caesar in 46 BC and used in Europe until the late 16th century in Catholic countries and even later in Protestant and Orthodox countries.

Malachy A saint who was the supposed author of a list of Latin mottoes, one for each pope through to the end of the papacy. After the motto of the current pope there are only two more mottoes and thus only two more popes before the demise of the papacy.

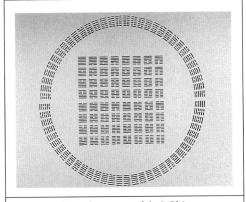
The 64 hexagrams of the I Ching

Metaplasmic Pertaining to the process of altering a word by the addition, removal, transposition or substitution of a letter or letters.

Midheaven The exact zodiacal degrees of the maximum elevation above the horizon at any particular time, most usually the time of a birth.

Millennium A period of 1000 years, usually measured since the birth of

The hawk of Horus and apes of Thoth

Christ, at the end of which a new age is to be ushered in.

Monophysitism A heresy which arose in the fifth century, denying the humanity of Christ. In 451 the Council of Chalcedon outlawed it, but nearly all Egyptian Christians refused to accept this ruling.

Mundane astrology The branch of judicial astrology which is concerned with the horoscopes and fate of cities and nations rather than those of individuals.

Necromancy The raising and questioning of the spirits of the dead.

Neoplatonists A school of philosophers, including Iamblichus, Proclus and Plotinus, centred around Alexandria in Egypt. Contemporaries of the early Christian Fathers, they founded their doctrines on the works of Plato.

Occult Relating to hidden or magical knowledge.

Precession of the Equinoxes A slow westward movement of the position of the

Equinoxes on the plane of the celestial Equator. The effect of this is that the signs of the zodiac no longer agree with the constellations with which they were first identified. In practical terms it means that the beginning of the first sign of the Zodiac (Aries) is now entering the constellation corresponding to Aquarius, hence the dawning of the Age of Aquarius.

Prophet A person who speaks or writes divinely inspired revelations of future events.

Quatrain A four-line rhyming verse used by Nostradamus to express his predictions. All are totally self-contained, and seldom relate to the adjoining quatrain.

Seer One who practises divination or who through natural talent sees revelations of the future which may not necessarily be divinely inspired.

Sortes Divination by lots, or by opening a sacred book at random and alighting upon a specific phrase which is construed as answering the question asked.

Tarot A pack of 78 cards used since the 13th century for play and also for divination.

Yang The male principle in Chinese cosmology, represented in the *I Ching* by an unbroken line.

Yin The female principle in Chinese cosmology, represented in the *I Ching* by a broken line.

171

An astrological consultation

173

ACKNOWLEDGEMENTS

The Publishers would like to thank the following for their kind permission to reproduce the photographs in this book:

The Bridgeman Art Library, London 122 bottom; /Bibliotheque Nationale, Paris 11 bottom left, 111 centre; /British Library, London 16 bottom; /Chateau de Versailles, France 26 bottom; /Cheltenham Art Gallery and Museums, Glos. 30; /Derby Museums and Art Gallery 129 top; /Giraudon 23, 28, 33 bottom, 36, 40, 42 top left and bottom right, 44, 45 top, 46, 48, 50 bottom, 56, 75; /Lauros-Giraudon 22; /Guildhall Art Gallery, Corporation of London 14, 34, 35; /Johnny van Haeften Gallery, London 24, 113, 168; /Hermitage, St. Petersburg 92; /Hotel Dieu, Beaune 5 bottom left; /House of Lords, Westminster, London 32; /The Imperial War Museum, London 64; /Lords Gallery, London 137; /Master and Fellows, Magdalene College, Cambridge 15 bottom right; /Roy Miles Gallery, London 21; /Museum Boymans-van Beuningen, Rotterdam 104; /Musee Conde, Chantilly 17; /Musee de la Ville de Paris, Musee Carnavalet 45 bottom; /Museum of the History of Science, Oxford 6 bottom left; /Museum of the Revolution, Moscow 68 bottom; /John Noott Galleries, Broadway, Worcs. 39; /Oriental Museum, Durham University 140 top; /Prado, Madrid 54; /Private Collection 29, 31, 63 top, 136 right,

145; /Raymond O'Shea Gallery, London 12; /State Collection, France 18 right; /Tate Gallery, London 74 bottom left, 154; /By courtesy of the Board of Trustees of the V&A 148 bottom; /Wallraf-Richartz Museum, Cologne 169.

ET Archive 2.

Mary Evans Picture Library 1, 3, 5 right of centre, 6 top left and top right, 7 bottom right and left, 8, 18 left, 19, 20, 26 top, 27, 37, 38 left and top right, 41, 43, 47, 49 top and bottom right, 50 top 51 top and bottom, 52, 53, 57 left and right, 58, 81, 91 top right, 93, 94, 107 bottom, 108 top and bottom, 111 right, 112 bottom, 119, 122 top, 124, 125, 127 bottom, 129 bottom, 134 top and bottom, 135 top and bottom, 138 top, 139 left and right, 140 bottom, 141, 144 bottom, 149 top, 150 top and bottom, 151 bottom, 159, 160, 163, 170 left, centre and right; /Sigmund Freud Copyrights/Sulloway 155 bottom.

Fortean Picture Library 80 bottom left.

Hulton Deutsch 5 top right, 9, 10 right, 11 top right, 13 bottom right, 15 top left, 16 top, 25, 33 top, 59 top and bottom, 60, 61, 62, 63 bottom, 68 top, 72 top and bottom, 76, 82, 83, 84 right, 99 bottom, 111 left, 117, 123, 133, 153, 170 right; /Bettmann 126 top, 127 top.

Images 5 top left, 7 top right, 10 left, 80 top right, 81, 91 bottom left, 121 left, 128, 146, 152, 153 bottom, 156, 157, 158, 161 top and bottom, 171 left and centre; /copyright US Games Systems Inc. New York 90; /Philip Daly 5 left of centre, 79.

The Kobal Collection 78, 80, 142 top, 144 top.

NASA 120.

Private Collection 138 bottom;

Rex Features 66 top right, 67, 69, 70, 71, 74 top right, 86, 87 top right, 89 top, 99 top, 105, 106, 107 top, 110, 111, 112 top, 114, 116 top and bottom, 121 right, 126 bottom, 136 left, 142 bottom, 143, 148 top, 155 top, 162, 164, 165; /C Aral 84 left, 103; /Cesare Bonazza 102; /Christopher Brown 73; /A Cavelli/Prisma 65; /Farnood 87 top left; /Tom Haley 66 bottom left; /Novosti/Sipa 88; /Rasmussen 95; /M Zihnioghi 55.

Science Photo Library/CDC 115; /Martin Land 101; /Los Almos National Laboratory 89 bottom; /Roger Ressmeyer 100; /Dr. Rob Stepney 147; /Andrew Syred 77.

Tony Stone 5 bottom right, 98, 118, 130, 131, 132, 166.